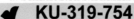

Taling Chan Floating Market (p47)
VIAJELEVE/SHUTTERSTOCK ©

Plan Your Trip
Thailand's Top 12

SOUTHTOWNBOY/GETTY IMAGES ©

Bangkok

Bangkok has it all in super-sized portions

This high-energy city loves neon and noise, chaos and concrete, fashion and the future. It's an urban connoisseur's dream: a city where the past, present and future are jammed into a steamy pressure cooker. Zip around town in the sleek, elevated BTS; watch the sun sink into the muddy Chao Phraya River on a commuter ferry; or get stuck in one of the city's famous traffic jams. Then pamper yourself with a top-notch spa treat. Above: Grand Palace (p39); Right: Chinatown (p59)

1

NOSSYTON/EYEEM/GETTY IMAGES ©

RUKSUTAKARN STUDIO/SHUTTERSTOCK ©

Chiang Mai

The cultural capital of the north

Chiang Mai is a cultural darling wearing its Lanna heritage with pride. Its old walled city is crowded with temples dating to the days of the teak boom. Bookshops and ethnic-chic stores outnumber glitzy shopping centres and the dining scene celebrates fresh and local produce. Country escapes are just an hour away. Nowhere else in Thailand has such a delightful mixture of big-city attractions with a provincial pace. Top: Thai meal (p211); Bottom: Wat Chedi Luang (p191)

2

Railay

Dramatic karst towers are the main event

Wade from a long-tail boat to the shore of this limestone-studded peninsula, and you'll see towering karst peaks hem in all sides, creating the illusion of a rocky fortress. Rock climbers turn the cliffs into vertical challenges, scrambling up for a high view of the karst-studded bay. Kayakers and snorkellers explore low-tide caves and peek at the marine life sheltered by islands. Above: Hat Tham Phra Nang (p118)

3

Chiang Rai

Ethnic diversity and dramatic
mountain scenery

The days of the Golden Triangle opium trade are over, but Chiang Rai still packs intrigue in the form of fresh-air fun such as hiking and self-guided exploration. It is also a great destination for unique cultural experiences, ranging from a visit to a hill-tribe village to a stay at the Yunnanese hamlet of Doi Mae Salong (pictured; p236). From the Mekong River to the mountains, Chiang Rai is arguably Thailand's most beautiful province.

Ayuthaya

Former capital packed with grand temples

Ayuthaya was once Siam's vibrant, glittering capital packed with temples and hosting seafaring merchants from the east and west. Today Ayuthaya has been ravaged by war and gravity but the brick-and-stucco ruins, which form a Unesco World Heritage Site, can be visited on a cycling tour that reveals their history and artistic legacy. Ayuthaya is an easy day trip from Bangkok or an alternative landing pad for city phobics. Right: Wat Mahathat (p89)

SAHO3P/SHUTTERSTOCK ©

PRETO PEROLA/SHUTTERSTOCK ©

Kanchanaburi

One of the country's easiest – and best – getaways

Given the jaw-dropping natural beauty of Kanchanaburi, it seems paradoxical that the region is best known for the horrors of WWII's Death Railway. The provincial capital's war memorials are a mandatory stop before heading deeper into the parks and preserves that comprise the Western Forest Complex, one of Asia's largest protected areas. The area is home to numerous waterfalls and caves as well as an array of lush riverside resorts. Above: Erawan National Park (p80)

6

VIKTORIYA KRAYN/SHUTTERSTOCK ©

Pai

Picture-perfect village in the northern hills

Atmospheric temples and a fun afternoon market in Pai (pictured; p270) are a reminder that the quaint hamlet has not forgotten its transnational status as a town with roots in Myanmar's Shan State, or that it is a crossroads for the ethnic minorities who live in the nearby hills. There are heaps of activities to keep visitors entertained and a relaxed vibe that makes some people wistfully fantasise about never leaving.

7

Sukhothai

Crumbling temples and picturesque countryside

Hop on a bicycle and explore Thailand's most impressive historical park, winding past crumbling temple ruins, graceful Buddha statues and fish-filled ponds. Worthwhile museums and good-value accommodation round out the package. Despite its popularity, Sukhothai rarely feels crowded, while nearby Si Satchanalai-Chaliang Historical Park attracts only a few history adventurers willing to scale its ancient stairways. Right: Sukhothai Historical Park (p174)

RCHATPHOTO GALLERY/SHUTTERSTOCK ©

VIEW APART/
SHUTTERSTOCK ©

9

Nong Khai

Riverside border town with laid-back charms

Nong Khai is not a usual stop on a quick country tour but it is worth the effort for its pretty Mekong River setting. A curious sculpture garden shelters an astounding collection of avant-garde art. The riverside market displays its Indochinese links. And visitors spend the rest of their visit cycling around town, past free-range chickens, uniformed school children and tropical fruit gardens. Far left: Mekong-side food stall; Left: Seven-headed serpent sculpture (p249) by Bunleua Sulilat, Sala Kaew Ku

Ko Pha-Ngan

Party hard, or take it easy

Famous for its Full Moon Parties, Ko Pha-Ngan has gone from sleepy
bohemian island to being a stop on the party circuit. In between lunar
festivities, it excels in laid-back island life accessible to everybody.
Backpackers can still find rustic, kick-back spots, and comfort seekers come here as an alternative to too-comfortable Ko Samui. Divers
are rewarded with easy access to some of the Gulf of Thailand's best
dive sites. Top: Full Moon Party, Hat Rin (p106); Above left and right: Ko Pha-Ngan beaches

LKUNL/SHUTTERSTOCK ©

Ko Samui

Grande dame of Thailand's island getaways

Ko Samui is like the oldest sibling among a family of islands who made it big. Here, high-class resorts operate with Swiss efficiency, lazy beaches washed by ultramarine waters stretch along tree-lined bays, and expat chefs plate up some of the yummiest food you can find in the Gulf of Thailand. Some would call it the quintessential seaside experience that offers something for everyone.
Above: Ang Thong Marine National Park (p160)

11

MAXIM TUPIKOV/SHUTTERSTOCK ©

Phuket

The ultimate beach escape

An international resort hub, Phuket is easy-peasy. You can fly in from Bangkok, cutting out the long land journey, and retreat into a five-star resort (pictured) or arty boutique hotel for a trouble-free tropical vacation. There are slinky stretches of sand, hedonistic party pits and all the mod cons needed for 21st-century rest and recreation. Mix it up with day trips to mangrove forests, charming Phuket Town, water sports and gibbon-rescue centres.

12

Plan Your Trip
Need to Know

When to Go

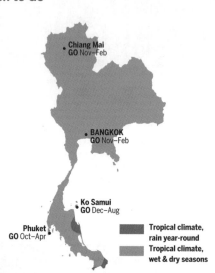

Chiang Mai
GO Nov–Feb

BANGKOK
GO Nov–Feb

Ko Samui
GO Dec–Aug

Phuket
GO Oct–Apr

Tropical climate, rain year-round

Tropical climate, wet & dry seasons

High Season (Nov–Mar)

○ A cool and dry season when the landscape is lush and temperatures are comfortable.

○ Christmas and New Year holidays bring crowds and inflated rates.

Shoulder Season (Apr–Jun, Sep & Oct)

○ April to June is hot and dry. Bangkok averages about 30°C.

○ The gulf islands are best for avoiding rain in September and October.

Low Season (Jul–Oct)

○ Monsoonal impact ranges from short, intense showers to major flooding.

○ Some islands shut down; boat service may be limited.

Currency
Thai baht (B)

Language
Thai

Visas
For visitors from 64 countries, visas are not required for stays of (mostly) up to 30 days.

Money
Cash is mostly preferred. Cards are accepted by travel agents, upmarket hotels, restaurants and shopping malls.

Mobile Phones
Thailand is on a GSM network through inexpensive prepaid SIM cards; 4G is widespread.

Time
GMT plus seven hours

Daily Costs

Budget: Less than 1000B

- Basic guesthouse room: 500–1000B
- Market/street stall meal: 40–100B
- Small bottle of beer: 80B
- Public transport around town: 20–50B

Midrange: 1000–4000B

- Flashpacker guesthouse or midrange hotel room: 1000–4000B
- Western lunches and seafood dinner: 150–350B
- Organised tour or activity: 1000–1500B
- Motorbike hire: 150–250B

Top End: More than 4000B

- Boutique hotel room: 4000B
- Meal at fine-dining restaurant: 350–1000B
- Private tours: 2000B
- Car hire: per day from 900B

Useful Websites

Thaivisa (www.thaivisa.com) Expat site for news and discussions.

Lonely Planet (www.lonelyplanet.com/thailand) Destination information, hotel bookings, traveller forum and more.

Richard Barrow (www.richardbarrow.com) Prolific blogger and tweeter focusing on Thai travel.

Tourism Authority of Thailand (TAT; www.tourismthailand.org) National tourism department covering info and special events.

Thai Language (www.thai-language.com) Online dictionary and Thai tutorials.

Opening Hours

Banks and government offices close for national holidays. Bars and clubs often close during elections and religious holidays.

Banks 8.30am–4.30pm Monday to Friday; ATMs 24-hour

Bars 6pm–midnight or 1am

Clubs 8pm–2am

Government offices 8.30am–4.30pm Monday to Friday

Restaurants 8am–10pm

Shops 10am–7pm

Arriving in Thailand

Suvarnabhumi International Airport (Bangkok) Airport Rail Link (45B, 30 minutes) to Phaya Thai station. Buses to Th Khao San (60B, one hour). Metered taxis (250B to 400B, one hour) run 24 hours.

Don Mueang International Airport (Bangkok) Four bus lines including Th Khao San (50B, one hour). Metered taxis (250B to 400B, one hour) run 24 hours. Free shuttle bus (one hour) to Suvarnabhumi.

Chiang Mai International Airport Taxis (150B, 15 minutes) to the city centre run 24 hours.

Phuket International Airport Buses (100B, one hour) to Phuket Town. Metered taxis (500B to 700B, 30 minutes to one hour) and minivans (200B to 300B, up to two hours) to beaches and Phuket Town.

Getting Around

Buses Extensive low-cost options connecting towns.

Air Cheap domestic connections on budget airlines.

Trains Slow but scenic routes across the country.

Car & motorcycle Easy to hire for local touring.

For more on **getting around**, see p306

Plan Your Trip
Hotspots for...

TUUL & BRUNO MORANDI/GETTY IMAGES ©

Beaches
Bliss out on a tropical beach surrounded by jewel-coloured waters and brooding jungle-clad mountains.

Ko Pha-Ngan (p99) Yoga centres, lunar parties, cooling waterfalls and remote beaches — pick one, or all!

Hat Rin
The beach (p106) for all-night lunar raves.

Railay (p113) Fairy-tale limestone formations tower over pristine sands and turquoise blue seas.

Hat Tham Phra Nang
Beautiful beach (p118) framed by karst cliffs.

Ko Samui (p155) Island paradise with a diverse bunch of beaches for every sort of beachaholic.

Hat Mae Nam
White beach (p162) along a sleepy coast.

EVGENY ERMAKOV/GETTY IMAGES ©

Historic Sites
Follow the cultural trail through the historic capitals, evolving art and architecture, and regional identities.

Ayuthaya (p85) Grand ruins of an ancient capital bring alive a pastoral riverside landscape.

Wat Chai Wattanaram
A grand and splendidly preserved temple (p89).

Sukhothai (p171) Explore melancholic 13th- and 14th-century temples harking back to Thailand's golden age.

Sukhothai Historical Park
Ideal historic site (p174) for aimless wandering.

Chiang Mai (p187) Lanna culture showcased within an ancient citadel boasting teak-lined temples.

Wat Phra Singh
Revered temple (p190) of the Lion Buddha.

Thai Food

Zesty spices and ingredients with a sting from chillies makes Thai food one of the globe's most beloved cuisines.

MOSAYMAY/GETTY IMAGES ©

Bangkok (p35) A culinary tour de force that unleashes the gastronome and the glutton in every visitor.

Saawaan
Red-hot restaurant (p66) for modern Thai fare.

Chiang Mai (p187) A delectable spread of ethnic cuisine and gourmet food rules the town's rich foodscape.

Lert Ros
Classic restaurant (p212) for northern-style meals.

Phuket (p123) Sumptuous Peranakan-style meals are easily Phuket's top gastronomic draw.

Kopitiam by Wilai
Popular shophouse (p144) for southern Thai food.

Shopping

An unofficial national pastime, shopping unfolds in exuberant street markets and high-end malls.

VASSAMON ANANSUKKASEM/SHUTTERSTOCK ©

Bangkok (p35) Burn your credit card as you weave through the capital's legendary malls and markets.

Chatuchak Weekend Market
A shopaholic's ultimate open-air market (p50).

Chiang Mai (p187) Thailand's handicrafts central makes you overspend on prized ethnic artefacts.

Night Markets
Buzzing bazaars (p197) for shopping and snacking.

Phuket (p123) Boho-chic boutiques and busy weekend markets set Phuket's shopping standards.

Walking Street
Sunday market (p143) for retro and artsy fare.

Plan Your Trip
Essential Thailand

HENN PHOTOGRAPHY/GETTY IMAGES ©

Activities

Thailand offers a wealth of activities for outdoorsy types. From swimming with whale sharks to visiting the Gulf of Thailand's premier dive spots in Krabi and Ko Pha-Ngan, water-based activities should be at the top of your holiday to-do list. If you prefer keeping your feet dry, Kanchanaburi Province offers historical sites, caves and national parks galore, while adrenaline junkies can scale the limestone crags or kayak the rocky monuments around Railay (also spelt Rai Leh). If hiking is more your thing, exploring the remote hill tribes of Chiang Rai might just be the tonic for you.

Shopping

Your wallet will get a serious retail workout in Thailand. The capital's mega-malls are packed with designer gear, unique gifts and home decor, and the daddy of all Thai markets – Chatuchak Weekend Market – should test your shopping muscles to the max. In Chiang Mai, the bustling Night Bazaar is filled with souvenirs and antiques, with boutique stores providing economic development opportunities for rural villagers with their handicrafts such as silk textiles and basketry. And don't forget to save room in your suitcase for the beautiful Lao-influenced weaving traditions of *mát·mèe,* to be found in the sleepy northeastern town of Nong Khai.

Eating

Thai food is super delicious and ridiculously cheap. Each region whips up its own variation of pungent, fiery and colourful curries, and you can learn the tricks of the trade at one of the cooking schools in Bangkok, Phuket or Chiang Mai. Hallowed dishes like grilled chicken and spicy green papaya salad have converts across the world, while new-age fine-dining restaurants in Bangkok constantly push the boundaries of Thai cuisine. Aromatic desserts and sweet-as-candy fruits can be plucked from colourful shop displays throughout the country.

TARAPATTA/SHUTTERSTOCK ©

Drinking & Nightlife

Be it international DJs spinning discs in ubercool clubs and cocktails flowing from the sky bars of Bangkok, the whisky-smothered Full Moon Parties and almighty hangovers nursed during lazy days on the beach at Ko Pha-Ngan, or carousing with hip uni students and boho NGOs in the beer-garden bars of Chiang Mai, the range of partying options in Thailand is as legendary as it is exhaustive.

Entertainment

There is no shortage of events to keep you entertained in Thailand. Traditional music and dance are performed in colourful street parades during local festivals in Chiang

★ **Best Cooking Courses**

Amita Thai Cooking Class (p61)

Cooking with Poo & Friends (p61)

Small House Chiang Mai Thai Cooking School (p210)

Phuket Thai Cookery School (p141)

Bangkok Bold (p61)

Mai, Chiang Rai or Nong Khai, you can experience Thai boxing champions sparring at the country's premier stadium in Bangkok, or catch an open-mic night, jazz jam session or Thai folk-music performance at cosy clubs in many places across the country.

From left: Climber on Hat Ton Sai, Railay (p116); Mango with sticky rice

Plan Your Trip
Month by Month

January

The weather is cool and dry, ushering in the peak tourist season.

✤ Chinese New Year

Thais with Chinese ancestry celebrate the lunar new year (*đrùt jeen*) with a week of house-cleaning and fireworks in late January (or early February).

February

Still in the high season; snowbirds flock to Thailand for sun and fun.

✤ Makha Bucha

One of most significant moments of the Buddha's life, Makha Bucha (*mah·ká boo·chah*) marks the day when 1250 enlightened Buddhists visited the Buddha and received Buddhist principles. The festival falls on the full moon of the third lunar month.

✤ Flower Festival

Chiang Mai displays its floral beauty during a three-day period. The festival highlight is the flower-decorated floats that parade through town.

March

Hot and dry season approaches and the beaches start to empty out.

✤ Kite-Flying Festivals

During the windy season, colourful kites battle it out over the skies of Sanam Luang in Bangkok and elsewhere in the country.

April

Hot, dry weather sweeps across the land, but the whole country is on the move for Songkran.

Above: Flower Festival

SATHITANONT N/SHUTTERSTOCK ©

🎋 Songkran

Thailand's traditional new year (13 to 15 April) starts out as a respectful affair then devolves into a water war. Morning visits to the temple involve water-sprinkling ceremonies. Afterwards, Thais load up their water guns and head out to the streets for battle.

🎋 Poy Sang Long

This Buddhist ordination festival is held in late March/early April in Chiang Mai and Pai. Young Shan boys are paraded in festive costumes.

May

Prices are low and tourists are few but it is still incredibly hot before the rains come in.

🎋 Royal Ploughing Ceremony

This royal ceremony employs astrology and ancient Brahman rituals to kick off the rice-planting season.

★ Best Festivals

Flower Festival, February

Kite-Flying Festivals, March

Songkran, April

Vegetarian Festival, September/October

Loi Krathong, November

🎋 Rocket Festival

In the northeast, where rain can be scarce, villagers craft bamboo rockets *(bâng fai)* that are fired into the sky to encourage precipitation. This festival is celebrated in Nong Khai.

🎋 Visakha Bucha

The holy day of Visakha Bucha *(wí·săh·kà boo·chah)* falls on the 15th day of the waxing moon in the sixth lunar month and commemorates the date of the Buddha's birth, enlightenment and *parinibbana* (passing away).

Above: Poy Sang Long

June

In some areas, the first rains are merely an afternoon shower. This month is a shoulder season.

July

The start of the rainy season ushers in Buddhist Lent, a period of reflection and meditation. Summer holidays bring an upsurge in tourists.

🎎 HM the King's Birthday

The current king's birthday is on 28 July, and is a public holiday.

🎎 Asanha Bucha

The full moon of the eighth lunar month commemorates the Buddha's first sermon, in which he described the religion's four noble truths. It is considered one of Buddhism's holiest days.

📅 Khao Phansaa

The day after Asahna Bucha marks the beginning of Buddhist Lent (the first day of the waning moon in the eighth lunar month), the traditional time for men to enter monasteries.

August

Overcast skies and daily showers mark the middle of the rainy season.

🎎 Mother's Day

The Queen Mother's Birthday (12 August) is a public holiday and national Mother's Day.

September

September is the wettest month in Bangkok. It's also a lean season for tourism.

October

Religious preparations for the end of Buddhist Lent begin. The monsoons are over in most places.

🎎 Vegetarian Festival

A holiday from meat is taken for nine days in adherence with Chinese beliefs of mind and body purification. In Phuket the festival gets extreme, while Bangkok's street-stall-laden Chinatown is dressed up in gorgeous yellow. Generally held in late September/early October.

🎎 Ork Phansaa

The end of Buddhist lent (three lunar months after Khao Phansaa) is followed by the *gà·tĭn* ceremony, in which new robes are given to the monks by merit-makers. In Nong Khai and other river towns, long-boat races are held.

🎎 King Chulalongkorn Day

Rama V is honoured on the anniversary of his death (23 October) at Bangkok's Royal Plaza in Dusit.

November

The cool, dry season has arrived; get here early to beat the tourist crowds. The beaches are inviting and the landscape is lush.

🎎 Loi Krathong

One of Thailand's most beloved festivals, Loi Krathong is celebrated on the first full moon of the 12th lunar month. Small origami-like boats (called *krathong* or *grà·tong*) festooned with flowers and candles are sent adrift in the waterways.

December

The peak of the tourist season has returned with fair skies, busy beach resorts and a holiday mood.

🎎 Father's Day

Honouring the former King Bhumibol's birthday on 5 December, this public holiday hosts parades and merit-making events.

Plan Your Trip
Get Inspired

ALEX KONON/SHUTTERSTOCK ©

Read

The Sad Part Was (Prabda Yoon; 2017) Satirical short stories about the lives of middle-class Thais in present-day Bangkok.

Bangkok Wakes to Rain (Pitchaya Sudbanthad; 2019) The lives of Bangkok residents collide in the past, present and future in this acclaimed novel.

Pisat (Evil Spirits) (Seni Saowaphong; 1957) Conflicts between the old and new generations.

Jasmine Nights (SP Somtow; 1994) An upbeat coming-of-age novel that fuses traditional ideas with Thai pop culture.

Married to the Demon King (Sri Daoruang; 2004) Adapts the *Ramakian*, the Thai version of the Indian epic *Ramayana*, into modern Bangkok.

Watch

How to Win at Checkers (Every Time) (Josh Kim; 2015) Eleven-year-old Oat deals with the military draft of his older (and gay) brother.

Tom-Yum-Goong (Prachya Pinkaew; 2005) Tony Jaa, the Thai Jackie Chan, stars in this martial arts movie, the most successful Thai film ever released in the US.

Last Life in the Universe (Pen-ek Ratanaruang; 2003) A spellbinding love story that established Thai new-wave cinema.

Paradoxocracy (2013) The country's political history is traced from the 1932 revolution on.

Listen

Dharmajāti (Bodyslam) Headlining alt-rock.

Best (Pumpuang Duangjan) The best from the late country diva.

Boomerang (Bird Thongchai) Album from the king of Thai pop.

Romantic Comedy (Apartment Khunpa) Leading post alt-rock.

Made in Thailand (Carabao) Thailand's classic classic-rock album.

The Sound of Siam: Leftfield Luk Thung, Jazz & Molam in Thailand (Soundway Records) Compilation of Thai tunes.

Above: A temple mural depicting the *Ramakian* (p276)

Plan Your Trip
Five-Day Itineraries

Bangkok to Chiang Mai

Touch down in Bangkok, jet to Chiang Mai and escape the urban grind with an excursion to the rural village of Pai.

FROM LEFT: PUMIDOL LEELERDSAKULVONG/500PX ©; BLUR LIFE 1975/SHUTTERSTOCK ©

Pai (p217) ③
Party, take a yoga course or get in touch with nature at the country's hottest inland backpacker destination.

Chiang Mai (p187) Visit the old city, explore the vibrant night markets, or visit an elephant sanctuary. 🚌 4 hrs to Pai

Bangkok (p35) Explore the capital's temples and restaurants, shop till you drop, then kick back at a rooftop bar. ✈ 1 hr to Chiang Mai

Bangkok to Kanchanaburi

See the best of what central Thailand has to offer with this itinerary that touches on Thailand's contemporary and ancient history.

Kanchanaburi (p73) WWII comes into vivid focus at the museums and monuments of this riverside town.
3

2 **Ayuthaya** (p85) Travel back in time to Thailand's golden age with a visit to Ayuthaya Historical Park.
🚌 2 hrs to Suphanburi, then 🚌 1½ hrs to Kanchanaburi

Bangkok (p35) Indulge in big-city excesses before downshifting to the provincial side of central Thailand.
🚌 1 hr to Ayuthaya **1**

Plan Your Trip
10-Day Itinerary

Ko Samui to Railay

Soak up the tropical scenery by surveying the beaches and islands of Thailand's famous coasts: the Gulf of Thailand and the Andaman Sea.

Ko Pha-Ngan (p99)
At full moon this relaxed island transforms into a party werewolf. 🚢 2½ hrs to Surat Thani, then 🚌 2½ hrs to Krabi, then 🚢 45 mins to Railay

Ko Samui (p155)
Fly into paradise and hit the beaches, or head offshore to the limestone crags of Ang Thong Marine National Park. 🚢 30-60 mins to Ko Pha-Ngan

Railay (p113)
It's worth the journey here to enjoy the stunning karst mountains jutting out of jewel-coloured seas; kayak among them or strap on a harness to climb the cliffs.

Plan Your Trip
Two-Week Itinerary

Sukhothai to Chiang Rai

Explore the facets of northern Thailand, from the ancient capital of Sukhothai to the contemporary cities of Chiang Mai and Chiang Rai.

Doi Mae Salong (p236) An ethnic Chinese community perched on the spine of a mountain; an easy day trip (or overnighter).

Chiang Rai (p229) Visit Wat Rong Khun, peruse Walking Street and take an NGO-led trekking tour over three or four days. 🚌 1½ hrs to Doi Mae Salong

Chiang Mai (p187) Leave three or more days for wandering around old city temples, handicraft shops and markets. 🚌 3-4 hrs to Chiang Rai

Sukhothai (p171) Spend a few days visiting the area's historical parks. 🚌 6 hrs to Chiang Mai

Plan Your Trip
Family Travel

Thais are so family focused that even grumpy taxi drivers want to pinch your baby's cheeks and play a game of peekaboo (*já ăir*). On crowded buses and skytrains, adults will stand so that children can sit, and hotel and restaurant staff willingly set aside chores to become a child's playmate.

Sights & Activities

Children will especially enjoy Thailand's beaches, as most are in gentle bays appropriate for novice swimmers. Some of the Gulf and Andaman islands have near-shore reefs for snorkelling.

Eco-tour projects and animal sanctuaries are good places to familiarise children with wildlife. Older children will enjoy jungle tours and other outdoor activities.

Families come to Chiang Mai in droves to expose their kids to culture, ziplining among gibbons and cycling about town. Phuket has activities galore (including child-friendly surf schools). There are several Andaman Coast islands where families can frolic in the sea.

Some kids might get nervous about the natural chaos of Thai cities. Consider giving your children a role: reading the map, setting up an itinerary or carrying water bottles. Staying at a hotel or resort with a pool will give kids a chance to exercise. Shopping malls offer air-conditioning, cinemas and play areas.

Kid-Friendly Eats

In Thailand, the vagaries of children's food preferences are further complicated by a cuisine known for its spiciness. Luckily, even Thai children are shielded from chillies and there's a handful of child-friendly dishes that every server can recommend. Because of the heat, remember to keep your little ones well hydrated, either with water or a variety of fruit juices, including fresh young coconuts or lime juice (a surprising hit with some kids).

Child-friendly meals include chicken in all of its nonspicy permutations – *gài yâhng* (grilled chicken), *gài tôrt* (fried chicken) and *gài pàt mét má·môo·ang* (chicken

AUNGKUL INTARAPRASONG/SHUTTERSTOCK ©

stir-fried with cashews). Helpful restaurant staff will recommend *kài jee·o* (Thai-style omelette), which can be made in a jiffy. If all else fails, tropical fruits and juices are ubiquitous and will keep the kids hydrated. Of course, most tourist centres also have Western restaurants catering to homesick eaters of any age.

Need to Know

Changing facilities Hard to find.

Cots By special request at top-end hotels.

Highchairs Occasionally available in resort areas.

Baby formula and nappies (diapers) Mini-markets and 7-Elevens carry small sizes; try Tesco Lotus or Tops Market for larger sizes.

Strollers Bring a compact umbrella stroller.

Transport Car seats and seat belts are not readily available.

★ Best Activities

Phuket Elephant Sanctuary (p141)

Queen Saovabha Memorial Institute (p61)

KidZania (p61)

Museum of Siam (p56)

Flight of the Gibbon (p210)

Health & Safety

Make kids drink lots of water. Regular hand washing should be enforced. Daily showers help with the heat. Avoid visiting in the rainy season (June to October) or the hottest months (April and May).

For more advice, check out Lonely Planet's *Travel with Children*.

From left: Elephants eating sugar cane; Ziplining, Chiang Mai (p210)

City Pillar Shrine

Emerald Buddha (p39)

Grand Palace (p39)

BANGKOK

N 0 —————— 2 km
0 —————— 1 miles

**Ko Ratanakosin &
Banglamphu**
Buddhist temples, royal
palaces, leafy lanes,
antique shophouses,
buzzing wet markets
and golden temples.

Chinatown
The streets are
crammed with bird's-
nest restaurants, gaudy
gold and jade shops, and
flashing neon signs in
Chinese characters.

**CHAO PHRAYA
RIVER**

JIM THOMPSON HOUSE

Hualamphong
Train
Station

WAT PHO

WAT PHRA KAEW & GRAND PALACE

Street-food market

Arriving in Bangkok

Suvarnabhumi International Airport
The Airport Rail Link (30 minutes) operates from 6am to midnight. Meter taxis make the run to town at all times.

Don Mueang International Airport
Meter taxis run into town 24 hours. Airport buses (one hour) into town are also available.

Where to Stay

Bangkok is home to a diverse spread of modern hostels, guesthouses and hotels. To make matters better, much of Bangkok's accommodation offers excellent value, and competition is so intense that fat discounts are almost always available.

For more information on the best neighbourhood to stay in, see p71.

Wat Phra Kaew

CHAIN45154/GETTY IMAGES ©

Wat Phra Kaew & Grand Palace

Bangkok's biggest tourist attraction is this fantastical complex, the spiritual core of Thai Buddhism and the monarchy, symbolically united in what is the country's most holy image, the Emerald Buddha.

Great For...

☑ Don't Miss

The *Ramakian* murals depicting the *Ramakian* (the Thai version of the Indian *Ramayana* epic) in its entirety.

The Complex

This ground was consecrated in 1782, the first year of Bangkok rule, and is today a pilgrimage destination for devout Buddhists and nationalists. The 94.5-hectare grounds encompass more than 100 buildings that represent 200 years of royal history and architectural experimentation.

Ramakian Murals

Outside the main *bòht* (ordination hall) of Wat Phra Kaew is a stone statue of the Chinese goddess of mercy, Kuan Im; nearby are two cow figures, representing the birth year of Rama I (King Phraphutthayotfa Chulalok; r 1782–1809). In the 2km-long cloister that defines the perimeter of the complex are 178 murals depicting the *Ramakian* in its entirety, beginning at the

Ramakian mural

NICEPIX/SHUTTERSTOCK ©

ℹ Need to Know

Wat Phra Kaew (วัดพระแก้ว; Map p58; Th Na Phra Lan; 500B; ⊙8.30am-3.30pm; 🚢Chang Pier, Maharaj Pier)

✕ Take a Break

Stop for a light bite at Ming Lee (p64), an old-school Thai eatery.

★ Top Tip

At Wat Phra Kaew and in the Grand Palace grounds, dress rules are strictly enforced. If you're wearing shorts or a sleeveless shirt you will not be allowed into the temple grounds.

north gate and moving clockwise around the compound.

If the temple grounds seem overrun by tourists, the mural area is usually mercifully quiet and shady.

Emerald Buddha

Upon entering Wat Phra Kaew you'll meet the *yaksha,* brawny guardian giants from the *Ramakian*. Beyond them is a courtyard where the central *bòht* houses the Emerald Buddha. The spectacular ornamentation inside and out does an excellent job of distracting first-time visitors from paying their respects to the image. Here's why: the

Emerald Buddha is only 66cm tall and sits so high above worshippers in the main temple building that the gilded shrine is more striking than the small figure it cradles. No one knows exactly where it comes from or who sculpted it, but it first appeared on record in 15th-century Chiang Rai (in northern Thailand).

Photography inside the *bòht* is not permitted.

Grand Palace

Adjoining Wat Phra Kaew is the Grand Palace (Phra Borom Maharatchawang), a former royal residence that is today only used on ceremonial occasions. Visitors can survey a portion of the Grand Palace grounds, but are not allowed to enter the palace buildings.

Wat Phra Kaew & Grand Palace

EXPLORE BANGKOK'S PREMIER MONUMENTS TO RELIGION & REGENCY

The first area tourists enter is the Buddhist temple compound generally referred to as Wat Phra Kaew. A covered walkway surrounds the area, the inner walls of which are decorated with the ❶ ❷ **murals of the Ramakian**. Originally painted during the reign of Rama I (r 1782–1809), the murals, which depict the Hindu epic the *Ramayana*, span 178 panels that describe the struggles of Rama to rescue his kidnapped wife, Sita.

After taking in the story, pass through one of the gateways guarded by ❸ **yaksha** to the inner compound. The most important structure here is the ❹ **bòht (ordination hall)**, which houses the ❺ **Emerald Buddha**.

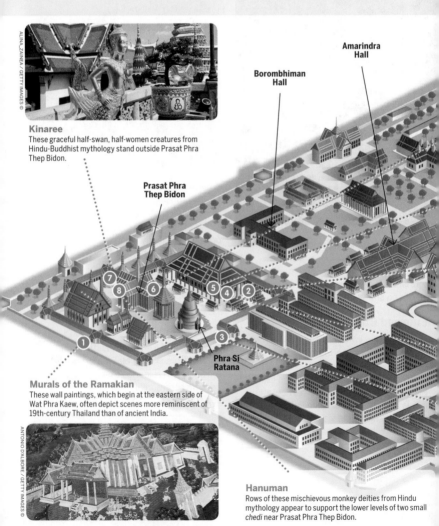

Kinaree
These graceful half-swan, half-women creatures from Hindu-Buddhist mythology stand outside Prasat Phra Thep Bidon.

Amarindra Hall

Borombhiman Hall

Prasat Phra Thep Bidon

Phra Si Ratana

Murals of the Ramakian
These wall paintings, which begin at the eastern side of Wat Phra Kaew, often depict scenes more reminiscent of 19th-century Thailand than of ancient India.

Hanuman
Rows of these mischievous monkey deities from Hindu mythology appear to support the lower levels of two small *chedi* near Prasat Phra Thep Bidon.

Head east to the so-called Upper Terrace, an elevated area home to the ❻ **spires of the three primary chedi.** The middle structure, Phra Mondop, is used to house Buddhist manuscripts. This area is also home to several of Wat Phra Kaew's noteworthy mythical beings, including beckoning ❼ **kinaree** and several grimacing ❽ **Hanuman.**

Proceed through the western gate to the compound known as the Grand Palace. Few of the buildings here are open to the public. The most noteworthy structure is ❾ **Chakri Mahaprasat.** Built in 1882, the exterior of the hall is a unique blend of Western and traditional Thai architecture.

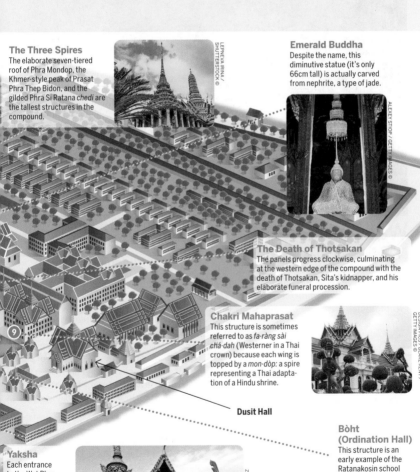

The Three Spires
The elaborate seven-tiered roof of Phra Mondop, the Khmer-style peak of Prasat Phra Thep Bidon, and the gilded Phra Si Ratana *chedi* are the tallest structures in the compound.

LEPNEVA IRINA / SHUTTERSTOCK ©

Emerald Buddha
Despite the name, this diminutive statue (it's only 66cm tall) is actually carved from nephrite, a type of jade.

ALEXEY STIOP / GETTY IMAGES ©

The Death of Thotsakan
The panels progress clockwise, culminating at the western edge of the compound with the death of Thotsakan, Sita's kidnapper, and his elaborate funeral procession.

Chakri Mahaprasat
This structure is sometimes referred to as *fa·ràng sài chá·dah* (Westerner in a Thai crown) because each wing is topped by a *mon·dòp:* a spire representing a Thai adaptation of a Hindu shrine.

DESIGN PICS / BLAKE KENT / GETTY IMAGES ©

Dusit Hall

Bòht (Ordination Hall)
This structure is an early example of the Ratanakosin school of architecture, which combines traditional stylistic holdovers from Ayuthaya along with more modern touches from China and the West.

Yaksha
Each entrance to the Wat Phra Kaew compound is watched over by a pair of vigilant and enormous *yaksha,* ogres or giants from Hindu mythology.

ZZVET / GETTY IMAGES ©

Reclining Buddha

Wat Pho

Of all Bangkok's temples, Wat Pho is arguably the one most worth visiting, for both its remarkable Reclining Buddha image and its sprawling, stupa-studded grounds.

Great For...

☑ Don't Miss

The Reclining Buddha, the granite statues and the massage pavilions within the complex.

Reclining Buddha

In the northwest corner of the site you'll find Wat Pho's main attraction, the enormous Reclining Buddha. The figure (46m long and 15m high) was originally commissioned by Rama III (King Phranangklao; r 1824–51), and illustrates the passing of the Buddha into nirvana. It is made of plaster around a brick core and finished in gold leaf, which gives it a serene luminescence that keeps you looking, and looking again, from different angles.

Phra Ubosot

Phra Ubosot, the compound's main *bòht* is constructed in Ayuthaya style and is strikingly more subdued than Wat Phra Kaew's. A temple has stood on this site since the 16th century, but in 1782 Rama I ordered the original Wat Photharam to

Wat Pho

FOTOS593/SHUTTERSTOCK ©

ℹ️ Need to Know

วัดโพธิ์/วัดพระเชตุพน, Wat Phra Chetuphon; www.watpho.com; Th Sanam Chai; 200B; ☺8.30am-6.30pm; 🚢Tien Pier

✗ Take a Break

Enjoy a Thai-themed cocktail and a spicy drinking snack at Err (p65).

★ Top Tip

Enter via Th Chetuphon or Th Sanam Chai to avoid the touts and tour groups of the main entrance on Th Thai Wang.

be completely rebuilt as part of his new capital. Rama I's remains are interred in the base of the presiding Buddha figure in Phra Ubosot. The images on display in the four *wí·hăhn* (sanctuaries) surrounding Phra Ubosot are worth investigation, as is a low marble wall with 152 bas-reliefs depicting scenes from the *Ramakian*.

Royal Chedi

On the western side of the grounds is a collection of four towering tiled *chedi* (stupa) commemorating the first four Chakri kings. The surrounding wall was built on the orders of Rama IV (King Mongkut; r 1851–68). Among the compound's additional 91 smaller *chedi* are clusters containing the ashes of lesser royal descendants.

Massage Pavilions

A small pavilion west of Phra Ubosot has Unesco-awarded inscriptions detailing the tenets of traditional Thai massage. These and other similar inscriptions led Wat Pho to be regarded as Thailand's first university. Today it maintains that tradition as the national headquarters for the teaching and preservation of traditional Thai medicine, including Thai massage. The famous school has two **massage pavilions** (Map p58; Thai massage per hr from 540B; ☺9am-4pm) located within the temple area.

Wat Pho

A WALK THROUGH THE BIG BUDDHAS OF WAT PHO

The logical starting place is the main *wí·hǎhn* (sanctuary), home to Wat Pho's centrepiece, the immense ❶ **Reclining Buddha**. In addition to its enormous size, note the ❷ **mother-of-pearl inlay** on the soles of the statue's feet. The interior walls of the *wí·hǎhn* are covered with murals that depict previous lives of the Buddha, and along the south side of the structure there are 108 bronze monk bowls; for 20B you can buy 108 coins, each of which is dropped in a bowl for good luck.

Exit the *wí·hǎhn* and head east via the two ❸ **stone giants** who guard the gateway to the rest of the compound. Directly south of these are the four towering ❹ **royal chedi**.

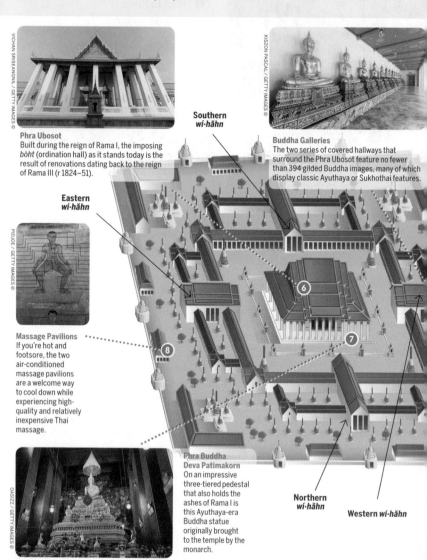

Southern *wí·hǎhn*

VICHAN SRISEANGNIL / GETTY IMAGES ©

KISZON PASCAL / GETTY IMAGES ©

Phra Ubosot
Built during the reign of Rama I, the imposing *bòht* (ordination hall) as it stands today is the result of renovations dating back to the reign of Rama III (r 1824–51).

Buddha Galleries
The two series of covered hallways that surround the Phra Ubosot feature no fewer than 394 gilded Buddha images, many of which display classic Ayuthaya or Sukhothai features.

Eastern *wí·hǎhn*

PIDJOE / GETTY IMAGES ©

Massage Pavilions
If you're hot and footsore, the two air-conditioned massage pavilions are a welcome way to cool down while experiencing high-quality and relatively inexpensive Thai massage.

Phra Buddha Deva Patimakorn
On an impressive three-tiered pedestal that also holds the ashes of Rama I is this Ayuthaya-era Buddha statue originally brought to the temple by the monarch.

Northern *wí·hǎhn*

Western *wí·hǎhn*

OASIZZ / GETTY IMAGES ©

Continue east, passing through two consecutive **⑤ galleries of Buddha statues** linking four *wí·hǎhn*, two of which contain notable Sukhothai-era Buddha statues; these comprise the exterior of **⑥ Phra Ubosot**, the immense ordination hall that is Wat Pho's second-most noteworthy structure. The base of the building is surrounded by bas-relief inscriptions, and inside is the notable Buddha statue, **⑦ Phra Buddha Deva Patimakorn**.

Wat Pho is often referred to as Thailand's first university, a tradition that continues today in an associated traditional Thai medicine school and, at the compound's eastern extent, two **⑧ massage pavilions**.

Interspersed throughout the eastern half of the compound are several additional minor *chedi* and rock gardens.

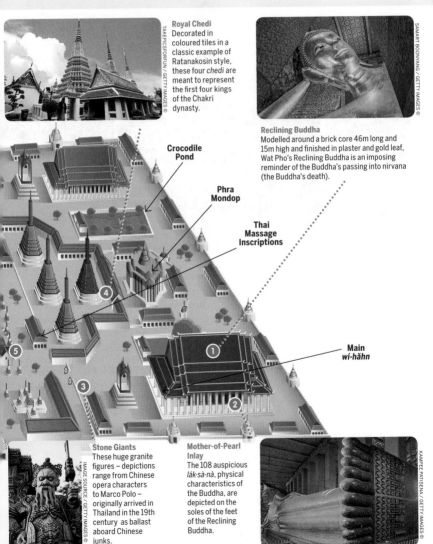

Royal Chedi
Decorated in coloured tiles in a classic example of Ratanakosin style, these four *chedi* are meant to represent the first four kings of the Chakri dynasty.

TAKEPICSFORFUN / GETTY IMAGES ©

SAMART BOONVANG / GETTY IMAGES ©

Reclining Buddha
Modelled around a brick core 46m long and 15m high and finished in plaster and gold leaf, Wat Pho's Reclining Buddha is an imposing reminder of the Buddha's passing into nirvana (the Buddha's death).

Crocodile Pond

Phra Mondop

Thai Massage Inscriptions

Main *wí·hǎhn*

Stone Giants
These huge granite figures – depictions range from Chinese opera characters to Marco Polo – originally arrived in Thailand in the 19th century as ballast aboard Chinese junks.

IMAGE SOURCE / GETTY IMAGES ©

Mother-of-Pearl Inlay
The 108 auspicious *lák·sà·nà*, physical characteristics of the Buddha, are depicted on the soles of the feet of the Reclining Buddha.

KAMPEE PATISENA / GETTY IMAGES ©

Wat Arun

MAKHH/SHUTTERSTOCK ©

Chao Phraya River

The River of Kings is the symbolic lifeblood of the Thai nation. Revered riverside temples stand sentry as boats and barges industriously move cargo and passengers, and cool breezes provide evening refreshment.

Great For...

☑ Don't Miss

Catch the Chao Phraya Express Boat as the sun sets across this throbbing metropolis.

Wat Arun

Claiming a powerful riverside position, **Wat Arun** (วัดอรุณฯ; Map p58; www.watarun.net; off Th Arun Amarin; 50B; ⊙8am-6pm; 🚢river-crossing ferry from Tien Pier, 🚤Chao Phraya Express Boat) marks the rebirth of the Thai nation after the fall of Ayuthaya to the invading Burmese army in the 1700s. The temple's facade is decorated with delicate porcelain mosaics, a common temple adornment from the days when Chinese porcelain was used for ship ballasts.

Thonburi's Canals

Bangkok's past as the Venice of the East lives, bathes and plays along Thonburi's network of canals, including Khlong Bangkok Noi and Khlong Mon. Traditional homes are built on stilts with front doors leading to the water.

Taling Chan Floating Market

PIU.PIU/SHUTTERSTOCK ©

❶ Need to Know

Tour the river and riverside attractions aboard chartered long-tail boats (1½ to two hours, 1300B to 1500B) or the Chao Phraya Express commuter boats.

✕ Take a Break

Make a dinner date with the river at Khinlom Chom Saphan (p68).

★ Top Tip

Women shouldn't sit in the last seats on the commuter boats; these are reserved for monks.

Royal Barges National Museum

Travel by boat used to be a majestic affair. Historic vessels dating back to the Ayuthaya period are on display at the **Royal Barges National Museum** (พิพิธภัณฑสถาน แห่งชาติเรือพระราชพิธี; Map p58; Khlong Bangkok Noi or 80/1 Th Arun Amarin; admission 100B, camera 100B; ⏰9am-5pm; ⛴Phra Pin Klao Bridge Pier). *Suphannahong* (the king's personal barge) is bestowed with a huge swan head carved into the bow. Lesser barges feature bows that are carved into other Hindu-Buddhist mythological shapes such as the *naga* (mythical sea serpent) and *garuda* (Vishnu's bird mount).

Floating Market

The nearly extinct floating markets (*đà·làht nám*) have been rescued by nostalgic Thais and tourists. **Taling Chan Floating Market** (ตลาดน้ำตลิ่งชัน; Map p87; Khlong Bangkok Noi, Thonburi; ⏰7am-4pm Sat & Sun; ⓢWongwian Yai exit 3 & taxi), located along Khlong Bangkok Noi, is a hybrid market with fruit vendors on the road and floating docks serving as informal dining rooms. Meals are prepared aboard tethered canoes.

Ko Kret

An easy rural getaway, Ko Kret is a car-free island and home to the Mon people, known for their hand-thrown terracotta pots. Locals flock to Ko Kret on weekends to snack and shop. Ko Kret is in Nonthaburi, about 15km north of central Bangkok. Take bus 166 from the Victory Monument or a taxi to Pak Kret, before boarding the cross-river ferry (from 5am to 9pm) that leaves from Wat Sanam Neua.

Jim Thompson House

COWARDLION/SHUTTERSTOCK ©

Jim Thompson House

The former home of an American silk entrepreneur is a beautiful repository for Thai art and architecture. On display are museum-quality examples of Thai craftsmanship, Buddhist sculpture and textiles.

Great For...

☑ **Don't Miss**

Wandering the lushly landscaped gardens.

A socialite and former spy, Jim Thompson's life is as intriguing as his belongings. He served briefly in the Office of Strategic Services (the forerunner to the CIA) in Thailand during WWII. Settling in Bangkok after the war, he established a successful Thai silk export business, introducing the textile to international fashion houses. He mysteriously disappeared in 1967 while out for a walk in Malaysia's Cameron Highlands. His disappearance was never explained and some suspect foul play.

Art

A collector with eclectic tastes, Thompson bought art and antiques from travelling merchants and neighbouring countries. He collected objects that were not well known at the time, including from the Dvaravati period.

ⓘ Need to Know

เรือนไทยจิมทอมป์สัน; Map p62; ☎02 218
7368; www.jimthompsonhouse.com; 6 Soi
Kasem San 2; adult/student 200/100B;
🕙9am-6pm, compulsory tours every 30min;
🚤klorng boat Sapan Hua Chang Pier,
🚇National Stadium exit 1

✕ Take a Break

Grab a bite at MBK Food Island (p66).

★ Top Tip

Beware of well-dressed touts outside.

Architecture

Thompson collected six teak houses
from different regions in the country as a
showcase for his art collection. Some of the
houses were brought from Ayuthaya, while
others were transported across the canal
from Baan Khrua. The homes were given a
landscaped jungle garden to further highlight Thailand's natural beauty. The home,
however, is organised like a Western residence with an entrance hall and all rooms
arranged on the same level overlooking the
terrace and the canal.

Baan Khrua

Just across the canal is the silk-weaving
community of **Baan Khrua** (บ้านครัว; Map
p62; 🚤klorng boat Sapan Hua Chang Pier,
🚇National Stadium exit 1). This neighbourhood was settled by Cham Muslims from
Cambodia and Vietnam, who relocated to
Bangkok after fighting on the side of the
Thai king during the wars of the end of
the 18th century. Their silk-weaving skills
attracted the attention of Jim Thompson
in the 1950s and '60s when he hired the
weavers for his burgeoning silk export
business. Since then commercial silk production and many of the original families
have moved elsewhere but two family-run
outfits, **Phamai Baan Krua** (ผ้าไหมบ้านครัว;
Map p62; www.phamaibaankrua.com; Soi 9, Soi
Phaya Nak; 🕙8.30am-5pm; 🚤klorng boat Sapan
Hua Chang Pier, 🚇National Stadium exit 1) and
Aood Bankrua Thai Silk (อู๊ดบ้านครัวไหม
ไทย; Map p62; Soi 9, Soi Phaya Nak; 🕙9am-8pm;
🚤klorng boat Sapan Hua Chang Pier, 🚇National
Stadium exit 1), continue the tradition. Baan
Khrua can be reached by the bridge over
the canal at the end of Soi Kasem San 3.

Chatuchak Weekend Market

Chatuchak Weekend Market

An outdoor market on steroids, Chatuchak Weekend Market sells everything under the sun. Vendors are packed into claustrophobic warrens creating a shopping obstacle course. It is crowded and chaotic but one of a kind.

Great For...

ℹ Need to Know

ตลาดนัดจตุจักร, Talat Nat Jatujak; www.chatuchakmarket.org; 587/10 Th Phahonyothin; ⊘9am-6pm Sat & Sun, 7am-6pm Wed & Thu plants, 6pm-midnight Fri wholesale; ⓂChatuchak Park exit 1, Kamphaeng Phet exits 1 & 2, ⓈMo Chit exit 1

★ **Top Tip**

Come early to beat the crowds and the heat.

A little pre-planning goes a long way. Nancy Chandler's *Map of Bangkok* has a handy schematic map and the clock tower provides an essential landmark.

Antiques, Handicrafts & Souvenirs

Section 1 is the place to go for Buddha statues, old LPs and other random antiques. More secular arts and crafts, such as musical instruments and hill-tribe items, can be found in Sections 25 and 26.

Clothing & Accessories

Clothing dominates much of Chatuchak, starting in Section 8 and continuing through the even-numbered sections to 24. Sections 5 and 6 deal in used clothing for every Thai youth subculture, from punks to cowboys; Soi 7, where it transects Sections 12 and 14, is heavy on hip-hop and skate fashions. Tourist-sized clothes and textiles are found in Sections 8 and 10. Sections 2 and 3, particularly the tree-lined Soi 2 of the former, is the Siam Sq of Chatuchak, and is home to heaps of cool, independent labels. Moving north, Soi 4 in Section 4 has several shops selling locally designed T-shirts. In fact, Chatuchak as a whole is a particularly good place to pick up interesting T-shirts of all types.

Housewares & Decor

The western edge of the market, particularly Sections 8 to 26, specialises in housewares, from cheap plastic buckets to expensive brass woks. This area is a particularly good place to stock up on inexpensive Thai ceramics, ranging from

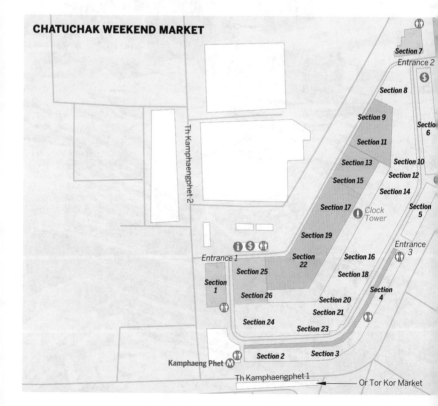

CHATUCHAK WEEKEND MARKET

celadon to the traditional rooster-themed bowls from Lampang. For less utilitarian goods, Section 7 is a virtual open-air gallery with stalls selling Bangkok-themed murals and other unique artwork. Burmese lacquerware can be found in Section 10, while Section 26 has dusty collections of real and reproduction antiques from Thailand and Myanmar.

☑ Don't Miss

More shopping at nearby **JJ Mall** (Th Kamphaeng Phet 2; ◷10am-7pm; ⓂKamphaeng Phet exits 1 & 2, Chatuchak Park exit 1, ⓈMo Chit exit 1).

✕ Take a Break

Sections 6 and 8 have food and drink vendors, a necessary antidote to Chatuchak fatigue.

Ⓢ Mo Chit

ak

Ⓓ Chatuchak Park

	Antiques, Handicrafts & Souvenirs
	Housewares & Decor
	Clothing & Accessories
	Pets
	Plants & Gardening

Plants & Gardening

The interior perimeter of Sections 2 to 4 features a huge variety of potted plants, flowers, herbs and fruits, and the accessories needed to maintain them. That apart, several gardening stalls spring up in the market area on Wednesdays and Thursdays (when the regular stalls stay shut) and trade in potted plants, saplings and gardening equipment through the day. Even if you can't buy potted plants, you can stock up on gardening accessories, as well as seeds for popular regional kitchen herbs such as coriander, Thai basil and chives.

Eating & Drinking

Lots of Thai-style eating and snacking will stave off Chatuchak rage, and numerous food stalls set up shop between Sections 6 and 8. Established standouts include Foontalop, a popular Isan restaurant; Café Ice, a Western-Thai fusion joint that does good, if overpriced, *pàt tai* (fried noodles) and tasty fruit shakes; Toh-Plue, which does all the Thai standards; and Saman Islam, a Thai-Muslim restaurant that serves a tasty chicken *biryani*. Viva 8 features a DJ and, when we stopped by, a chef making huge platters of paella. As evening draws near, down a beer at Viva's, a cafe-bar that features live music.

Walking Tour: Bangkok

Stroll around the former royal district of Ko Ratanakosin. Start early to beat the heat, dress modestly for the temples, and ignore shopping advice from well-dressed touts.

Start Wat Phra Kaew & Grand Palace
Distance 5km
Duration Three hours

5 Wander along Trok Mahathat, the alley leading to the **Amulet Market** (p57).

Thammasat University

Th Phra Chan

Th Maha Rat

5

4

Silpakorn University

Th Na Phra Lan

Th Maha Rat

Take a Break

Savoey (www.savoey.co.th; 1st fl, Maharaj Pier, Th Maha Rat ; mains 125-1800B; ☉10am-10pm) provides an air-conditioned rest stop.

Mae Nam Chao Phraya

4 Explore the classic architecture in the narrow alleyway of **Trok Tha Wang**.

3 Catch the cross-river ferry from Tien Pier to the military-looking **Wat Arun** (p46).

3

N
0   1 km
0   0.5 miles

6 Continue east until you reach **Sanam Luang (Royal Field)**, the location of elaborate, albeit infrequent, royal cremations, and seasonal festivals.

Th Na Phra That

Sanam
Luang

6
FINISH

Th Ratchadamnoen Nai

KO RATANAKOSIN

Th Sanam Chai

Th Kanlaya Namit

1
START

Saranrom
Royal
Garden

Th Thai Wang

Th Charoen Krung

2

Th Chetuphon

Th Maha Rat

Classic Photo: Wat Phra Kaew

1 Start with the architecturally flamboyant and domestically revered **Wat Phra Kaew & Grand Palace** (p38).

2 Head to **Wat Pho** (p42) to see the Reclining Buddha and visit the massage pavilions.

1 DNAI AMPORNDANAI/SHUTTERSTOCK © 2 MQA99/GETTY IMAGES © 3 PHUWADACH PATTANAIMON/SHUTTERSTOCK © 5 PKITTYWONGSAKUL/SHUTTERSTOCK ©

◎ SIGHTS

◎ Ko Ratanakosin & Banglamphu

National Museum · Museum

(พิพิธภัณฑสถานแห่งชาติ; Map p58; 4 Th Na Phra That; 200B; ⏰9am-4pm Wed-Sun; 🚢Chang Pier, Maharaj Pier) Thailand's National Museum is home to an impressive collection of items dating from throughout the country's glittering past. Most of the museum's structures were built in 1782 as the palace of Rama I's viceroy, Prince Wang Na. Rama V turned it into a museum in 1874, and today there are three permanent exhibitions spread out over several buildings. The principal exhibition, **Gallery of Thai History**, is home to some of the country's most beautiful Buddha images and sculptures of Hindu gods.

The **history wing** has made impressive bounds towards contemporary curatorial aesthetics with a succinct chronology of prehistoric, Sukhothai-, Ayuthaya- and Bangkok-era events and figures. Gems include King Ramkhamhaeng's inscribed stone pillar, said to be the oldest record of Thai writing (although this has been contested); King Taksin's throne; the Rama V section; and the screening of a movie about Rama VII, *The Magic Ring*.

The **decorative arts and ethnology exhibit** covers seemingly every possible handicraft including traditional musical instruments, ceramics, clothing and textiles, woodcarving, regalia and weaponry. The **archaeology and art history wing** has exhibits ranging from prehistory to the Bangkok period.

In addition to the main exhibition halls, the **Bhuddhaisawan (Phutthaisawan) Chapel** includes some well-preserved murals and one of the country's most revered Buddha images, Phra Phuttha Sihing. The northern **Chariot Hall** houses the ornate funeral chariots of past royalty.

Museum of Siam · Museum

(สถาบันพิพิธภัณฑ์การเรียนรู้แห่งชาติ; Map p58; Th Maha Rat; 200B; ⏰10am-6pm Tue-Sun; 🚻; 🚢Tien Pier) This fun museum's collection employs a variety of media to explore the origins of the Thai people and their culture.

National Museum

THEBIGLAND/SHUTTERSTOCK ©

Housed in a European-style 19th-century building that was once the Ministry of Commerce, the exhibits are presented in a contemporary, engaging and interactive fashion not typically found in Thailand's museums. They are also refreshingly balanced and entertaining, with galleries dealing with a range of questions about the origins of the nation and its people.

Each room has an informative narrated video started by a sensory detector, keeping waiting to a minimum. An Ayuthaya-era battle game, a room full of traditional Thai toys and a street vending cart where you can be photographed pretending to whip up a pan of *pàt tai* will help keep kids interested for at least an hour, adults for longer. Check out the attached shop for some innovative gift ideas.

Amulet Market   Market

(ตลาดพระเครื่องวัดมหาธาตุ; Map p58; Th Maha Rat; ⏱7am-5pm; 🚢Chang Pier, Maharaj Pier) This arcane and fascinating market claims both the footpaths along Th Maha Rat and Th Phra Chan, as well as a dense network of covered market stalls that runs south from Phra Chan Pier. The easiest entry point is clearly marked 'Trok Maha That'. The trade is based around small talismans highly prized by collectors, monks, taxi drivers and people in dangerous professions.

Potential buyers, often already sporting many amulets, can be seen bargaining and flipping through magazines dedicated to the amulets, some of which command astronomical prices. It's a great place to just wander and watch men (because it's rarely women) looking through magnifying glasses at the tiny amulets, seeking hidden meaning and, if they're lucky, hidden value.

Wat Suthat   Buddhist Temple

(วัดสุทัศน์; Th Bamrung Meuang; 100B; ⏱8.30am-9pm; 🚢klorng boat Phanfa Leelard Pier) Other than being just plain huge and impressive, Wat Suthat also holds the highest royal temple grade. Inside the *wí·hăhn* are intricate *Jataka* (stories of the Buddha) murals and the 8m-high **Phra Si Sakayamuni**, Thailand's

Thanon Khao San

Th Khao San, better known as Khao San Rd, is genuinely unlike anywhere else on earth. It's an international clearing house of people either entering the liberated state of travelling in Southeast Asia or returning to the coddling bonds of 'real' life, all coming together in a neon-lit melting pot in Banglamphu. The anthropological canvas here includes first-time backpackers, hippies, hipsters, nerds, glamazons, package tourists, global nomads, weekend trippers and gap-year explorers. The strip anticipates every traveller need: meals to soothe homesickness, cafes and bars for swapping travel tales, tailors, travel agents, teeth whitening, secondhand books, hair braiding and, of course, the obligatory 'been-there' tattoo studio.

Hawker selling pàt tai

largest surviving Sukhothai-period bronze, cast in the former capital of Sukhothai in the 14th century. The ashes of Rama VIII (King Ananda Mahidol; r 1935–46) are contained in the base of the image.

Golden Mount   Buddhist Temple

(ภูเขาทอง, Phu Khao Thong; off Th Boriphat; summit admission 50B; ⏱7.30am-5.30pm; 🚢klorng boat Phanfa Leelard Pier) Even if you're wát-ed out, you should tackle the brisk ascent to the Golden Mount. Serpentine steps wind through an artificial hill shaded by gnarled trees, some of which are signed in English, and past graves and pictures of wealthy

Ko Ratanakosin, Banglamphu & Chinatown

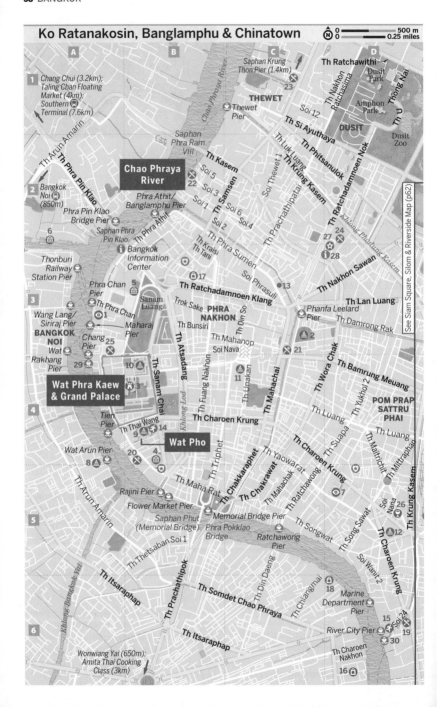

N

0   500 m
0   0.25 miles

Ko Ratanakosin, Banglamphu & Chinatown

benefactors. At the peak, you'll find a breezy 360-degree view of Bangkok's most photogenic side.

The hill was created when a large stupa, under construction by Rama III, collapsed because the soft soil beneath would not support it. The resulting mud-and-brick hill was left to sprout weeds until Rama IV built a small stupa on its crest. Rama V (King Chulalongkorn; r 1868–1910) added to the structure and housed a Buddha relic from India (given to him by the British government) in the stupa. The concrete walls were added during WWII to prevent the hill from eroding.

In November there's a festival in the grounds that includes an enchanting candlelight procession up the Golden Mount.

⊙ **Chinatown**

Wat Traimit (Golden Buddha)   Buddhist Temple

(วัดไตรมิตร, Temple of the Golden Buddha; Map p58; Th Mittaphap Thai-China; 40B; ⊗8am-5pm; 🚢Marine Department Pier, Ⓜ Hua Lamphong

exit 1) The attraction at Wat Traimit is undoubtedly the impressive 3m-tall, 5.5-tonne, **solid-gold Buddha image**, which gleams like, well, gold. Sculpted in the graceful Sukhothai style, the image was 'discovered' some 65 years ago beneath a stucco/plaster exterior, when it fell from a crane while being moved within the temple compound. It's speculated that the covering was added to protect it from marauding Burmese invaders, during a siege either in the late Sukhothai period or the Ayuthaya period.

The temple itself is said to date from the early 13th century. Donations and a constant flow of tourists have proven profitable, and the statue is now housed in an imposing four-storey marble structure called Phra Maha Mandop. The 2nd floor of the building is home to the **Yaowarat Chinatown Heritage Center** (ศูนย์ประวัติศาสตร์เยาวราช; 100B; ⊗8am-5pm Tue-Sun), a small but engaging museum with multimedia exhibits on the history of Bangkok's Chinatown and its residents, while the 3rd floor is home to the **Phra Buddha Maha Suwanna Patima-korn Exhibition** (นิทรรศการพระพุทธมหาสุวรรณปฏิมากร; 100B; ⊙8am-5pm Tue-Sun), which has exhibits on how the statue was made.

Talat Mai   Market
(ตลาดใหม่, New Market; Soi Yaowarat 6/Charoen Krung 16; ⊙6am-6pm; ⚓Ratchawong Pier, Ⓜ Hua Lamphong exit 1 & taxi) With some two centuries of commerce under its belt, New Market is no longer an entirely accurate name for this strip of commerce. Regardless, this is Bangkok's quintessential Chinese market, and the dried goods, seasonings, spices and sauces will be familiar to anyone who's ever spent time in China. Even if you're not interested in food, the hectic atmosphere (watch out for motorcycles squeezing between shoppers) and exotic sights and smells create a somewhat surreal sensory experience for curious wanderers.

While much of the market centres on cooking ingredients, the section north of Th Charoen Krung (equivalent to Soi 21, Th Charoen Krung) is known for selling incense, paper effigies and ceremonial

sweets – the essential elements of a traditional Chinese funeral.

◎ Siam Square, Silom & Riverside

Lumphini Park   Park
(สวนลุมพินี; Map p62; bounded by Th Sarasin, Rama IV, Th Witthayu/Wireless Rd & Th Ratchadamri; ⊙4.30am-9pm; ⚑; Ⓜ Lumphini exit 3, Si Lom exit 1, Ⓢ Sala Daeng exit 3/4, Ratchadamri exit 2) Named after the Buddha's birthplace in Nepal (Lumbini), Lumphini Park is central Bangkok's largest and most popular park. Its 58 hectares are home to an artificial lake surrounded by broad, well-tended lawns, wooded areas, walking paths and startlingly large resident monitor lizards to complement the shuffling citizens. It's the best outdoor escape from Bangkok without actually leaving town. The park was originally a royal reserve but in 1925 Rama VI (King Vajiravudh; r 1910–25) declared it a public space.

One of the best times to visit is early morning (or late evenings), when the air is relatively fresh (or pleasantly balmy)

Lumphini Park

and legions of Thai-Chinese are practising t'ai chi, or doing their best to mimic the aerobics instructor, or doing the half-run half-walk version of jogging that makes a lot of sense in oppressive humidity. There are paddleboats for lovers, playgrounds for the kids and ramshackle weightlifting areas for stringy elderly men.

Cold drinks are available at the entrances and street-food vendors set up tables outside the park's northwest corner from about 5pm. Late at night, it's a slightly dodgy scene with the borders of the park being frequented by streetwalking sex workers, both male and female.

Queen Saovabha
Memorial Institute
Zoo

(สถานเสาวภา, Snake Farm; Map p62; cnr Rama IV & Th Henri Dunant; ☉9.30am-3.30pm Mon-Fri, to 1pm Sat & Sun; 🚻; Ⓜ️Si Lom exit 2, Ⓢ Sala Daeng exit 1/3) FREE Founded in 1923, Asia's oldest snake farm gathers antivenom by milking snakes, injecting it into horses, and then harvesting and purifying the antigens the equines produce. Milking sessions (11am Monday to Friday) and snake-handling performances (2.30pm Monday to Friday and 11am weekends) are held at the outdoor amphitheatre. The latter is quite a spectacle – picture a 3m king cobra furiously lashing at a handler as he deftly demonstrates his handling capabilities. Leave a donation for the snakes at the office.

Bangkok Art &
Culture Centre
Gallery

(BACC; หอศิลปวัฒนธรรมแห่งกรุงเทพมหานคร; www.bacc.or.th; cnr Th Phayathai & Rama I; ☉10am-9pm Tue-Sat; Ⓢ National Stadium exit 3) FREE This large, modern building in the centre of Bangkok has become one of the more significant players in the city's contemporary arts scene. As well as its three floors and 3000 sq metres of gallery space, the centre also contains shops, private galleries, cafes and an art library. Visit the website to see what exhibitions are on when you're in town.

Cooking
Courses

Amita Thai Cooking Class (📞02 466 8966; www.amitathaicooking.com; 162/17 Soi 14, Th Wutthakat, Thonburi; classes 3000B; ☉9.30am-1pm Thu-Tue; 🚤klorng boat from Maharaj Pier) A course at this charming canalside cooking school includes a romp through the kitchen garden and instruction in four dishes.

Cooking with Poo & Friends (📞080 434 8686; www.cookingwithpoo.com; classes 1500B; ☉8.30am-1pm; 🚻) Started by a native of Khlong Toey's slums. Courses, which must be booked in advance, span three dishes and include a visit to Khlong Toey Market.

Bangkok Bold (Map p58; 📞098 829 4310; www.boldbangkok.wordpress.com; 503 Th Phra Sumen; classes 2500-4500B; ☉11am-2pm; 🚤klorng boat Phanfa Leelard Pier) Offers daily courses in three Thai dishes, with lessons conducted in a chic shophouse setting.

DEXTAIRPHOTOGRAPHY/SHUTTERSTOCK ©

⊕ ACTIVITIES
Health Land
Massage

(Map p68; 📞02 261 1110; www.healthlandspa. com; 55/5 Soi 21/Asoke, Th Sukhumvit; Thai massage from 600B; ☉9am-11pm; Ⓜ️Sukhumvit exit 1, Ⓢ Asok exit 5) A winning formula of affordable prices, expert treatments and pleasant facilities has created a small empire of Health Land centres across Bangkok.

KidZania
Play Centre

(Map p62; 📞02 683 1888; www.bangkok.kidza nia.com; 991/1 Rama I, 5th fl, Siam Paragon; adult 640-800B, child 700-1350B; ☉10am-

Siam Square, Silom & Riverside

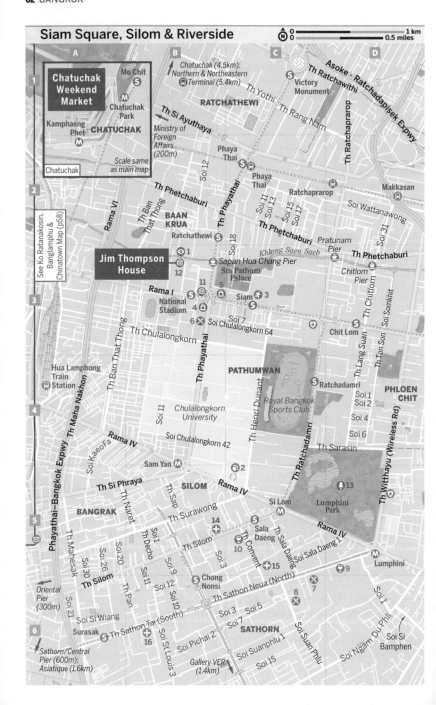

0 1 km
0 0.5 miles

Chatuchak (4.5km);
Northern & Northeastern
Terminal (5.4km);

Asoke - Ratchadapisek Expwy

Mo Chit

**Chatuchak
Weekend
Market**

Chatuchak
Park

Kamphaeng
Phet

CHATUCHAK

Th Si Ayutthaya

Ministry of
Foreign
Affairs
(200m)

RATCHATHEWI

Th Yothi

Th Rang Nam

Victory
Monument

Th Ratchawithi

Th Ratchaprarop

Scale same
as main map

Chatuchak

Rama VI

Th Phetchaburi

Th Ban That Thong

BAAN
KRUA

Ratchathewi

Phaya
Thai

Phaya
Thai

Th Phayathai

Soi 12

Soi 18

Ratchaprarop

Soi 11
Soi 13
Soi 15
Soi 17

Th Phetchaburi

Soi Wattanawong

Makkasan

Soi 31

Th Phetchaburi

See Ko Ratanakosin, Banglamphu & Chinatown Map (p58)

**Jim Thompson
House**

⊙1

⌂12

Rama I

National
Stadium

11

5

⌂

4 ⌂

6 ✖

Sapan Hua Chang Pier

Sra Pathum
Palace

Siam ✪3

Soi 7

Soi Chulalongkorn 64

Khlong Saen Saeb

Pratunam
Pier

Chitlom
Pier

Th Phetchaburi

Th Chitlom

Th Ton Son

Th Somkhit

Th Chulalongkorn

Th Ban That Thong

Th Phayathai

Chit Lom

Th Lang Suan

Hua Lamphong
Train
Station

Th Maha Nakhon

Soi 11

Chulalongkorn
University

Soi Chulalongkorn 42

PATHUMWAN

Th Henri Dunant

Royal Bangkok
Sports Club

Ratchadamri

PHLOEN
CHIT

Soi 1
Soi 2

Soi 4

Soi 6

Th Ratchadamri

Th Witthayu (Wireless Rd)

Rama IV

Soi Kaeofa

Sam Yan

✪2

Th Si Phraya

SILOM

Rama IV

Th Sarasin

Si Lom

Lumphini
Park

13

BANGRAK

Th Naret

Th Sap

Th Surawong

Th Decho

Th Silom

14

✚

10

Sala
Daeng

Th Sala Daeng

Rama IV

Lumphini

Th Mahesak

Soi 30

Soi 26

Soi 20

Th Silom

Soi 1

Soi 9

Soi 3

Th Silom

Th Convent

15 ✚

Soi Sala Daeng 1

✖9

Soi 11

Soi 12

Soi 10

Chong
Nonsi

8

7 ✖

Oriental
Pier
(300m)

Soi 21

Soi Si Wiang

Th Pan

Th Sathon Neua (North)

Soi 3   Soi 5

Soi 1

Surasak

Th Sathon Tai (South)

16

St Louis 3

Soi Pichai 2

Soi 7

SATHORN

Soi Suanphlu 1

Soi Suan Phlu

Soi Ngam Du Phli

Soi Si
Bamphen

Sathorn/Central
Pier (600m);
Asiatique (1.6km)

Gallery VER
(1.4km)

Soi 15

Siam Square, Silom & Riverside

5pm Mon-Fri, 10.30am-8pm Sat & Sun; ⓢSiam exit 3/5) Kids can have their first mock experience of piloting a plane, recording an album, making sushi, repairing a car or even performing root canal surgery at this well-designed and impressive learn-and-play centre.

◎ SHOPPING

MBK Center   Shopping Centre
(Map p62; cnr Rama I & Th Phayathai; ☺10am-10pm; ⓢNational Stadium exit 4) This eight-storey market in a mall has emerged as one of Bangkok's top attractions. On any given weekend half of Bangkok's residents (and most of its tourists) can be found here combing through a seemingly inexhaustible range of small stalls, shops and merchandise.

MBK is Bangkok's cheapest place to buy mobile phones and accessories (4th floor). It's also one of the better places to stock up on camera gear (ground floor and 5th floor), and the expansive food court (6th floor) is one of the best in town.

Siam Discovery   Shopping Centre
(Map p62; www.siamdiscovery.co.th; cnr Rama I & Th Phayathai; ☺10am-10pm; ⓢSiam exit 1) With an open, almost-market-like feel and an impressive variety of unique goods ranging

from housewares to clothing (including lots of items by Thai designers), the fashionable Siam Discovery is hands down the most design-conscious mall in town. Alongside established stores, don't forget to check out the kiosks, which often display some excellent locally designed merchandise.

Asiatique   Market
(Soi 72-76, Th Charoen Krung; ☺4pm-midnight; ⚤Sathorn/Central Pier & mall shuttle boat) Considered one of Bangkok's most popular night markets, Asiatique is housed within restored warehouses next to the Chao Phraya River. Expect clothing, handicrafts, souvenirs, several dining and drinking venues, and a 60m-high Ferris wheel. To get here, take one of the frequent, free shuttle boats from Sathorn (Central) Pier that run from 4pm to 11.30pm.

ICONSIAM   Mall
(www.iconsiam.com; 299 Charoen Nakhon Rd; ☺10am-10pm; ⚤Sathorn/Central Pier & mall shuttle boat) This megamall on the Chao Phraya River has six floors dedicated to luxury shopping encompassing everything from high-end to high street. It also rolls in two food courts to suit all palates and budgets. Adding to its diversity are speciality restaurants, a conjoined multilevel Japanese department store, a much-touted River Museum on the 8th floor, and a 12-theatre cinema.

To get here, hop onto the free shuttle boat that operates from Sathorn/Central Pier during the mall's business hours.

Khao San Market   Gifts & Souvenirs

(Th Khao San; ⏰10am-midnight; 🚤Phra Athit/ Banglamphu Pier) The main guesthouse strip in Banglamphu is a day-and-night shopping bazaar peddling all the backpacker 'essentials': profane T-shirts, bootleg DVDs of popular films and TV series, hemp clothing, knock-off designer wear, selfie sticks, orange juice and – of course – those wooden frogs that croak when you rub a stick down their spine. Cheap shopping thrills couldn't be better defined.

Lhong 1919   Shopping Centre

(248 Th Chiangmai, Khlong San; ⏰10am-10pm; 🚤mall shuttle boat from Sathorn/Central Pier, 🚆Krung Thonburi exit 1/3 & taxi) Spanning a group of restored defunct Chinese warehouses on the western bank of the Chao Phraya River, this concept shopping complex combines the old-world charm of its 19th-century premises with an artsy shopping experience promised by a line of designer stores and boutiques housed within the buildings. A few good restaurants thrown along the property's riverside promenade complete the evening-out experience.

✖ EATING

✖ Ko Ratanakosin & Banglamphu

Thip Samai   Thai $

(Map p58; 313 Th Mahachai; mains 50-250B; ⏰5pm-2am, closed alternate Wed; 🚤klorng boat to Phanfa Leelard Pier) This institution reputedly serves the definitive version of *pàt tai* – period. Every evening, scores of eager diners queue on the pavement for a table (the queue moves fast, so don't walk away in despair if you see 50-odd people ahead of you). Your patience is duly rewarded in the end with a delicious platter of the iconic dish.

Ming Lee   Thai, Chinese $

(Map p58; 28-30 Th Na Phra Lan; mains 70-100B; ⏰11.30am-4pm; 🚤Chang Pier, Maharaj Pier) Hidden in plain sight across from Wat Phra Kaew is this decades-old shophouse

From left: Thip Samai; Jay Fai; Lhong 1919

restaurant. The menu spans Western/
Chinese dishes (eg stewed tongue) and
Thai standards (such as 'beef spicy sal-
ad'). There's no English sign; it's the first
shophouse in the lime-washed commercial
building across the road from Wat Phra
Kaew's northern wall as you walk in from
Chang Pier.

Err
Thai $$

(Map p58; ☏02 622 2292; off Th Maha Rat;
mains 100-350B; ⏰11am-4pm & 5-9pm Tue-Sun;
❄; ⛴Tien Pier) Think of all those different
smoky, spicy, crispy, meaty bites you've
encountered on the street. Now imagine
them assembled in one hip, retro-themed
locale, and coupled with tasty Thai-themed
cocktails and domestic microbrews. If Err
(a Thai colloquialism for agreement) seems
too good to be true, allow us to insist that
it's indeed true.

Jay Fai
Thai $$$

(Raan Jay Fai; Map p58; 327 Th Mahachai; mains
200-1000B; ⏰2pm-2am Tue-Sat; ⛴klorng boat
Phanfa Leelard Pier) Wearing ski goggles
and furiously cooking over a charcoal fire,
septuagenarian Jay Fai is renowned for
serving Bangkok's tastiest (and priciest)
crab omelettes and *pàt kêe mow* (wide rice
noodles fried with seafood and Thai herbs).
The price, however, is justified by copious
fresh seafood, plus a distinct frying style
resulting in an almost oil-free finished dish.
The restaurant is located in a virtually
unmarked shophouse, but walking down
the road, it's quite impossible to miss the
sight of the one-Michelin-star chef cooking
away with superhero fervour in the open
kitchen.

✖ Chinatown

Hua Seng Hong
Chinese $$

(Map p58; 371-373 Th Yaowarat; mains 80-350B;
⏰9am-9pm; ❄; ⛴Ratchawong Pier, Ⓜ Hua
Lamphong exit 1) 🍴 Hua Seng Hong's varied
menu, including braised goose feet, sea-
food hotpot, soft-shell crab in curry pow-
der, crab fried rice and a variety of noodles,
makes it a handy destination for anybody
craving good Chinese food. Order a lavish
dim sum spread for lunch, choosing from
the wide range of dumplings on offer.

Vendor in MBK Food Island

80/20 International $$

(☎099 118 2200; 1052-1054 Th Charoen Krung; mains 250-450B; ☺6-11pm Tue-Sun; ❋☎; ⛴Si Phraya/River City Pier, ⓂHua Lamphong exit 1) Freshly renovated in 2019, 80/20 continues to excel at what it has always done with perfection – blending Thai and Western ingredients and dishes to arrive at something altogether unique. The often savoury-leaning desserts are especially worth the trip. It's a progressive breath of air in an otherwise conservative Chinatown dining scene.

✖ Siam Square, Silom & Riverside

MBK Food Island International $

(Map p62; cnr Rama I & Th Phayathai, 6th fl, MBK Center; mains 50-150B; ☺10am-9pm; ❋✍; ⓈNational Stadium exit 4) With dozens of vendors offering exceedingly cheap and tasty regional Thai, international and even vegetarian dishes, MBK Food Island fiercely clings to its crown as the grandaddy of Bangkok food courts.

Saawaan Thai $$$

(Map p62; ☎02 679 3775; www.saawaan. com; 39/19 Soi Suan Phlu; set menu 2450B; ☺6pm-midnight; ❋; ⓈChong Nonsi exit 5) Two exceptionally talented chefs run what can easily be called one of the finest Thai restaurants in the world. Its name meaning 'heaven', this chic address has a seven-course tasting menu themed on cooking methods, featuring dishes that are inherently Thai but are executed with the fancy, finesse and flair worthy of a Michelin-starred restaurant (which it is).

Expect dishes conjured from sea urchins, wild betel leaves or rice paddy crabs, and wacky desserts (such as bitter chocolate with a hint of the stinky durian fruit). Advance bookings – and smart attire – essential.

nahm Thai $$$

(Map p62; ☎02 625 3333; www.comohotels.com; 27 Th Sathon Tai/South, ground fl, Metropolitan Hotel; set dinner 2500B, mains 300-700B; ☺noon-2pm & 6.30-10pm; ❋; ⓂLumphini exit 2) In the modern-day melee of top-notch restaurants here, nahm may no longer be on top of the competition, but it's still one of Bangkok's nicest Thai restaurants. Helmed by the talented female chef Pim, counted among the city's leading chefs, it consistently serves up creative and classy dishes, such as black grouper in tamarind and ginger broth, or the stir-fried 'angry beef'.

If you're expecting bland, gentrified Thai food meant for foreigners, prepare to be surprised — dishes here are as spicy and pungent as they need to be. Reservations essential.

Thanon Sukhumvit
Soul Food Mahanakorn Thai $$
(Map p68; ☎02 714 7708; www.soulfoodmahan akorn.com; 56/10 Soi 55/Thong Lor, Th Sukhumvit; mains 150-350B; ◷5.30pm-midnight; ❄☕; ⓢThong Lo exit 1/3) This contemporary Thai diner is a favourite go-to place for a comfort meal. The menu – incorporating tasty interpretations of rustic Thai dishes – has not changed over several years, but the top quality of the food hasn't wavered either. The bar serves deliciously boozy, Thai-influenced drinks, as well as cocktails and a few craft beers. Reservations recommended.

Sri Trat Thai $$
(Map p68; ☎02 088 0968; www.facebook.com/sritrat; 90 Soi 33, Th Sukhumvit; mains 200-450B; ◷noon-11pm Wed-Mon; ❄; ⓢPhrom Phong exit 5) This fabulous restaurant specialises in the unique fare of Thailand's eastern provinces, Trat and Chanthaburi. What this means is lots of rich, slightly sweet, herbal flavours, fresh seafood and dishes you won't find anywhere else in town. That's also because it's a family operation, and most of the recipes originate in the family kitchen.

Thewet & Dusit
Likhit Kai Yang Thai $
(off Th Ratchadamnoen Nok; mains 50-200B; ◷10am-8.30pm; ❄☎; ⓔThewet Pier, ⓢPhaya Thai exit 3 & taxi) Located just behind Rajadamnern Stadium (p69), this decades-old restaurant is where locals come for a

Dinner Cruises

A dinner cruise along the Chao Phraya River is touted as an iconic Bangkok experience, and several companies cater to this. Yet it's worth mentioning that, in general, the vibe can be somewhat cheesy, with loud live entertainment and mammoth boats so brightly lit inside you hardly know you're on the water. The food, typically served as a buffet, usually ranges from mediocre to forgettable. But the atmosphere of the river at night, bordered by illuminated temples and skyscrapers, and the cool breeze chasing the heat away, is usually enough to trump all of this.

A good one-stop centre for all your dinner cruise needs is the **River City Boat Tour Check-In Center** (Map p58; www.rivercity.co.th; ground fl, River City; ◷10am-10pm; ⓔSi Phraya/River City Pier), where tickets can be purchased for several cruise offerings. For something slightly more upmarket, consider **Manohra Cruises** (☎02 476 0022; www.manohracruises.com; Anantara Riverside Resort & Spa; cruises 2300B; ⓔSathorn/Central Pier & hotel shuttle boat) or **Supanniga Cruise** (Map p58; ☎02 714 7608; www.supannigacruise.com; River City; cocktail/dinner cruises 1250/3250B; ◷cruises 4.45-5.45pm & 6.15-8.30pm; ⓔSi Phraya/River City Pier), which are both more upscale and private (and pricier) compared to the other cruises – they also get positive feedback for their food.

Chao Phraya River dinner cruise
ARJAN ARD STUDIO/SHUTTERSTOCK ©

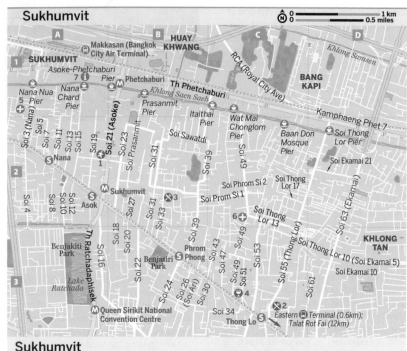

Sukhumvit

northeastern-style meal before a Thai boxing match. The friendly English-speaking owner will steer you through the ordering, but don't miss the deliciously herbal, eponymous 'charcoal roasted chicken'. There's no English-language sign; look for the bright pink shopfront and an overwhelming grilled garlic smell emanating from inside.

Krua Apsorn   Thai $$

(www.kruaapsorn.com; 503-505 Th Samsen; mains 150-400B; ⊙10.30am-8pm Mon-Sat; ❄️🛜; 🚤Thewet Pier) This is the original branch of this homey, award-winning and royally patronised restaurant. Expect a clientele of large families and middle-aged ladies, and

a cuisine revolving around full-flavoured, largely seafood- and vegetable-heavy central and southern Thai dishes. The crab meat in curry powder remains a public favourite, as does the green curry with fishballs. No reservations. Last orders at 7.30pm.

Khinlom Chom Saphan   Thai $$

(Map p58; ☏02 628 8382; www.khinlomchom saphan.com; 11/6 Soi 3, Th Samsen; mains 150-450B; ⊙11.30am-midnight; 🚤Thewet Pier) Patrons come to this open-air restaurant for the combination of riverfront views and tasty, seafood-based eats. It also doubles quite neatly as a pub. It's popular with locals, especially large families, so be sure to call ahead to book a riverfront table.

DRINKING & NIGHTLIFE

Moon Bar
Bar

(Vertigo; Map p62; www.banyantree.com; 21/100 Th Sathon Tai/South, 61st fl, Banyan Tree Hotel; ⏰5pm-1am; Ⓜ Lumphini exit 2) An alarmingly short barrier at this rooftop bar is all that separates patrons from the street, 61 floors down. Moon Bar claims to be among the highest alfresco bars in the world. It's a great place to meet, greet and generally hang out with friends old and new. The hoppy house beer, called Banyan Tree IPA, is a must-try.

WTF
Bar

(Map p68; www.wtfbangkok.com; 7 Soi 51, Th Sukhumvit; ⏰6pm-1am Tue-Sun; 🌐; Ⓢ Thong Lo exit 3) This cool and friendly neighbourhood bar also packs in a gallery space. Arty locals and resident foreigners come for the old-school cocktails, live music, DJ events, poetry readings, art exhibitions and tasty bar snacks. And we, like them, give WTF our top rating. The negroni here comes with a dash of spice, and is easily the best in Bangkok.

Tep Bar
Bar

(Map p58; 69-71 Soi Nana; ⏰7pm-midnight Tue-Sun; Ⓜ Hua Lamphong exit 1) No one ever expects to find a bar this sophisticated – yet this fun – in Chinatown. Tep hits the spot with Thai-tinged, contemporary interiors and boozy signature cocktails; it also stocks a few delicious local rice-based brews. There are tasty drinking snacks on the side, and raucous live folk music performances from Thursday to Sunday.

Vesper
Bar

(www.vesperbar.co; 10/15 Th Convent; ⏰5.30pm-1am; 🌐; Ⓜ Si Lom exit 2, Ⓢ Sala Daeng exit 2) This deceptively classic-feeling bar-restaurant is one of the most popular watering holes in Bangkok's business district. As the name unequivocally suggests, the emphasis here is on cocktails, including several revived classics and mixed drinks

mellowed by ageing for six weeks in white-oak barrels. Call ahead for a table if you're planning to visit over the weekend.

ENTERTAINMENT

Rajadamnern Stadium
Spectator Sport

(สนามมวยราชดำเนิน; Map p58; www.rajad amnern.com; off Th Ratchadamnoen Nok; tickets 3rd class/2nd class/club class/ringside 1000/1500/1800/2000B; ⏰matches 6.30pm Mon, Wed & Thu, 3pm & 6.30pm Sun; 🚤Thewet Pier, Ⓢ Phaya Thai exit 3 & taxi) Rajadamnern Stadium is Bangkok's oldest and most venerable venue for moo·ay tai (Thai boxing; also spelt muay Thai). Be sure to buy tickets from the official ticket counter or online, not from touts and scalpers who hang around outside the entrance.

Major Cineplex
Cinema

(☎02 129 4635; www.majorcineplex.com; Th Rama I, 5th fl, Siam Paragon; Ⓢ Siam exits 3/5) In addition to housing Thailand's largest IMAX screen, Major Cineplex' options include the Blue Ribbon Screen, a cinema with a maximum of 72 seats, where you're plied with pillows, blankets, complimentary snacks and drinks and a 15-minute massage; and Enigma, where, in addition to a sofa-like love seat designed for couples, you'll be served cocktails and food.

ℹ INFORMATION

Bangkok Information Center (Map p58; ☎02 225 7612-4; 17/1 Th Phra Athit; ⏰8am-7pm Mon-Fri, 9am-5pm Sat & Sun; 🚤Phra Athit Pier) City-specific tourism office providing maps, brochures and directions. Seldom-staffed kiosks and booths are found around town; look for the green-on-white symbol of a mahout on an elephant.

ℹ GETTING THERE & AWAY

AIR

Suvarnabhumi International Airport (BKK; p306), located 30km east of Bangkok, has international and domestic services to countries around the world.

ARTAPARTMENT/SHUTTERSTOCK ©

Chinatown (p59)

Don Mueang International Airport (DMK; p306), 25km north of Bangkok, handles international (Terminal 1) and domestic (Terminal 2) operations.

TRAIN

Hua Lamphong (☎call centre 1690; www. railway.co.th; off Rama IV; Ⓜ Hua Lamphong exit 2), Bangkok's main train station, has connections across Thailand. To check timetables, destinations and fares, visit the official website of the State Railway of Thailand (www.railway. co.th/main/index_en.html).

❶ GETTING AROUND

Bangkok may seem chaotic and impenetrable at first, but its transport system is gradually improving. No matter how much you ride the BTS, MRT or ferry systems, you'll almost certainly find yourself stuck in road traffic at some point during your visit.

- **BTS** The elevated Skytrain runs from 6am to midnight. Tickets 16B to 52B.

- **MRT** The Metro runs from 6am to midnight. Tickets 16B to 42B.

- **Taxi** Outside of rush hours, Bangkok taxis are a great bargain. Flagfall 35B.

- **Chao Phraya Express Boat** Runs 6am to 8pm, charging a flat 15B. A tourist boat ride costs 60B.

- **Klorng boat** Bangkok's canal boats run from 5.30am to 8pm most days. Tickets 9B to 19B.

- **Bus** Cheap but a slow and confusing way to get around Bangkok. Tickets 10B to 25B.

- **Tûk-tûk** Available across town. Rides cost 50B to 200B (bargain hard). Beware of drivers who offer 'special day' 20B rides (usually a prelude to a scam).

Where to Stay

Because Bangkok is a sprawling metropolis, it is best to pick your neighbourhood and then shop within your budget range. Otherwise pick a spot on the BTS for easy neighbourhood-hopping.

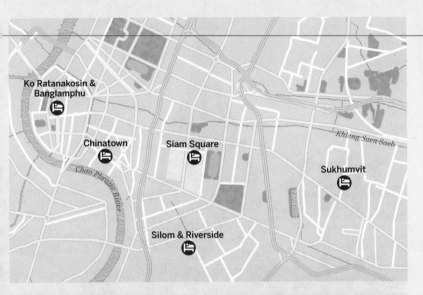

Neighbourhood	Atmosphere
Ko Ratanakosin & Banglamphu	Close to sights, old-school Bangkok feel; lots of touts and tourists.
Chinatown	Interesting budget and midrange options, easy access to sights and train station; noisy and hectic.
Siam Square	Convenient access to shopping and BTS; overly commercial; lack of dining and entertainment.
Silom & Riverside	Upscale accommodation, convenient to transport, lots of dining and nightlife; noisy and hectic.
Sukhumvit	Sophisticated hotels, easy access to BTS and MRT; international dining and bars; touristy, sexpat hang-outs.

KANCHANABURI

Kanchanaburi at a Glance...

Kanchanaburi has an array of lush riverside resorts, and is a gateway to pristine national parks. During WWII, Japanese forces used Allied prisoners of war and Asian labourers to build a rail route between Thailand and Myanmar. The harrowing story became famous after the publication of Pierre Boulle's book The Bridge Over the River Kwai. War cemeteries, museums and the chance to ride a section of the so-called 'Death Railway' serve as reminders of this time.

Two Days in Kanchanaburi

Travel back in time at Kanchanaburi's **Death Railway Bridge** (p76) and its various WWII museums. On day two, take the train to **Hellfire Pass Memorial** (p79). Take in the river with dinner at **Blue Rice** (p82).

Four Days in Kanchanaburi

With more time, you can explore the sights outside of the city centre such as the cave temples of **Wat Tham Khao Pun** (p80) and **Wat Tham Seua** (p80), or the waterfalls at **Erawan National Park** (p80). Take a cooking course at **Apple & Noi Thai Cooking** (p80).

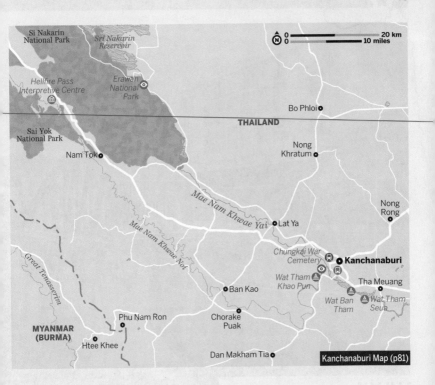

Kanchanaburi Map (p81)

Arriving in Kanchanaburi

Bus station Located in the centre of town.

Train station Located in the middle of town.

Where to Stay

Accommodation is plentiful along Th Mae Nam Khwae. Budget and mid-range digs sit alongside the river. A few high-end resorts exist in town but the best are in the surrounding countryside (where it's a good idea to have a car). Many Bangkokians arrive for the weekend; reserve well ahead.

Death Railway Bridge

LITTLEKOP/GETTY IMAGES ©

WWII History

Beyond its hectic modern centre and river views, Kanchanaburi has a dark history, paid tribute to at excellent memorials and museums.

Great For...

☑ Don't Miss

For Thais, a photo on the so-called Death Railway Bridge is a must-do.

Death Railway Bridge

This 300m-long **bridge** (สะพานข้ามแม่น้ำ แคว, Bridge Over the River Kwai; ⊘24hr) [FREE], made famous by the movie *The Bridge on the River Kwai* (1957), is heavy with the history of the Thailand–Burma Railway, the construction of which cost thousands of imprisoned labourers their lives.

The 425km railway was built by hard labour during the WWII Japanese occupation of Thailand (1941–45). Japan's Allied prisoners of war (POWs) and conscripted workers were armed only with basic tools and dynamite as they toiled. Well over 12,000 POWs and as many as 90,000 recruited and forced labourers (many of them Malay, Chinese and Indian) died due to disease, poor hygiene, lack of medical equipment and brutal treatment by camp guards. Many Thais risked their lives to aid

ℹ Need to Know

Kanchanaburi's famous bridge was destroyed in 1945; only the outer curved spans are original.

✕ Take a Break

Don't leave Kanchanaburi without dining at one of its charming riverside restaurants.

★ Top Tip

You should call it the River Khwae (sounds like 'square' without the 's' and 'r'), not Kwai (sounds like 'why').

the bridge, so the site can have a jarring, funfair-like atmosphere; come early or late to avoid the scrum.

If you'd like to see more, it's possible to take a train to Hellfire Pass Memorial (p79), a museum and memorial trail that pay tribute to those who died building the railway.

Thailand–Burma Railway Centre

This excellent **museum** (ศูนย์รถไฟไทย-พม่า; 📞034 512721; www.tbrconline.com; 73 Th Jaokannun; adult/child 150/70B; ⏰9am-5pm) balances statistics and historical context with personal accounts of the conditions endured by POWs and other imprisoned labourers forced to build the railway. Kanchanaburi's role in WWII is thoroughly explained, but most of the museum traces the journey of railway workers from transport in cramped boxcars to disease-ridden labour camps in the jungle, as well as survivors' fates after the war. Allow time for the poignant video with testimony from both POWs and Japanese soldiers.

Galleries upstairs display wartime artefacts, and there's a 3m-deep diorama showing how Hellfire Pass got its name. Allow at least an hour for your visit.

Kanchanaburi War Cemetery

Immaculately maintained by the Commonwealth War Graves Commission, this **cemetery** (สุสานทหารพันธมิตรดอนรัก, Allied War Cemetery; Th Saengchuto; ⏰daylight hours)

the POWs, most of whom were Australian, American, British and Dutch, but they could offer only limited help.

The objective of the railway was to secure an overland supply route to Burma (Myanmar) for the Japanese conquest of other Asian countries. Because of the mountainous landscape, 688 bridges were built along the route. Most were wooden trestle bridges, such as those at the oft-visited Tham Krasae. The Death Railway Bridge was the only steel bridge built in Thailand; Burma had seven. It was bombed several times by the Allies, but the POWs were sent to rebuild it. When the war's tide turned, the railway became an escape path for Japanese troops.

You're free to roam over the bridge; stand in a safety point if a train appears. Food and souvenir hawkers surround

FREE is right in town. Of the 6982 soldiers buried here, nearly half were British; the rest came mainly from Australia and the Netherlands. As you stand at the cemetery entrance, the entire right-hand side contains British victims, the front-left area contains Australian graves, the rear left honours Dutch and unknown soldiers, and those who were cremated lie at the furthest spot to the left.

Chung Kai War Cemetery

Smaller and less visited than the war cemetery in town (but just as well maintained), **Chung Kai War Cemetery** (สุสานทหาร พันธมิตรช่องไก่; Rte 3228; ⊘daylight hours; P) **FREE** honours 1400 Commonwealth and 300 Dutch soldiers. This was the site of one of the biggest Allied POW camps. Prisoners built their own hospital and church close by

and the majority of those buried here died at the hospital.

The cemetery is near the river, 2.5km southwest of the Wat Neua bridge. It's easily reached by bicycle.

JEATH War Museum

This small, open-air **museum** (พิพิธภัณฑ์ สงคราม; cnr Th Wisuttharangsi & Th Pak Phraek; 50B; ⊘8am-5pm) displays correspondence and artwork from former POWs involved in the building of the Death Railway. Their harsh living conditions are evident in the many photos on display alongside personal effects and war relics, including an unexploded Allied bomb dropped to destroy the bridge. One of the three galleries is built from bamboo in the style of the shelters (called *attap*) the POWs lived in; another has a 10-minute video presentation.

Kanchanaburi War Cemetery (p77)

JEATH is an acronym of the warring countries involved in the railway: Japan, England, Australia/USA, Thailand and the Netherlands. The museum is run by the monks of the adjacent **Wat Chai-chumphon** (วัดไชยชุมพลชนะ; Th Pak Phraek; ⊙daylight hours; P) FREE.

WWII Museum

Though well-intentioned, the dispersed (and usually context-free) displays at this **museum** (พิพิธภัณฑ์สงครามโลกครั้งที่สอง; Art Gallery & War Museum; Th Mae Nam Khwae; 40B; ⊙8am-6pm) have limited educational value. Still, you'll see trains, Japanese motorcycles, anchors and old helmets, plus the museum has a great view of the bridge (the tower in the northwest corner has the best viewpoint).

THALERNGSAK MONGKOLSIN/SHUTTERSTOCK ©

Life-sized statues of soldiers recreate the harsh conditions endured by prisoners building the Thailand–Burma Railway, though the overall impression is of a museum of horrors rather than a historical display.

Hellfire Pass Memorial

A poignant **museum and memorial trail** (พิพิธภัณฑ์ช่องเขาขาด; ☎034 919605; Hwy 323; ⊙museum 9am-4pm, grounds daylight hours; P) FREE pay tribute to those who died building the Thailand–Burma Railway. Begin at the museum and ask for the free audio guide, which provides historical detail and fascinating first-person accounts from survivors. Then descend behind the museum to a trail following the original rail bed. The infamous cutting known as Hellfire Pass was the largest along the railway's length and the most deadly for the labourers forced to construct it.

The museum is 80km northwest of Kanchanaburi on Hwy 323 and can be reached by Sangkhlaburi and Thong Pha Phum buses (45B to 65B, two hours, every 30 minutes). The last bus back to Kanchanaburi passes here around 5pm.

◎ SIGHTS

Heritage Walking Street Area
(ถนนปากแพรก; Th Pakprak) A stroll along this city centre street offers a glimpse of a bygone Kanchanaburi. Many buildings date to the 1920s and '30s and their Sino-Portuguese, Thai, Vietnamese and Chinese styles have been preserved; faded yellow signs reveal the history, architecture and present owners of about 20 of them. WWII buffs should include this on their pilgrimage because some of the structures are connected to the construction of the Death Railway.

Erawan National Park National Park
(อุทยานแห่งชาติเอราวัณ; ☎034 574222; adult/child 300/200B, car/motorbike 30/20B; ⊙park gate 8am-4pm; waterfall levels 1-3 8.30am-5pm, levels 4-7 8.30am-4pm; P) Splashing in emerald-green pools under **Erawan Falls** is the highlight of this very popular 550-sq-km park. Seven tiers of waterfall tumble through the forest, and bathing beneath these crystalline cascades is equally popular with locals and visitors. Reaching the first three tiers is easy; beyond here, walking shoes and some endurance are needed to complete the steep 2km hike but it's undoubtedly worth it.

Wat Tham Khao Pun Buddhist Temple
(วัดถ้ำเขาปูน; Rte 3228; 30B; ⊙6am-6pm; P) The nearest cave temple to Kanchanaburi town is a fun labyrinth of illuminated passageways. The marked trail is a bit of a squeeze in some places (and can be slippery), but ducking beneath limestone protrusions to discover these subterranean shrines is a special experience. It's a stop on the standard boat tour, but still rarely busy, so it might just be you and some fluttering bats. The temple is 4km southwest of town, beyond Chungkai War Cemetery (p78).

Wat Tham Seua Buddhist Temple
(วัดถ้ำเสือ; Tambon Muang Chum; ⊙daylight hours; P) FREE The centrepiece of this hilltop temple is a striking 18m-high Buddha covered in golden mosaic. One of the merit-making ceremonies for devotees is to place coins in small trays on a conveyor belt that drops donations into a central bowl with a resounding clang. It's fun to ride the steep cable car (20B per person) to the top of the temple, but you can also climb the stairs.

Wat Ban Tham Buddhist Temple
(วัดบ้านถ้ำ; Tambon Khao Noi; ⊙temple daylight hours, stairway 8am-5pm; P) FREE In the countryside around Kanchanaburi, cave temples are almost as common as convenience stores are inside the city, but this is one of the most interesting, in part because you walk up steps and into a dragon's mouth to reach the large main cave.

Wat Ban Tham is 10km southeast of town (4km before Wat Tham Seua) on the south bank of the river .

Sri Nakarin Dam National Park National Park
(อุทยานแห่งชาติเขื่อนศรีนครินทร์; Khuean Srinagarindra National Park; ☎082 290 2466; adult/child 300/200B, car/motorbike 30/20B; ⊙waterfall trail 6.30am-5pm; P) Visitors to Erawan National Park often find themselves wondering what the waterfall would be like without the hordes. The answer is **Namtok Huay Mae Khamin**.

Despite access on a good sealed road just 45km northwest of Erawan, this stunning cerulean waterfall at the heart of the 1532-sq-km park is usually peaceful and private. While Erawan might win a straight-out beauty contest, when you add atmosphere to the equation, Huay Mae Khamin unquestionably comes out on top.

✪ ACTIVITIES

Apple & Noi Thai Cooking Cooking
(☎062 324 5879, 034 512017; www.applenoi kanchanaburi.com/apple-noi-cooking; Blue Rice restaurant, Mu 4, Ban Tamakham; per person 1950B; ⊙Tue, Wed, Fri & Sat) If you don't know your *sôm·đam* from your *đôm yam*, Khun Noi can assist. Her very popular one-day course has an emphasis on local recipes and seasonal produce, beginning at the

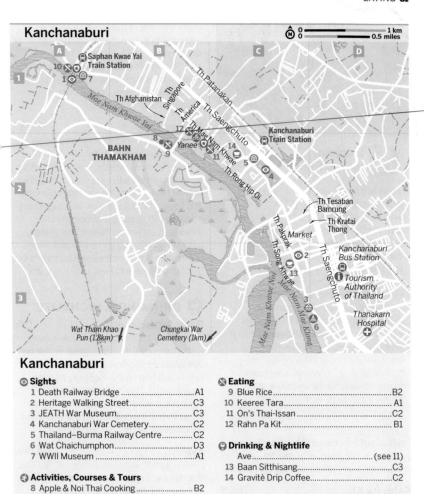

Kanchanaburi

local market and ending, four dishes later, at the dining table. Book well ahead.

SUP Hire Thailand   Water Sports
(📱090 975 9718; www.supkanchanaburi.com; Hwy 323, Tambon Kaeng Sian; ⊗hours vary) This responsible outfit has standup paddle-boarding (SUP) lessons, trips and rentals with good instructors and equipment. Short and long trips are available, and for the uninitiated there's a two-hour 'taster session' (per person 450B, private lesson 800B) on a beautiful stretch of Mae Nam

Kwae Yai just outside town. Also offers guided bike rides with high-quality hybrids, which can be combined with paddling.

⊗ EATING

On's Thai-Issan   Vegetarian $
(📱087 364 2264; www.onsthaiissan.com; Th Mae Nam Khwae; mains 70-80B; ⊗10am-9pm; ❄📷) Not your typical Thai-style vegan ('jay') restaurant, On and her daughter make their Thai (and a few Isan) dishes not only

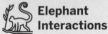

Elephant Interactions

Tours around Kanchanaburi often include elephant trekking. For the wellbeing of the elephants, we strongly advise against this, no matter how good the tour company tells you the elephant camp is. If you do join one of those tours, you always have the option to walk alongside the elephant or go down to the river to bathe it instead of riding it.

The only place in Kanchanaburi that we can recommend for elephant interaction is **Elephant Haven** (☏053 272855; www.elephantnaturepark.org; Sai Yok; 1-day adult/child 2500/1250B, 2 days 5800/2900B) 🖉, a genuine sanctuary where the elephants' welfare is the primary concern.

XIEBIYUN/SHUTTERSTOCK ©

healthy, but fully flavourful and as spicy as you want it. Big plates of ginger tofu and massaman curry are served with brown rice.

Rahn Pa Kit Thai $

(Th Mae Nam Khwae; mains 30-80B; ⊗7am-8pm) To escape the mediocrity of guesthouse Thai food, look for the yellow 'Thai Food' sign at the entrance to Blue Star Guesthouse. The pair of women running this tiny street-side shop do all the standard foods exceptionally well.

Blue Rice Thai $$

(www.applenoikanchanaburi.com/our-apples-restaurants; Mu 4, Ban Tamakham; mains from 135B; ⊗10.30am-3pm, 5-10pm, evenings only in low season; P🖉) Masterful spice blends, a creative menu and peaceful river views

make this one of the most irresistible restaurants in Kanchanaburi. The signature massaman curry is perfectly balanced, and Chef Apple puts a gourmet spin on Thai classics such as *yam sôm oh* (pomelo salad) and chicken-coconut soup with banana plant.

Keeree Tara Thai $$

(☏034 513855; www.facebook.com/keereeTara; 431/1 Th Mae Nam Khwae; mains 75-450B; ⊗10am-midnight, last order 9.30pm; P) This refined riverside eatery is ever so slightly upriver from the melee around the bridge, and has a pretty good view of it, especially from the raft seating that opens in the evening. It serves upmarket Thai dishes, both standards and some regionally popular dishes like giant freshwater prawns in tamarind sauce and river snail red curry.

🍷 DRINKING & NIGHTLIFE

Baan Sitthisang Cafe

(Th Pakprak; ⊗8am-6pm; 🛜) Hunker down with a bit of history – plus great coffee and dainty baked goods – in this primrose-yellow building on the Heritage Walking Street (p80). This house (built in 1920) has been owned by the same family for generations; it's one of the best-preserved buildings along this storied street.

Ave Craft Beer

(Th Mae Nam Khwae; ⊗noon-midnight; 🛜) This little spot with great people-watching seats eschews the cheap-drinks, loud-music standard for this area and instead provides dozens of craft beers, most from Thai brewers. Staff greet you with a smile and there's a food menu with all the Thai standards.

Gravitè Drip Coffee Coffee

(www.facebook.com/gravitedrip; 3/17 Th Mae Nam Khwae; ⊗9am-7pm; 🛜) Serious about coffee, this small, quiet, owner-managed shop just up from the Thailand-Burma Railway Center brings in new beans from new places (Laos to Guatemala) every week. It has good brownies too.

Namtok Huay Mae Khamin (p80)

INFORMATION

Tourism Authority of Thailand (TAT; ☎034 511200; tatkan@tat.or.th; Th Saengchuto; ⊗8.30am-4.30pm) Provides free maps of the town and province, along with friendly advice.

GETTING THERE & AWAY

BUS & MINIVAN

Kanchanaburi's **bus station** (☎034 515907; Th Lak Meuang) is in the centre of town by the clock tower. Minivans to Bangkok depart until around 7pm.

TRAIN

Trains to Bangkok's Thonburi station (three hours) depart **Kanchanaburi** (☎034 511285; Th Saengchuto) at 7.19am and 2.48pm.

GETTING AROUND

Bikes (per day 50B) and motorcycles (200B) can be hired at dozens of guesthouses and shops along Th Mae Nam Khwae.

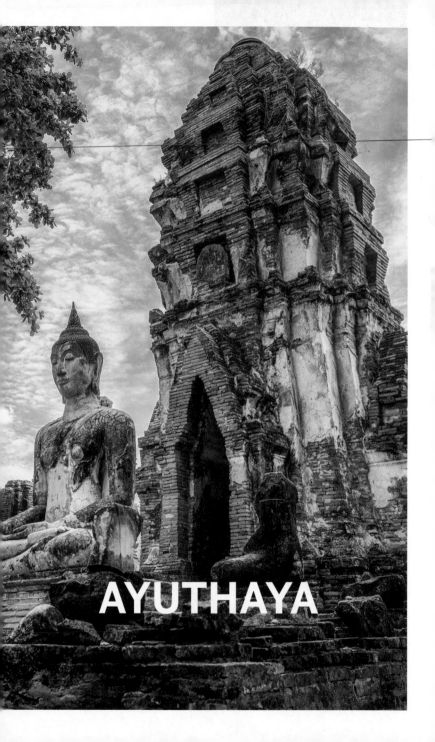

AYUTHAYA

Ayuthaya at a Glance...

Ayuthaya reigned as the Siamese capital for more than 400 years. The island city was regaled at the time for its golden temples and architectural splendour. After frequent wars with the Burmese, the city eventually fell in 1767. War, looting and gravity took their toll on Ayuthaya's once great temples and today the remaining ruins are designated as a Unesco World Heritage Site.

Two Days in Ayuthaya

Visit the interactive exhibition at the **Ayutthaya Tourist Center** (p90). Cycle around **Ayuthaya Historical Park** (p88), stopping at **Lung Lek** (p95) for the best noodles in town. The following day, wander among the ruins then finish your visit with a feast at **Pae Krung Gao** (p95).

Four Days in Ayuthaya

On your third day head out of the city to visit **Bang Pa In Palace** (p92). On the way back, drop by at **Wat Phanan Choeng** (p90) to ensure good luck by releasing fish back into the river and return to the island in time to visit the nostalgic **Million Toy Museum** (p94).

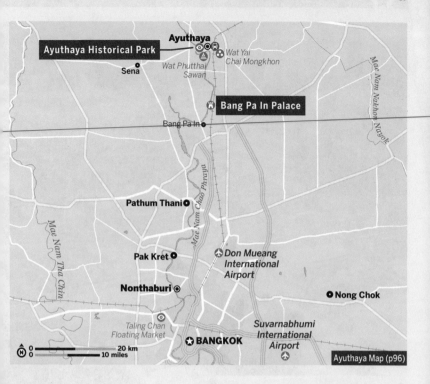

Ayuthaya

Ayuthaya Historical Park

Sena

Wat Phutthai
Sawan

Wat Yai
Chai Mongkhon

Bang Pa In Palace

Bang Pa In

Mae Nam Nakhon Nayok

Pathum Thani

Mae Nam Chao Phraya

Mae Nam Tha Chin

Pak Kret

Nonthaburi

Taling Chan
Floating Market

Don Mueang
International
Airport

Nong Chok

BANGKOK

Suvarnabhumi
International
Airport

0   20 km
0   10 miles

Ayuthaya Map (p96)

Arriving in Ayuthaya

Bus stop Most visitors arrive via bus or minivan from Bangkok. The bus stop is in the centre of town.

Train station Services from Bangkok connect to the train station across the river from the centre of town.

Where to Stay

The primary guesthouse zone is on the island around Soi 2, Th Naresuan – a convenient location with easy access to the historical park, restaurants, markets and transport – and there are also budget options close to the train station. Midrange and top-end hotels typically congregate around the river.

Wat Mahathat

THANAN KONGDOUNG/SHUTTERSTOCK ©

Ayuthaya Historical Park

At its zenith, Ayuthaya was home to over 400 temples. Today dozens of them have been partially restored, leaving the naked stupas, roofless chapels and headless Buddha images to evocatively tell the kingdom's tale of war with enemies and time.

Great For...

☑ **Don't Miss**

At night the ruins are dramatically lit, providing great photo ops.

The historical park is divided into two parts: sites on the island and sites off the island. You can visit the island on a bicycle but will need a motorcycle or chartered transport to go beyond.

Wat Phra Si Sanphet

One of the holiest sites, **Wat Phra Si Sanphet** (วัดพระศรีสรรเพชญ์; 50B, 6-temple ticket 220B; ◷8am-6.30pm) has three magnificent stupas and served as the model for Bangkok's Wat Phra Kaew. The temple was built in the late 15th century inside the palace grounds. It was Ayuthaya's largest temple and once contained a 16m-high standing Buddha (Phra Si Sanphet) covered with approximately 143kg of gold.

❶ Need to Know

ศูนย์ท่องเที่ยวอยุธยา; ☎035 246076; Th Si Sanphet; ⊘8.30am-4.30pm; P FREE

✗ Take a Break

Lung Lek (p95) serves old-fashioned style 'boat noodles', a recipe from the days of floating markets.

★ Top Tip

The temple ruins are revered symbols of royalty and religion; dress modestly and behave respectfully.

Wihan Phra Mongkhon Bophit

Next to Wat Phra Si Sanphet, this **sanctuary hall** (วิหารพระมงคลบพิตร; ⊘8am-5pm) FREE houses one of Thailand's largest bronze Buddha images. The 12.5m-high figure (17m with the base) was badly damaged by a lightning-induced fire around 1700, and again when the Burmese sacked the city. The Buddha and the building were repaired in the 20th century.

Wat Mahathat

Founded in 1374, during the reign of King Borom Rachathirat I, **Wat Mahathat** (วัดมหาธาตุ; Th Chee Kun; 50B, 6-temple ticket 220B; ⊘8am-6.30pm; P) was the seat of the supreme patriarch and the kingdom's most important temple. Today the ruins are best known for a curious interplay between

nature and art: a sandstone Buddha head is held above the ground by entangled bodhi tree roots.

Wat Ratchaburana

The *prang* (Khmer-style stupa) in this **temple** (วัดราชบูรณะ; Th Chee Kun; 50B, 6-temple ticket 220B; ⊘8am-6.30pm; P) is one of the best extant versions in the city, with detailed carvings of lotus and mythical creatures. You can climb inside it to visit the brightly painted crypt, if you aren't afraid of heights, small spaces or bats. The temple was founded in 1424 by King Borom Rachathirat II on the cremation site for his two brothers who died fighting each other for the throne.

Wat Chai Wattanaram

This is the most impressive off-island **site** (วัดไชยวัฒนาราม; Rte 3469; 50B, 6-temple ticket 220B; ⊘8am-6.30pm; P) thanks to its 35m-high central *prang* and overall good condition. It was built by King Prasat Thong beginning in 1630 (and taking around 20 years) to honour his mother.

Wat Phanan Choeng

A bevy of popular merit-making ceremonies makes this **temple** (วัดพนัญเชิง; Rte 3477; 20B; ⊙daylight hours, buildings 8am-5pm; P) a bustling place on weekends. The temple marks the historic location of a Chinese community who settled in Ayuthaya in the 14th century and is often associated with Zheng He (known as Sam Po Khong in Thailand), the Chinese emissary who explored Southeast Asia in the 15th century.

The signature attraction is the 19m-high Phra Phanan Choeng Buddha, which was created in 1324 and sits inside a sanctuary surrounded by 84,000 small Buddha images. The Chinese shrine facing the river is especially colourful.

Wat Na Phra Men

This **temple** (วัดหน้าพระเมรุ; Tambon Lum Phli; 20B; ⊙daylight hours, buildings 8am-5pm; P) was one of the few to escape the wrath of Myanmar's invading army in 1767 since it served as their main base. The *bòht* (ordination hall) is massive, larger than most modern ones, and the very holy main Buddha image wears royal attire, which was very common in the late Ayuthaya era. Despite what the English sign inside says, it's made of bronze, not gold.

Ayutthaya Tourist Center

This multipurpose building houses the tourist information centre on the ground floor. But the reason for a visit is the excellent upstairs museum, which puts Ayuthaya history into context with displays about the

Wat Phanan Choeng Buddha

temples and daily life. Also upstairs is the tiny but interesting Ayutthaya National Art Museum.

Ayuthaya Historical Study Centre

This modern **museum** (ศูนย์ศึกษาประวัติศาสตร์ อยุธยา; ☎035 245123; Th Rotchana; adult/child 100/50B; ⏰9am-4.30pm Mon-Fri, to 5pm Sat & Sun; P) funded by Japan features exhibitions on the lives of traditional villagers and the foreign communities during the Ayuthaya kingdom, plus a few dioramas of the city's former glories.

★ **Did You Know?**

Bicycles are a great way of getting around more rural, less-trafficked corners of Thailand such as Ayuthaya Historical Park.

IMPAKPRO/GETTY IMAGES ©

Chao Sam Phraya National Museum

The largest **museum** (พิพิธภัณฑสถานแห่งชาติ เจ้าสามพระยา; ☎035 241587; Th Rotchana; 150B; ⏰9am-4pm Tue-Sun; P) in the city displays many of the treasures unearthed during excavations of the ruins, including the golden treasures found in the crypts of Wat Mahathat and Wat Ratchaburana. Despite these treasures, the building lacks English signs and is a bit outdated.

Wat Yai Chai Mongkhon

King U Thong founded this **temple** (วัดใหญ่ ชัยมงคล; Rte 3477; 20B; ⏰6am-6pm; P) in 1357 to house monks returning from ordination in Sri Lanka. In 1592 King Naresuan built its fantastic bell-shaped *chedi* (stupa) after a victory over the Burmese. The landscaped gardens make this one of Ayuthaya's most photogenic ruins. There's a 7m-long reclining Buddha near the entrance and the local belief is that if you can get a coin to stick to the Buddha's feet, good luck will come your way.

Phu Khao Thong

Phu Khao Thong (เจดีย์ภูเขาทอง; off Hwy 309; ⏰daylight hours; climbing stupa 8am-6pm; P) FREE is a huge white stupa built by the Burmese to commemorate their occupation of Ayuthaya in 1569. The larger-than-life statue is a memorial to the all-conquering Thai King Naresuan, who ousted the Burmese. Surrounding him are reliefs of his heroic exploits, including wrestling a crocodile, and dozens of statues of fighting cockerels.

✕ **Take a Break**

Drop in to **Bang Ian Night Market** (Th Bang Ian; mains from 30B; ⏰4.30-10pm; P) if you're visiting the park in the late afternoon to evening.

Phra Thinang Wehut Chamrun

HAMDAN YOSHIDA/SHUTTERSTOCK ©

Bang Pa In Palace

A former summer palace for the Thai kings, Bang Pa In is an eclectic assortment of architectural styles ranging from Chinese throne rooms to Gothic churches.

Bang Pa In was built beside the Chao Phraya River in the 17th century during the reign of King Prasat Thong. The palace was abandoned by the Ayuthaya kings and later revived by the Bangkok kings. The European formal gardens, statuary and residences were introduced by Rama V (King Chulalongkorn; r 1868–1910), an enthusiast of Western art and architecture. At the time of use, the property was divided into two sectors by an artificial lake – the outer was for ceremonial use and the inner for the royal family only.

Saphakhan Ratchaprayun

A striking European-style residence originally built for the king's brothers now houses a small history museum about the palace.

Great For...

☑ **Don't Miss**

Feeding fish that live in the palace lake is an act of merit-making for Thai Buddhists.

❶ Need to Know

พระราชวังบางปะอิน; 100B; ⊘8am-5pm, last entrance 4pm; Ⓟ

✕ Take a Break

Drinks and snacks are served at the small cafe by the Therawat Khanlai Gate.

★ Top Tip

This is royal property so dress modestly.

Phra Thinang Warophat Phiman

Built in 1876, this neoclassical building served as King Rama V's residence and throne hall. Historical paintings decorate the chambers. During the current royal family's rare visits, they stay here.

Aisawan Thiphya-At

A classical Thai-style pavilion is scenically situated in the palace lake. Inside is a statue of King Rama V.

Phra Thinang Wehut Chamrun

A grand Chinese-style palace, known as the 'Residence of Heavenly Light', was a gift to King Rama V from the Chinese Chamber of Commerce in 1889. On the ground floor is an ornate throne room.

Ho Withun Thatsana

'Sages' Lookout' is a brightly painted lookout tower. Climb the spiral staircase to reach King Rama V's favourite viewpoint.

Wat Niwet Thamaprawat

King Rama V loved mixing Thai and Western styles. This Buddhist temple located on an island across the river is a Gothic-church replica complete with stained-glass windows, a steeple and statues of knights in shining armour standing among Buddha images. Take the cable car across the river.

Memorial to Queen Sunanda

A marble obelisk remembers King Rama V's consort Queen Sunanda, who drowned on the boat journey to the palace. Thai law forbade courtiers from touching the queen, so nobody dared jump in to save her. The law was later changed.

◎ SIGHTS

Baan Hollanda   Museum
(บ้านฮอลันดา; ☏035 245683; www.baanhollanda.
org; Soi Khan Rua, Mu 4; ☺9am-4pm Wed-Sun;
ℙ) FREE The little 'Dutch House' features a
concise but informative exhibition of Dutch
history in Thailand from 1604, when the
Dutch East India Company (VOC) arrived
in Ayuthaya, up to the present. Out the
back are the excavated foundations of the
second trading office, built in 1634. Just as
interesting is the adjacent boatyard with
many classic wooden craft.

Million Toy Museum   Museum
(พิพิธภัณฑ์ล้านของเล่นเกริกยุ้นพันธ์; ☏081 890
5782; www.milliontoymuseum.com; Th U Thong;
50B; ☺9.30am-4pm Tue-Fri, 9.30am-5pm Sat &
Sun; ℙ) Thousands of toys from across the
decades are amassed in this jam-packed
private museum. Rare porcelain elephants,
wooden Japanese *kokeshi* dolls, wind-
up robots and retro racing cars are filed
alongside mass-produced Santa Claus
and Shrek figurines. It isn't just toys; the
impressively large and diverse collection
includes the likes of ancient pottery and old
coconut scrapers.

☉ TOURS

Most guesthouses can arrange tours,
though you'll usually get more options and
flexibility by talking to a travel agency such
as **Tour With Thai** (☏035 958226, 086 982
6265; http://tour-with-thai.business.site; Naresuan Soi 2; ☺8.30am-7pm).

    The most promoted trip is a two-hour
afternoon boat tour (200B per person)
circling the island and stopping at Wat
Phanan Choeng (p90), **Wat Phutthai
Sawan** (วัดพุทไธศวรรย์; Rte 3469; ☺temple daylight hours, prang 8am-5.30pm; ℙ) FREE and
Wat Chai Wattanaram (p89); it's a convenient, though rushed, way to see these three
great off-island sites. You can also hire a
boat on your own starting around 700B per
hour: head up to the northeast corner of
the island and look for one of the 'boat trip'
signs near the **immigration office** (☏035
328411; Th U Thong; ☺8.30am-noon & 1-4.30pm
Mon-Fri).

Wat Putthai Sawan

PAKIN SONGMOR/GETTY IMAGES ©

Ayutthaya Boat & Travel (🖄081 733 5687; www.ayutthaya-boat.com; cnr Th Chee Kun & Th Rotchana; ⊙9am-5pm Mon-Sat) offers lunch and dinner cruises on a teak rice barge, as well as longer cycling and boat tours, some with homestay accommodation.

Recreational Ayutthaya Biking (🖄021 072500; www.ayutthayabiking.com; 141 Mu 1, Rte 3053; ⊙8am-5pm) also has a few bike tours.

For a personal guided visit to the ruins, **Mr Pok** (🖄081 253 9037; per hr 300B) comes highly recommended.

🍴 EATING

Sainam Pomphet   Thai $
(Th U Thong; mains 70-400B; ⊙10am-10pm; 🅿️📶) Spider crab – either steamed or fried with curry powder (*ƀoo pàt pŏng gà·rèe*) – is the house speciality at this small riverside restaurant. Fish 'steamboat' dishes (in a simmering tureen) are also immensely popular. Those who aren't fans of seafood can tuck into a range of other Thai fare: try pineapple spare ribs or the spicy frog salad.

Lung Lek   Noodles $
(Th Chee Kun; mains 20-50B; ⊙8am-4pm Mon-Fri, 8am-4.30pm Sat & Sun) This locally adored hole-in-the-wall serves some of the most notable *gŏo·ay dĕe·o reu·a* (boat noodles: a pork noodle soup with a complex soy and pig's blood broth) in town. Uncle Lek has been filling bowls for more than four decades.

> *This hole-in-the-wall serves some of the most notable boat noodles in town.*

Pae Krung Gao   Thai $$
(Th U Thong; mains 60-700B; ⊙10am-8pm; 🅿️📶) A wonderfully cluttered restaurant serving top-notch Thai food. Seemingly half the punters are here for grilled river prawns, though the *gaang kĕe·o wăhn* (green curry) and lotus stem salad are just as tasty.

🍽️ Dessert Doyenne

A half-Japanese, half-Portuguese chef from Ayutthaya is fondly remembered for her contribution to tooth-tingling Thai desserts. Madame Maria Guyomar de Pinha (aka Thao Thong Kip Ma) rose to local fame as the head of the royal dessert kitchen in King Narai's court thanks to her Portuguese-inspired sweets recipes, which she disseminated among ladies of the court. Guyomar is credited with creating numerous classic desserts, so spare a thought for this 17th-century chef when you nibble on *thong yot* (syrupy golden droplets of flour and egg) and *fŏy torng* (sweet threads made from duck egg yolk).

Thong yot
YODASWAJ/GETTY IMAGES ©

🍸 DRINKING & NIGHTLIFE

Most travellers limit their nightlife to the pack of street-side bars on Naresuan Soi 2 (Soi Farang). For a wholly Thai night out, there's the oddly named **Coffee House** (Th Naresuan; ⊙6pm-midnight; 📶) bar with live music nightly.

ℹ️ INFORMATION

Tourism Authority of Thailand (TAT; 🖄035 246076; tatyutya@tat.or.th; Th Si Sanphet; ⊙8.30am-4.30pm) Has an information counter with maps and good advice at the Ayutthaya Tourist Center (p90).

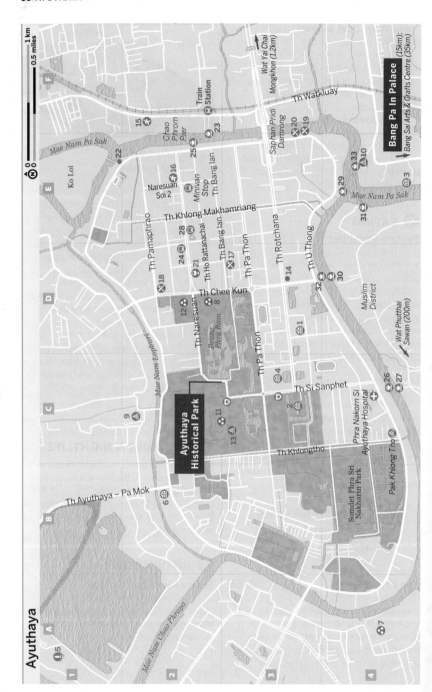

Ayuthaya

Ayuthaya Historical Park

Bang Pa In Palace

Bang Sai Arts & Crafts Centre (35km); (15km);

1 km
0.5 miles

Mae Nam Pa Sak

Ko Loi

Train Station

Chao Phrom Pier

Th Watkluay

Wat Yai Chai Mongkhon (1.2km)

Saphan Pridi Damrong

Th Bang Ian

Th Bang Ian

Naresuan Soi 2

Minivan Stop

Th Khlong Makhamriang

Mae Nam Pa Sak

Th Pamaphrao

Th Ho Rattanachai

Th Bang Ian

Th Pa Thon

Th Rotchana

Th U Thong

Muslim District

Wat Phutthai Sawan (200m)

Th Chee Kun

Th Naresuan

Beung Phra Ram

Th Pa Thon

Th Si Sanphet

Phra Nakorn Si Ayuthaya Hospital

Th Khlongtho

Pak Khlong Tho

Somdet Phra Sri Nakharin Park

Th Ayuthaya – Pa Mok

Mae Nam Lophuri

Mae Nam Chao Phraya

Ayuthaya

GETTING THERE & AWAY

BUS & MINIVAN

Ayuthaya has two minivan stations. The one just south of the backpacker strip serves Suphanburi (transfer here for Kanchanaburi). A block and a half west is the **station** (Th Naresuan) for all destinations in Bangkok.

TRAIN

Ayuthaya's **train station** (☏035 241521; Rte 3053) is located just across the river from the island, and has connections to Bangkok.

GETTING AROUND

Cycling is the ideal way to see the city. Many guesthouses hire bicycles (per day 50B) and motorcycles (200B).

KO PHA-NGAN

Ko Pha-Ngan at a Glance...

Hippie-at-heart Ko Pha-Ngan has become so synonymous with the wild Full Moon Party that the rest of the island gets eclipsed. After the werewolves of the Full Moon leave, Ko Pha-Ngan returns to its hammock hanging. The island is carved into sandy coves with offshore reefs and a thick jungle crown in the interior. The gentle coral-fringed bays make it perfect for families. And a diversity of accommodation makes this tropical island a well-rounded holiday companion.

Two Days in Ko Pha-Ngan

Savour the great diversity of the ocean's blues and greens from one of Ko Pha-Ngan's many beautiful beaches. Go for a beach snorkel or a **dive** (p104). Check out the shacks on **Hat Rin** (p106) for a sundowner, or more.

Four Days in Ko Pha-Ngan

Start day three exploring the eastern side of the island for castaway fantasies. Then do a full-day **dive tour** (p105) of the gulf's famous dive spots. Lounge around and do nothing on your last day.

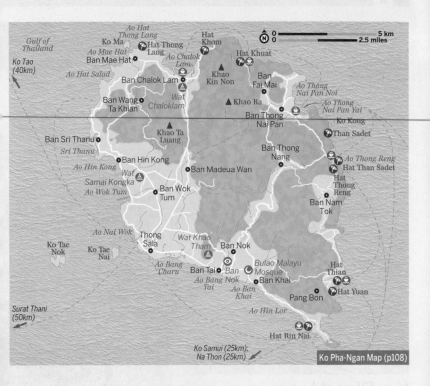

Ko Pha-Ngan Map (p108)

Arriving on Ko Pha-Ngan

Thong Sala Boats connect Ko Pha-Ngan with Ko Samui, Chumphon and Surat Thani. *Sŏrng·tăa·ou* (pick-up minibuses) meet passengers for hotel transfers.

Where to Stay

Hat Rin is the busy party beach with a huge selection of accommodation. The west coast has a diverse range of places. There's limited lodging at the north coast beaches. The east coast beaches have minimal development; transport is limited.

Full Moon Party, Hat Rin (p106)

4FR/GETTY IMAGES ©

Ko Pha-Ngan Party Scene

Throngs of whisky bucket–sippers and fire twirlers gather on Hat Rin (Sunrise Beach) for the infamous Full Moon Parties. Full-on debauchery rages until the sun replaces the moon in the sky.

No one knows exactly when or how these crazy parties started – most believe they began in 1988, but accounts of the first party range from an Australian backpacker's going-away bash to a group of hippies escaping Samui's 'electric parties'. None of that is relevant now: today thousands of bodies converge for an epic trance-a-thon. Crowds can swell to an outrageous 40,000 partiers during high season, while the low season still sees a respectable 5000 pilgrims.

Great For...

☑ Don't Miss

Transforming yourself into a walking day-glo stick – it's *the* thing to do.

Party Tips

If your trip doesn't coincide with a full moon, fear not. Enterprising locals have organised a slew of other reasons to get sloshed. There are Black Moon Parties, Half Moon Parties and Moon-set Parties to name a few.

❶ Need to Know

Party dates vary so check ahead. A 100B fee is charged for post-party clean-up.

✕ Take a Break

Chicken corner is a street stall area to load up on pre-party stamina.

★ Top Tip

Make accommodation reservations in advance as lodging fills up fast.

○ Don't sample the drug buffet, nor swim in the ocean under the influence of alcohol.

○ Stay in a group of people, especially if you're a woman, and especially when returning home at the end of the evening.

Party Places

The Full Moon Party unfolds on the soft sands of Hat Rin (p106). Surrounding bars also have their own periphery parties.

Rock (p111) Superb views of the party from the elevated terrace on the far southern side of the beach are matched by the best cocktails in town.

Sunrise (☏077 375144; www.sunrisephang an.com; 136 Mu 6, Hat Rin; ⊗8am-2am; 🛜) Claims a spot on the sand where trance beats shake the graffitied walls, with drum 'n' bass coming into its own at Full Moon.

Tommy (☏077 375215; www.tommyresort. net; Hat Rin; ⊗8am-2am; 🛜) Hat Rin's largest venue with blaring Full Moon trance music. Drinks are dispensed from a large ark-like bar.

Some critics claim the party scene has lost its carefree flavour after increasing violence (assaults, thefts and injuries). Precautions should be followed to ensure personal and property safety.

○ Secure all valuables, especially when staying in budget bungalows.

○ Wear protective shoes during the sandy celebration, unless you want a tetanus shot.

BILL45/SHUTTERSTOCK ©

Diving in Ko Pha-Ngan

Everyone will tell you to go to nearby Ko Tao to learn to dive. But Ko Pha-Ngan enjoys a much quieter, more laid-back diving scene focused on fun diving.

Great For...

☑ Don't Miss

Hit the near-shore snorkelling spots early in the morning.

Dive Sites

A major perk of diving from Ko Pha-Ngan is the proximity to Sail Rock (Hin Bai) and Chumphon Pinnacle, the premier dive sites in the Gulf of Thailand.

Chumphon Pinnacle (36m maximum depth) has a colourful assortment of sea anemones along the four interconnected pinnacles. The site plays host to schools of giant trevally, tuna and large grey reef sharks. Whale sharks are known to pop up once in a while.

Sail Rock (40m maximum depth) features a massive rock chimney with a vertical swim-through, and large pelagics like barracuda and kingfish. This is one of the top spots in Southeast Asia to see whale sharks; in the past few years they have been seen year-round, so there's no

ⓘ Need to Know

Three dives cost 4000B and include a full lunch. Two dives cost around 2500B to 3000B.

✖ Take a Break

Grab a sundowner at Amsterdam (p111) with tourists and locals alike.

★ Top Tip

Ko Pha-Ngan is now competitive with Ko Tao for Open Water certification prices.

clear season. An abundance of corals and large tropical fish can be seen at depths of 10m to 30m.

Like the other islands in the Samui Archipelago, Pha-Ngan has several small reefs dispersed around the island. The clear favourite is **Ko Ma**, a small island in the northwest connected to Ko Pha-Ngan by a sandbar. There are also some rock reefs of interest on the eastern side of the island. Hiking and snorkelling day trips to Ang Thong Marine National Park (p160) generally depart from Ko Samui, but recently tour operators are starting to shuttle tourists from Ko Pha-Ngan as well. Ask at your accommodation for details about boat trips as companies often come and go due to unstable petrol prices.

Dive Companies

Group sizes tend to be smaller on Ko Pha-Ngan than on Ko Tao since the island has fewer divers in general. But be warned that demand goes up before and after the Full Moon Parties because there are more tourists.

The most popular trips departing from Ko Pha-Ngan are three-site day trips, stopping at Chumphon Pinnacle, Sail Rock and one of the other premier sites in the area.

Lotus Diving (☏077 374142; www.lotus diving.com; Ban Chalok Lam; ☺7am-6pm) and **Haad Yao Divers** (☏086 279 3085; www. haadyaodivers.com; Hat Yao Rd; snorkelling/ diving from 1200/1400B) are the main operators on the island with a solid reputation.

⊙ SIGHTS

Hat Than Sadet   Beach

(หาดธารเสด็จ; **P**) This lovely beach of leaning coconut trees has the royal seal of approval, literally. Behind the collection of shacks that line the sands and azure waters are large boulders (signposted) where three Thai kings, Rama V, VII and IX, carved their insignia, affirming their love for this dreamy cove at the mouth of Than Sadet. Consider walking the wooden bridge at the south end beyond the stilted shacks to **Hat Thong Reng** (หาดท้องเหรง). The swimming is good at both beaches.

Hat Rin   Beach

(หาดริ้น, Hat Rin Nok; Baan Haad Rin) Also known as Sunrise Beach, aka Full Moon Party Beach, this is actually one of Ko Pha-Ngan's cleanest and most pleasant beaches, because much of the money from the monthly partying admission charge goes towards the (necessary) cleaning of the sands. Its reputation as party central keeps many people away, so it can be surprisingly crowd-free at times.

Hat Khuat   Beach

(หาดขวด, Bottle Beach) This lovely, secluded cove has a stretch of soft sand overlooked by green hills and is a superb choice for a relaxing day of swimming and snorkelling. With no proper roads leading to the beach, there is a genuine sense of exclusivity. Most people arrive by water taxi from **Hat Khom** (หาดขอม; **P**) or they pack a bottle of water and don a pair of walking shoes and a sun hat to do the Chalok Lam to Bottle Beach Trek through the jungle.

Yang Na Yai Tree   Landmark

(ต้นยางนาใหญ่; Ban Nok) Thrusting 54m into the heavens near Wat Pho, Ko Pha-Ngan's tallest Yang Na Yai (*dipterocarpus alatus*; ยางนา), said to be over 400 years old, is an astonishing sight in the heart of **Ban Nok** (ตำบล บ้านนอก) village. The aesthetically pleasing giant of nature is deemed by Ban Nok villagers to be sacred, which is why there are several small shrines near the foot of the tree and it is often garlanded with colourful ribbons.

Hat Rin

✈ ACTIVITIES

Chalok Lam to Bottle Beach Trek — Hiking

This moderate 5km trek through light jungle over the ridge of the northern headland is highly rewarding. As you follow the blue and yellow arrows beneath the jungle's canopy, the trail periodically opens up to stunning vistas over the gulf – the finest are from atop a sheer rock face looking out over jungle-covered hills sliding into the azure waters. The route is tricky in parts, so solid footwear is a must, as too is water and a sun hat.

Samma Karuna — Yoga

(☏077 377049; www.sammakaruna.org; Hin Kong Rd; ⊗8am-8pm) Samma Karuna has a serene, landscaped garden, with the sound of running water gently cascading down to a private beach where several open spaces such as the Buddha Hall and Osho Hall sit facing the blue sea. This is where daily sessions (some free) of yoga, tantra, tai chi, reiki and a host of other alternative wellbeing practices take place.

The Phangan Thai Cooking Class — Cooking

(☏087 278 8898; 101/13 Mu 1, Thong Sala; classes 1200-1500B) Located along the main road in Thong Sala, this cooking school is run by the very likeable and laid-back Chef Oy. You start your session by heading to the market and picking out the raw, local ingredients before a seriously fun class learning to master Thai culinary skills in a very homely kitchen.

Wat Pho Sauna — Health & Fitness

(ซาวน่าวัดโพธิ์; Wat Pho, Ban Tai; sauna 110B; ⊗noon-7pm) With a dazzling gateway and extensive temple grounds, Wat Pho, near Ban Nok village, is noted for its herbal saunas (110B), which use a traditional local method that involves heating lemongrass and tamarind leaves on a log fire and is said to have health benefits. It also offers Thai massages for 300B.

Temples & Mosques

Ko Pha-Ngan's temples provide a tranquil sanctuary and an opportunity for reflection. One of the most intriguing shrines on the island is the colourful **Guan Yin Temple** (ศาลเจ้าแม่กวนอิม เกาะพะงัน; 40B; ⊗6am-6pm; P), dedicated to the Buddhist goddess of compassion. It's also worth checking out **Wat Khao Tham** (วัดเขาถ้ำ; ☏087 974 9465; www. kowthamcenter.org; ⊗daylight hours) **FREE**, which sits among the dense foliage of trees high on a tranquil hill near Ban Tai. Other temples on the island include the oldest, **Wat Phu Khao Noi** (วัดภูเขาน้อย; Ban Wok Tum; ⊗daylight hours; P) **FREE**, Wat Pho, which offers herbal saunas, quiet **Wat Chaloklam** (วัดโฉลกหลำ; Chalok Lam; ⊗daylight hrs; P) **FREE**, and the intriguing **Wat Samai Kongka** (วัด สมัยคงคา; ☏094 603 3651; ⊗daylight hours; P) **FREE**, home to clay model scenes of the Buddhist vision of hell. The reportedly 100-year-old **Bulao Malayu Mosque** (มัสยิดบูเลามะลายู; Taladkao Rd, Ban Khai; ⊗daylight hours), resembling a wooden Chinese house on stilts, is an example of indigenous Thai Islam. Check out the colourful prayer rugs and ornate wooden pulpit inside.

When visiting temples or mosques, remember to dress modestly with nontransparent clothes reaching below the knees and elbows, and remove your shoes on entry. For mosques, women should also wear a headscarf.

Wat Samai Kongka
PHOTOALIONA/GETTY IMAGES ©

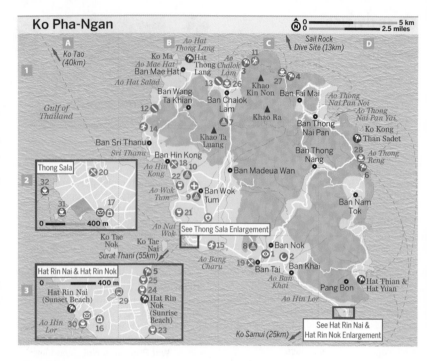

Ko Pha-Ngan

See Thong Sala Enlargement

See Hat Rin Nai & Hat Rin Nok Enlargement

🔒 SHOPPING

Thong Sala Walking Street   Market

(Taladkao Rd, Thong Sala; ⊙4-10pm Sat) When Thong Sala's Walking Street market comes around every Saturday from 4pm, the terrific choice of street food, souvenirs, gifts, handicrafts and clothes, and the swarm of tourists, make this one of the most buzzing spots in town. Even if you're not shopping, pop along to hang out, snack on a tasty satay or simply absorb the atmosphere.

Fusion Fashion   Clothing

(☎089 868 1938; 94/17, Hat Rin; ⊙11am-10pm) The Swedish owner of this cute little boutique imports all her wares from India, making this one of the few shops worth stopping in along the main drag in Hat Rin. Opened in 2003, the colourful store is littered with attractive and eye-catching lines of boho and colourful gossamer blouses, skirts, hot pants, bags and jewellery.

🍴 EATING

Chaloklum Food Market   Market $

(Chaloklum Pier; dishes 40B; ⊙4-11pm Sun) Ko Pha-Ngan's most authentically local food market is in the far north, where every Sunday in front of the village **pier** (Chalok Lam), a series of red tables and chairs appear beside a stage where locals play live. This is surrounded by stalls serving food you will not see in any of the 'night markets' elsewhere. Be brave and get stuck in. Try the deep-fried fish patty, or the fish in spiced coconut – grilled inside a banana leaf tube.

Chana Masala   Indian $

(☎081 622 3374; Ban Hin Kong; mains 120B; ⊙11am-10pm Sun-Fri; ❄🎵🍴) Classic Bollywood hits play and wooden faces of Hindu gods Kali and Baghvan peer down at you inside this spacious venue decked out in Indian teak serving the best Indian vegetarian food on the island. If they haven't sold out,

Ko Pha-Ngan

Sights
1 Ban Nok C3
2 Bulao Malayu Mosque C3
3 Hat Khom C1
4 Hat Khuat C1
5 Hat Rin B3
Hat Than Sadet .... (see 6)
6 Hat Thong Reng D2
7 Shrine of Our Lady Guanyin Phangan C1
8 Wat Khao Tham C3
9 Wat Phu Khao Noi B2
10 Wat Samai Kongka B2
Yang Na Yai Tree .... (see 1)

Activities, Courses & Tours
11 Chalok Lam to Bottle Beach Trek C1
12 Haad Yao Divers B1
13 Lotus Diving B1
14 Samma Karuna B2
15 The Phangan Thai Cooking Class B3
Wat Pho Sauna .... (see 1)

Shopping
16 Fusion Fashion A3
17 Thong Sala Walking Street A2

Eating
18 Chana Masala B2
19 Fisherman's Restaurant C3
Fruitarian Experience .... (see 14)
20 Phantip Food Market A2
Pura Vida .... (see 12)

Drinking & Nightlife
21 Amsterdam B2
22 Jam Bar B2
23 Rock B3
24 Sunrise B3
25 Tommy B3

Transport
26 Chaloklum Pier C1
27 Long-tail Boats Hat Khuat (Bottle Beach) C1
28 Long-tail Boats Hat Than Sadet D2
29 *Sŏrng·tăa·ou* to Thong Sala B3
30 Thong Nai Pan Express A3
31 Thong Sala Pier A2
32 Thong Sala Pier A2

go for the excellent value *thali* (platter), but if they have, then the *dosas* (rice crepe) are a great substitute.

Phantip Food Market Market $
(Mu 1, Thong Sala; dishes 60B; ⌚1-11pm) Thong Sala's terrific food market is a must for those looking for doses of culture while nibbling on low-priced street food. Wander the galaxy of stalls and grab a spicy sausage, satay-style kebab, spring roll, Hainanese chicken rice or coconut ice cream. There are even a few vegetarian and Italian options at the back.

Pura Vida Cafe $
(☎094 827 7641; Hat Yao Rd; breakfast from 70B; ⌚8.30am-5pm Mon-Sat; 📶) This charming and bright Portuguese cafe is an alluring choice as you head up the west coast. Breakfasts are excellent, especially the pancakes and natural yoghurt, or you can go the whole hog with a full brekkie. There are also delicious burgers, sandwiches and panini and we love the 'Eat Well, Travel Often' campervan painting.

Fisherman's Restaurant Seafood $$
(☎084 454 7240; www.fishermansphangan.com; 30/6 Mu 1 Ban Tai; mains 250B; ⌚1.30-10pm; 📶) Sit in a long-tail boat looking out over the sunset and a rocky pier. Lit up at night, this is one of the island's nicest settings, and the food, from the yellow-curry crab to the massive seafood platter to share, is as wonderful as the ambience. Reserve ahead, especially when the island is hopping during party time.

DRINKING & NIGHTLIFE

Every month, on the night of the full moon, pilgrims pay lunar tribute to the party gods with dancing, wild screaming and glow-in-the-dark body paint. For something mellower, the west coast has several excellent bars, where you can raise a loaded cocktail glass to a blood-orange sunset from a hilltop or over mangrove trees at the water's edge. Thong Sala has a couple of decent bars too and the island's coffee is also excellent, so look out for several cool, hipster caffeine spots scattered around the island.

Amsterdam
Bar

(☏095 018 4891; Ao Plaay Laem; ⊗noon-1am; 📶) The rooftop swimming pool staring out to glorious sunsets is the key draw at this popular hillside bar, perched high up on the west coast. Arrive early to avoid the crowds, bring your swimsuit, slip into the warm waters, grab yourself a beer (Chang 70B), and enjoy the crimson Pha-Ngan sun descending into the blue ocean.

Jam Bar
Bar

(Hin Kong; ⊗7pm-2am Sun & Thu) Sit beneath a starry sky at this pop-up stage and bar where it's live DIY music, with anyone welcome to get up and jam. The action is usually kicked off by host Robert, who belts out a few rock classics to get things going. His friendly nightspot on the west coast is now a popular fixture for tourists.

Rock
Bar

(☏093 725 7989; 130/4 Mu 6, Hat Rin; ⊗8am-late; 📶) Offering superb views of the Full Moon Party from an elevated terrace – and excellent panoramas at all other times – this bar at the southern end of the Hat Rin beach has super cocktails and a mixed menu of plates at reasonable prices even during the lunar lunacy.

INFORMATION

Ko Pha-Ngan Hospital (☏077 377034; www. kpho.go.th; 6 Mu 4, Ban Wok Tum; ⊗24hr) About 2.5km north of Thong Sala, this government hospital offers 24-hour emergency services.

Ko Pha-Ngan Police Station (☏077 377114, 191; www.suratthani.police.go.th) The island's main police station is 2km northeast of Thong Sala.

GETTING THERE & AWAY

Transport via the sea is the only way to arrive on Ko Pha-Ngan. Boats from the mainland, Ko Samui and Ko Tao arrive daily at the piers in Thong Sala, and there are also boats arriving directly from Ko Samui to Haad Rin.

GETTING AROUND

Pick-up trucks and *sŏrng·tăa·ou* chug along the island's major roads, and the riding rates double after sunset. Long-tail boats depart from Thong Sala, Chalok Lam (p108) and Hat Rin, heading to far-flung destinations such as Hat Khuat (Bottle Beach; from 600B) and Hat Than Sadet (from 600B).

RAILAY

Railay at a Glance...

Fairy-tale limestone crags come to a dramatic climax at Railay (also spelt Rai Leh), a mountainous peninsula of Krabi Province that is only reached by boat. Rock climbers scramble up huge limestone towers for amazing clifftop views while kayakers and snorkellers take on amphibious adventures. The wind-down scene has a Thai-Rasta vibe that enthusiastically toasts the sunsets and welcomes new acolytes.

Two Days in Railay

Take a two-day **rock-climbing course** (p117) to master the vertical cliffs and embrace endless sea views. Get your dose of choice seafood dishes at **Sunset Restaurant** (p119).

Four Days in Railay

Hire a long-tail boat to go **snorkelling** (p119) at the nearby islands. Do a sweaty hike to **Sa Phra Nang** and **Hat Tham Phra Nang** (p118); remember your bug spray. Reward breaking a sweat with a cocktail at **Last Bar** (p119) and dinner at **The Terrace** (p119).

Previous page: Hat Tham Phra Nang (p118)
MAXIM TUPIKOV/SHUTTERSTOCK ©

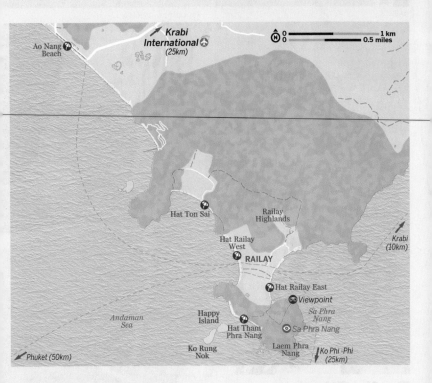

Krabi
International ✈
(25km)

Ao Nang
Beach

N 0 |————| 1 km
0 |————| 0.5 miles

Hat Ton Sai

Railay
Highlands

Hat Railay
West

RAILAY

Krabi
(10km)

Hat Railay East

Viewpoint

Sa Phra
Nang

Andaman
Sea

Happy
Island

Hat Tham
Phra Nang

Sa Phra Nang

Ko Rung
Nok

Laem Phra
Nang

Ko Phi-Phi
(25km)

Phuket (50km)

Arriving in Railay

Long-tail boats run from Krabi's Tha
Khong Kha (45 minutes). There's also
a year-round ferry from Phuket (2¼
hours).

Where to Stay

There aren't a lot of lodging options.
Railay Highlands and Hat Ton Sai favour
backpackers while Railay East and
Railay West have midrange and top-end
options. Book in advance in December
and January.

Rock climbing in Railay

KING ROPES ACCESS/SHUTTERSTOCK ©

Rock Climbing

Railay is one of Southeast Asia's top climbing spots and continues to gain in popularity. The routes are varied in technical challenge and have rewarding sea views.

With over 1000 bolted routes, ranging from beginner to advanced, all with unparalleled clifftop vistas, you could spend months climbing and exploring. Deep-water soloing, where free-climbers scramble up ledges over deep water, is incredibly popular.

Climbing Routes

Most climbers start off at **Muay Thai Wall** and **One, Two, Three Wall**, at the southern end of Hat Railay East (p118), where there are at least 40 routes graded from 4b to 8b on the French system. The mighty **Thaiwand Wall** sits at the southern end of Hat Railay West, offering a sheer limestone cliff with some of the most challenging climbing routes, graded from 6a to 7c+.

Other top climbs include **Hidden World**, with its classic intermediate routes; **Wee's Present Wall** (Hat Railay West), an overlooked

Great For...

☑ **Don't Miss**

Try deep-water soloing; if you fall you'll probably just get wet.

Ao Nang
Tower

Wee's Present
Wall

Diamond
Cave

RAILAY Hat Railay East

Thaiwand
Wall

One, Two,
Three Wall

*Andaman
Sea*

Muay Thai Wall Hidden World

ⓘ Need to Know

Climbing courses cost 1200B for a half-day and 2000B for a full day.

✕ Take a Break

Talk bolts and ropes at Highland Rock Climbing (p120), a popular hang-out.

★ Top Tip

Chalk is obligatory for avoiding sweaty palms in this tropical climate.

If climbing independently, you're best off bringing your own gear, including nuts and cams as backup for thinly protected routes. Some climbing schools sell a limited range of imported gear.

Climbing Outfitters

Recommended companies include the following:

Basecamp Tonsai (⌂095 284 7354; www.tonsaibasecamp.com; Hat Ton Sai; half-/full day 900/1800B, 3-day course 6000B; ⊗8.30am-4pm & 6-9pm)

Hot Rock (⌂085 641 9842; www.railayadventure.com; Hat Railay East; half-/full day 1200/2000B, 3-day course 6500B; ⊗9am-8pm)

King Climbers (⌂081 797 8923; www.railay.com; Walking St; half-/full day 1200/2000B, 3-day course 6500B; ⊗8.30am-9pm Mon-Fri, to 6pm Sat & Sun)

Highland Rock Climbing (⌂084 443 9539; www.highlandrockclimbingthailand.weebly.com; Railay Highlands; half-/full day 1000/1800B, 3-day course 6000B; ⊗8am-10pm)

7c+ winner; **Diamond Cave**, a busy beginner-to-intermediate favourite; and **Ao Nang Tower**, a three-pitch climbing wall reached only by boat.

There's excellent climbing information at www.railay.com. *Rock Climbing in Thailand and Laos* (2014; Elke Schmitz) is an up-to-date guide to the area.

Courses & Gear

Beginners can start with a half- or full-day session. Private sessions are also available. Three-day courses involve lead climbing, where you clip into bolts on the rock face. Experienced climbers can rent gear sets for two people from the climbing schools for around 1200B per day (quality varies); the standard set consists of a 60m rope, two climbing harnesses and climbing shoes.

⊙ SIGHTS

Hat Railay East
Beach

(หาดไร่เลย์ตะวันออก) Railay's most developed beach, this shallow, muddy, mangrove-lined bay recedes to mudflats during low tide, gets steamy hot if the breezes aren't blowing and isn't appealing for swimming. But it's lined with affordable hotels, guesthouses and restaurants and is only a five-minute walk to better beaches.

Hat Railay West
Beach

(หาดไร่เลย์ตะวันตก) This beach is a near-flawless white wonder and is the best place in Railay to swim, join an afternoon pick-up football game or watch a fiery sunset. It's all tasteful midrange and top-end resorts here, but rates can drop by up to 50% in low season. Long-tail boats to/from Ao Nang pick up and drop off here.

Hat Tham Phra Nang
Beach

(หาดถ้ำพระนาง) A genuine candidate for Thailand's most beautiful beach, Hat Tham Phra Nang is on the southwest side of the headland and has a crescent of pale, golden sand, framed by cave-carved karst cliffs and Ko Kai (Chicken Island) and Ko Poda peeking out of the cerulean sea. There's only one place to stay here – the peninsula's most exclusive resort, Rayavadee (www.rayavadee.com).

Sa Phra Nang
Lagoon

(สระพระนาง, Holy Princess Pool) Halfway along the trail linking Hat Railay East to Hat Tham Phra Nang, a sharp 'path' leads up the jungle-cloaked cliff wall to this hidden lagoon. The first section is a steep 10-minute uphill climb with ropes for assistance. Fork right for the lagoon, reached by sheer downhill climbing. If you fork left, you'll quickly reach a dramatic cliff-side **viewpoint** offering fine vistas over the peninsula; this is a strenuous but generally manageable, brief hike.

✈ ACTIVITIES

Railay Dive Center
Diving

(☎075 819417; www.railay-divecenter.com; Walking St; 2 dives 3700B) This is the only dive centre on Railay, and it offers everything

Sa Phra Nang

from fun dives to Open Water courses (14,900B) to dive trips to Koh Phi-Phi, as well as guided snorkelling trips (from 1500B). Prices don't include national park entry fees.

Freebird Paddle Kayaking

(☑061 953 9913; www.gofreebird.com; Walking St; kayak tour per person day/night 800/1800B; ☺10am-9pm) See what lies beneath in these tours' see-through kayaks and experience bioluminescent plankton on the night tours. Aslo offered are stand-up paddleboarding (SUP) tours (day/night tours 800/1800B).

❌ EATING

The beachfront resort restaurants at Hat Railay West are the best, and the most expensive, on Railay. You'll find more affordable Thai and Western options inland.

Sunset Restaurant Seafood $$

(www.krabisandsea.com; Hat Railay West; mains 180-400B; ☺11am-9pm; 🛜) Attached to the Sand Sea Resort (www.krabisandsea.com) and with a fine beachfront location, this is a popular place to sample fresh seafood while gazing out to sea. It also does a full range of Thai classics: curries, stir-fries and salads.

Mangrove Restaurant Thai $$

(Walking St; mains 80-350B; ☺10am-10pm; 🛜) This humble, heaving, local-style place, set beneath a stilted thatched roof between Railay's east and west beaches, turns out all the Thai favourites, from glass-noodle salad and cashew-nut stir-fry to curries, spicy *sôm·dam* (spicy green papaya salad) and the wonderful creation that is egg-grilled sticky rice.

The Terrace Asian $$$

(Hat Tham Phra Nang; mains 450-1890B; ☺11am-11pm; ☑) An upscale pan-Asian menu – of Japanese, Vietnamese, Indian and Thai dishes – is served on a terrace overlooking Hat Tham Phra Nang. It does decent cocktails, too.

Diving & Snorkelling

Dive operations in Railay run trips out to local dive sites. Two dives cost 3700B; an Open Water dive course is 14,500B. There are also dive trips to Ko Phi-Phi and **King Cruiser Wreck** (ซากเรือคิงครุยเซอร์; Ko Phi-Phi Don) for 4900B. Most Ao Nang–based dive operators (where there's more choice) will pick up from Railay. You will also pay a national park entry fee (adult/child 400/200B) valid for three days, as well as a dive fee (200B per day).

Full-day, multi-island snorkelling trips to Ko Poda, Ko Hong, Ko Kai and beyond can be arranged through resorts and agencies from 1200B, or you can charter a long-tail (half-/full day 1800/2800B) from Hat Railay West. One-day snorkelling tours to Ko Phi-Phi cost 2400B. If you're just snorkelling off Railay, most resorts rent mask sets and fins for around 150B each.

Coral in King Cruiser Wreck
METHANON/SHUTTERSTOCK ©

🍸 DRINKING & NIGHTLIFE

Last Bar Bar

(Hat Railay East; ☺11am-late) This is a reliably packed-out multilevel tiki bar that rambles to the edge of the mangroves, with bunting, balloons and cushioned seats on one deck, candlelit dining tables on another, live music out the back and waterside fire shows.

Tew Lay Bar Bar

(Hat Railay East; ☺11am-midnight; 🛜) Kick back at this chill-out open-air bar decked out with tree platforms, hammocks, lounge

Beach life

cushions and fairy lights. Its superb and isolated waterfront location on a rocky headland offers lazy views of Hat Railay East. It's the perfect place to escape the hustle. It's located 200m east of the Last Bar (p119).

Highland Rock Climbing — Cafe

(☎084 443 9539; Railay Highlands; ⊗8am-8pm; 🛜) Part climbing school (p117), part cafe, this driftwood-clad place sources beans from sustainable farms in Chiang Rai and serves some of the peninsula's best coffee.

❶ GETTING THERE & AROUND

Long-tail boats run to Railay from Krabi's Tha Khong Kha and from the seafront at Ao Nang and Ao Nam Mao. To Krabi, **long-tails** (⊗7.45am-6pm) leave from Hat Railay East. Boats in both directions leave between 7.45am and 6pm when they have eight people (150B, 45 minutes). Chartering the boat costs 1200B.

Boats to Hat Railay West from the southeastern end of Ao Nang (15 minutes) cost 100B from 8am to 6pm or 150B from 6pm to midnight. Boats don't leave until eight people show up. Private charters cost 1200B. Services stop as early as 5pm May to October. **Long-tails** (⊗8am-6pm) return to Ao Nang from Hat Railay West on the same schedule.

A year-round ferry runs to Ko Phi-Phi (450B, 1¼ hours). In high season, from October to April, it leaves from Hat Railay West at 9.45am and 2.45pm; long-tails motor over to meet it. In low season it leaves from the **ferry jetty** (Hat Railay East) at 9.45am. Boats to Ko Lanta (550B, two hours, 10.45am daily) operate only during the high season. For Phuket (650B, 2¼ hours), there's a year-round ferry at 3.15pm. Some ferries pick up off Hat Railay West.

Where to Stay

There are four beaches around Railay, or you can sleep up on the headland.

Area	Atmosphere
Hat Railay East (Hat Sunrise)	This shallow, steamy, muddy bay is lined with affordable hotels, guesthouses and restaurants and is only a five-minute walk to better beaches.
Hat Railay West	An almost perfect white beach and the best place for a swim or to watch the sun set. You'll find tasteful midrange and top-end resorts here. Long-tail boats to/from Ao Nang.
Hat Tham Phra Nang	One of the world's most beautiful beaches; there's only one place to stay here – the peninsula's most exclusive resort, Rayavadee. Anyone can drop a beach towel.
Hat Ton Sai	The grittier climbers' and budgeteers' retreat. Bars and bungalows are nestled further back in the jungle and it's a lively, fun scene. To get to the other beaches you'll need to take a long-tail (50B), scramble over rocks at low tide, or hike 30 minutes through the jungle.
Railay Highlands	About 500m inland from Hat Railay West or East. Lodgings are good value.

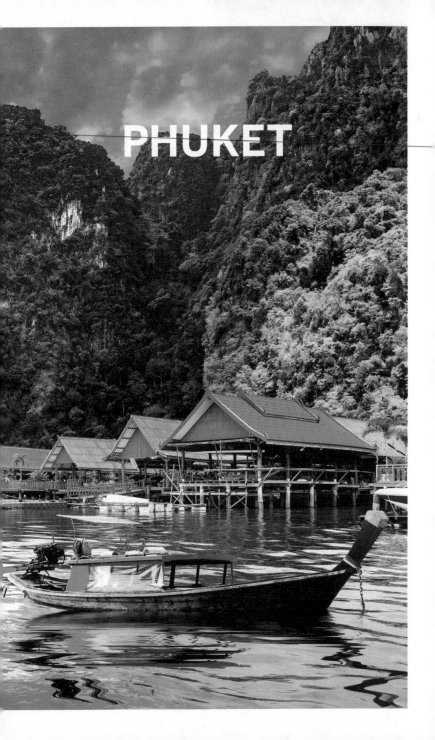
PHUKET

Phuket at a Glance...

Branded the 'pearl of the Andaman', Phuket doesn't feel like an island at all. It's 49km long, the biggest in Thailand, and the sea feels secondary to the city that is now the country's premier resort and expat retirement destination. The busy town of Patong attracts beachaholics, while other beaches are more refined with luxury hotels, restaurants and spas.

Two Days in Phuket

Break up the beach routine with a **walking tour** (p136) through Phuket Town's old Sino-Portuguese architecture. Enjoy fabulous fusion cuisine at **Suay** (p144). Party hard in Patong with a stop at good old **Nicky's Handlebar** (p147). Or drink up the cocktails and quirkiness at **Art Space Cafe & Gallery** (p146).

Four Days in Phuket

Devote one day to **Ao Phang-Nga National Park** (p132), a protected bay cluttered with more than 40 peaked karst islands. Take the kids to activity spots such as **Soi Dog** (p140) and **Kiteboarding Asia** (p140).

Previous page: Phuket coastal view
CARLOS CASTILLA/SHUTTERSTOCK ©

Ao Phang-Nga

Phuket Town Map (p139)
Phuket Map (p142)

Arriving in Phuket

Phuket International Airport Located 30km northwest of Phuket Town.

Phuket Bus Terminal 2 Located 4km north of Phuket Town.

Tha Rassada For boats to Ko Phi-Phi and Krabi (Railay); 3km southeast of Phuket Town.

Where to Stay

The island is packed with fashionable resorts and boutique hotels. Save your penny-pinching for other locations. Book hotels well in advance during the busy high season (November to April) and hunt online for discounts.

Kata

ALEKSANDAR TODOROVIC/SHUTTERSTOCK ©

Phuket Beaches

Phuket's beaches are stunning stretches of sand with emerald waters. Like a big family, each beach has its own personality. And the island's modern roads make it easy to explore the island looking for your best match.

Patong

Patong is *not* the poster child of sophistication. In fact it makes its bread and butter from knock-off T-shirts, girly bars for those in midlife crisis and slapdash commercialism of mediocre quality but immense quantity.

But past the brash beach village is a breathtaking crescent bay. In Thailand, the pretty beaches get all of the attention, for better or worse.

Karon

The next beach south of Patong is Hat Karon, which is a spillover for Patong's hyperactive commercialism. The beach village is a harmless mess of local food, Russian signage, low-key girly bars, T-shirt vendors and pretty Karon Park, with its artificial lake and

Great For...

☑ Don't Miss

Sampling the beaches until you've found a favourite – it's a Phuket tradition.

❶ Need to Know

High season runs from November to February. The monsoon runs from May to October.

✕ Take a Break

Sabai Corner (Map p142; ☎089 875 5525; www.sabaicornerphuket.com; Soi Laem Mum Nai, off Rte 4233; mains 160-490B; ☺10am-10pm; 🛜) has a mouth-watering view and satisfying Thai and international standards.

★ Top Tip

Get a bird's-eye view of Phuket from Laem Promthep, a cape to the southwest.

mountain backdrop. Southern Karon takes on more sophistication.

On the beach, Karon has a broad golden beach that culminates at the northernmost edge (accessible from a rutted road past the roundabout) with glass-like turquoise waters. Megaresorts dominate the beach and there's still more sand space per capita here than at Patong or Kata.

Kata

The classiest of the popular west coast beaches, Kata attracts travellers of all ages and walks of life. While you won't bag a secluded strip of sand, you'll still find lots to do. Be careful of riptides and undercurrents while splashing in the sea.

Kata has surfing in the shoulder and wet seasons (a rarity in Thailand), terrific day spas, fantastic food and a top-notch yoga

studio. The gold-sand beach is carved in two by a rocky headland. **Hat Kata Yai** (หาด กะตะใหญ่; Map p142) lies on the northern side; more secluded **Hat Kata Noi** (หาด กะตะน้อย; Map p142) unfurls to the south. The road between them is home to Phuket's original millionaire's row.

Rawai

Now this is a place to live, which is exactly why Phuket's rapidly developing south coast is teeming with retirees, artists, Thai and expat entrepreneurs, and a service sector that, for the most part, moved here from somewhere else.

The region is defined not just by its beaches but also by its lush coastal hills that rise steeply and tumble into the Andaman Sea, forming Laem Phromthep (p140), Phuket's beautiful southernmost point. For a more secluded sunset spot, seek out the secret **Windmill Viewpoint** (มุมมอง; Map p142;

Rte 4233) 1.5km north. These hills are home to neighbourhoods knitted together by just a few roads – though more are being carved into the hills each year and you can almost envision real-estate money chasing away all the seafood grills and tiki bars. Even with the growth you can still feel nature, especially when you hit the beach.

Ask a Phuket local or expat about their favourite beach and everyone's answer is **Hat Nai Han**, one of Rawai's great swimming spots (be careful of rips in low season).

Kamala

A chilled-out beach hybrid, Kamala lures in a mix of long-term, low-key visitors, families and young couples. The bay is magnificent and serene. Palms and pines mingle on the rocky northern end, where the water is a rich emerald green and the snorkelling around the rock reef is halfway decent. Flashy new resorts are carved into the southern bluffs and jet skis make an appearance, but Kamala is quiet and laid-back, by Phuket standards.

Laem Singh, 1km north of Kamala, conceals one of the island's most beautiful beaches. Park on the headland and clamber down a steep jungle-frilled path, or charter a long-tail from Hat Kamala. It gets crowded.

Surin

With a wide, blonde beach, water that blends from pale turquoise in the shallows to a deep blue on the horizon, and lush, boulder-strewn headlands, Surin could easily attract visitors on looks alone. Day passes are available at **Catch Beach Club**

Laem Singh beach

(Map p142; 📱065 348 2017; www.catchbeach
club.com; 202/88 Mu 2, Hat Bang Thao; day pass
2000B; ⊙9am-late), one of Surin's swishest
resorts.

Ao Bang Thao

Stunning, and we mean 'stunning', 8km-
long, white-sand Bang Thao is the glue that
binds this area's disparate elements. The
southern half of the region is dotted with
three-star bungalow resorts. Further inland
is an old fishing village laced with canals,
upstart villa subdivisions and some stellar
restaurants. If you see a herd of water buffalo grazing beside a gigantic construction

> ★ **Top Tip**
>
> Jamie's Phuket (www.jamiesphuket
> blog.com) is a fun insider's blog by a
> long-time Phuket expat.

site...well, that's how fast Bang Thao has
developed.

Smack in the centre of it all is the somewhat bizarre Laguna Phuket complex, a
network of five four- and five-star resorts
tied together by an artificial lake (patrolled
by tourist shuttle boats) and a paved nature trail. At the northern end, Mother Nature reasserts herself, and a lonely stretch
of powder-white sand and tropical blue sea
extends past the bustle into the peaceful
bliss you originally had in mind.

Sirinat National Park

Comprising the exceptional beaches of Nai
Thon, Nai Yang and Mai Khao, along with
the former Nai Yang National Park and Mai
Khao wildlife reserve, **Sirinat National
Park** (อุทยานแห่งชาติสิรินาถ; Map p142; 📱076
327152, 076 328226; www.portal.dnp.go.th;
89/1 Mu 1, Hat Nai Yang; adult/child 200/100B;
⊙6am-6pm) 🏖 encompasses 22 sq km of
coastline and 68 sq km of sea, stretching
from the northern end of Ao Bang Thao to
Phuket's northernmost tip. This is one of
the sweetest slices of the island. The whole
area is 15 minutes from Phuket International Airport.

IGOR BUKHLIN/SHUTTERSTOCK ©

> ★ **Did You Know?**
>
> Phuket Yacht Haven Marina, on Phuket's
> northeasterly tip, boasts 320 high-tech
> berths with deep-water access, availa-
> ble to boats up to 60m in size.

Diving in Phuket

SUNTORN SUNTORNRAT/SHUTTERSTOCK ©

Phuket Water Sports

Ride the waves, the winds or the underwater currents in Phuket's ocean playground. The island has access to some of the Andaman's most famous dive sites. Monsoon weather turns surfing and kiteboarding into adrenalin sports.

Great For...

☑ Don't Miss

Take this opportunity to learn a new sport, if you've never mastered the waves.

Diving

Phuket enjoys an enviable location central to the Andaman's top diving destinations.

Most Phuket operators take divers to the nine decent sites near the island, including **Ko Raya Noi** and **Ko Raya Yai** (Ko Racha Noi and Ko Racha Yai), but these spots rank lower on the wow-o-meter. The reef off the southern tip of Raya Noi is the best spot, with soft corals and pelagic fish species, though it's usually reserved for experienced divers. Manta and marble rays are frequently glimpsed here and occasionally a whale shark. Snorkelling here is better than elsewhere on the island.

From Phuket, you can join a huge range of liveaboard diving expeditions to the Similan Islands and Myanmar's Mergui Archipelago. Recommended dive schools:

Sea Fun Divers (Map p142; ☎081 367 4542; www.seafundivers.com; 29 Soi Karon Nui; 2-/3-dive trip 3900/4400B; ⊗9am-6pm)

Rumblefish Adventure (Map p142; ☎095 441 8665; www.rumblefishadventure.com; 98/79 Beach Centre, Th Kata/Patak West; 2-dive trip 3500-4500B; ⊗9am-7pm)

Sunrise Divers (Map p142; ☎084 626 4646, 076 398040; www.sunrise-divers.com; 269/24 Th Patak East; 3-dive trip 3700B, liveaboard per day from 4900B; ⊗10am-6pm daily Nov-Apr, to 4pm Mon-Fri May-Oct)

ⓘ Need to Know

Diving is good from November to April, surfing from June to September and kitesurfing nearly all year.

✖ Take a Break

Nikita's (Map p142; ☎076 288703; www.nikitas-phuket.com; Hat Rawai; ⊗9.30am-11pm; ☏) offers Rawai sea views if you are a better spectator than athlete.

★ Top Tip

Be aware of rip tides and undercurrents. Red flags usually indicate hazardous conditions.

Kitesurfing

The best kitesurfing spots are Hat Nai Yang from April to October and Rawai from mid-October to March. **Kite Zone** (Map p142; ☎083 395 2005; www.kitesurfthailand.com; Hat Friendship; 1hr lesson 1600B, 3-day course 10,000-15,000B; ⊗hours vary) has all the gear and classes to get you started.

Surfing

With the monsoon's mid-year swell, glassy seas fold into barrels. **Nautilus Dive & Surf Shop** (Map p142; ☎076 330229; www.phuketsurfing.com; 186/1 Th Kata Noi, Hat Kata Yai; class 1200B, board rental per hr/day 200/800B; ⊗9am-6pm) is a good spot for break information and gear rental.

Kata Yai and Hat Nai Han both have surf spots but beware of the vicious undertows. Hat Kalim is sheltered and has a consistent 3m break, considered one of the best breaks on the island. Other spots can be found at Hat Kamala and Laem Singh. Hat Nai Yang has a consistent (if soft) wave that breaks more than 200m offshore. Hat Nai Thon gets better shape.

Ko Panyi

Ao Phang-Nga

Between turquoise bays peppered with craggy limestone towers, brilliant-white beaches and tumbledown fishing villages, Ao Phang-Nga is one of the Andaman's most spectacular landscapes. It can be visited on a day trip from Phuket or with an overnight at Ko Yao.

Great For...

☑ Don't Miss

Keep an eye out for the monitor lizard, a small dinosaur lookalike.

Ao Phang-Nga National Park

Established in 1981, 400-sq-km Ao Phang-Nga National Park is famous for its classic karst scenery. Huge vertical cliffs frame 42 islands, some with caves accessible only at low tide and leading into hidden *hôrng* (semi-submerged island caves). The bay is composed of large and small tidal channels, which run north to south through vast mangroves functioning as aquatic highways for fisherfolk and island inhabitants. These are Thailand's largest remaining primary mangrove forests.

In high season (November to April), the bay becomes a clogged package-tourist superhighway. But if you explore in the early morning (ideally from Ko Yao) or stay out later, you'll have more opportunity to enjoy the curious formations and natural splendour.

Ko Khao Phing Kan

INDAHS/GETTY IMAGES ©

Ao Phang-Nga
National Park

Andaman
Sea

Phuket
Town

❶ Need to Know

Ao Phang-Nga National Park (อุทยาน
แห่งชาติอ่าวพังงา; ☎076 481188; www.dnp.
go.th; adult/child 300/100B; ☺8am-4.30pm)

✗ Take a Break

If you're headed to Ko Yao, the pier
at Bang Rong has vendors for quick
snacks. Just watch out for the monkeys.

★ Top Tip

The best way to explore the bay is by
kayak.

Ko Khao Phing Kan ('Leaning on Itself
Island') is the bay's top tourist draw.
The Thai name efficiently describes the
massive rock formation surrounded by a
small spit of sand but it is Hollywood that
made it famous. In the James Bond film
The Man with the Golden Gun, this rocky
island starred as Scaramanga's hidden
lair. Most tour guides refer to the island as
'James Bond Island' and photo-snapping
visitors and souvenir-hawking vendors have
turned the impressive natural feature into
something of a circus.

A stilted Muslim village clings to **Ko
Panyi,** a popular lunch stop for tour groups.
It's busy, but several Phang-Nga town tours
enable you to stay overnight and soak up
the scenery without the crowds.

Keep an eye out in the mangroves for
Ao Phang-Nga's marine animals including

monitor lizards, two-banded monitors
(reminiscent of crocodiles when swimming), flying lizards, banded sea snakes,
shore pit vipers and Malayan pit vipers.
Mammals include serows, crab-eating
macaques, white-handed gibbons and
dusky langurs.

Although it's nice to create your own Ao
Phang-Nga itinerary by chartering a boat,
it's easier (and cheaper) to join a tour from
either Phuket or Ko Yao. From Phuket, John
Gray's Seacanoe (p141) is the top choice
for kayakers.

Ko Yao

Soak up island living with a quick escape
from Phuket to the Yao Islands. With mountainous backbones, unspoilt shorelines,
varied bird life and a population of friendly
Muslim fisherfolk, Ko Yao (Ko Yao Yai and
Ko Yao Noi) are laid-back vantage points
for soaking up Ao Phang-Nga's beautiful
karst scenery. The islands are part of Ao
Phang-Nga National Park, but most easily
accessed from Phuket (30km away).

The relative pipsqueak, **Ko Yao Noi** is the main population centre, with fishing, coconut farming and tourism sustaining its small, year-round population. Most resorts occupy the bays on the east coast that recede to mudflats at low tides but the views of the otherworldly rock formations are incredible.

Scenic beaches include gorgeous Hat Pasai, on the southeast coast, and Hat Paradise, on the northeast coast. Hat Tha Khao, on the east coast, has its own dishevelled charm. Hat Khlong Jark is a beautiful sweep of sand with good sleeping options.

Ko Yao Yai is wilder, more remote and less developed; it's twice the size of Yao Noi with a fraction of the infrastructure. The most accessible beaches are slightly developed Hat Lo Pared, on the southwest coast, and powder-white Hat Chonglard on the northeast coast.

Ko Yao can be reached from Phuket's Tha Bang Rong (30 minutes, nine daily departures).

Activities

Touring around the sandy trails is a great way to get to know the island. You can rent bicycles from resorts and guesthouses. And if you don't have time to overnight here, **Amazing Bike Tours** (Map p142; ☎087 263 2031; www.amazingbiketoursthailand.asia; half-/full-day trip 1900/3200B; ⊗9am-8pm) runs popular small-group day trips to Ko Yao Noi from Phuket. And you can tackle the water with a kayak, widely available on Ko Yao Noi.

There are over 150 rock-climbing routes in the area. **Mountain Shop Adventures**

Yoga on Ko Yao Noi

(☎083 969 2023; www.themountainshop. org; Tha Khao, Ko Yao Noi; half-day 3200B; ⊙9am-7pm) arranges beginner to advanced outings that involve boat travel to remote limestone cliffs.

Ko Yao is so serene, you will want to harness that energy with a yoga class. **Island Yoga** (☎087 387 9475; www.thailandyogaretreats.com; 4/10 Mu 4, Hat Tha Khao, Ko Yao Noi; classes 600B) has popular drop-in classes.

Eating

There are several options in Ao Phang-Nga that combine accommodation with restaurants. Some of the best include the following:

> ★ **Top Tip**
>
> Respect local beliefs and dress modestly away from the beaches.

Rice Paddy (☎082 331 6581, 076 410233; www. ricepaddy.website; Hat Pasai, Ko Yao Noi; mains 180-890B; ⊙noon-10pm & 6-10pm May-Oct; 🛜🌿) The flash-fried *sôm-dam* (spicy green papaya salad), falafel and hummus, and spicy, fruit-enhanced curries at this German-owned kitchen are all delicious.

Sabai Corner Restaurant (☎076 597497; Hat Khlong Jark, Ko Yao Noi; mains 95-300B; ⊙8am-10pm; 🛜) This chilled-out waterside restaurant is a bubbly place to hang out over cocktails, and the Thai and Italian dishes are good (if small) too.

Ko Yao Island Resort (☎076 597474; www. koyao.com; 24/2 Mu 5, Hat Khlong Jark, Ko Yao Noi; villas 7400-19,900B; ❄@🛜≋) There's a snazzy bar-restaurant area and the service is stellar.

Chaba Café (☎087 887 0625; Hat Khlong Jark, Ko Yao Noi; mains 80-220B; ⊙9am-5pm Mon-Sat; 🌿) Rustic-cute with pastel-painted prettiness, driftwood walls, mellow music and a small gallery. Organic-oriented offerings include juices, shakes, tea and home-baked paninis, cookies and cakes, and Thai dishes.

Rock Art in Ao Phang-Nga

Many of Ao Phang-Nga's limestone islands have prehistoric rock art painted on or carved into cave walls and ceilings, rock shelters, cliffs and rock massifs. You can see rock art at Khao Khian, Ko Panyi, Ko Raya, Tham Nak and Ko Phra At Thao. Images at **Khao Khian** (the most visited cave-art site) contain human figures, fish, crabs, prawns, bats, birds and elephants, as well as boats, weapons and fishing equipment, seemingly referencing some communal effort tied to the all-important sea harvest. Most rock paintings are monochrome, though some have been traced in orange-yellow, blue, grey and black.

> ★ **Did You Know?**
>
> The national park can be visited on two- to three-hour tours.

Walking Tour: Phuket Town

A walk through Phuket Town's core will lead you past the mid-19th-century architectural legacies, grand mansions and narrow shophouses of the Baba (also known as Peranakan or Straits-Chinese) people.

Start Memory at On On Hotel
Distance 2km
Duration Two hours

6 The early-20th-century **Phra Pitak Chinpracha Mansion** (96 Th Krabi) has been immaculately restored and now houses a restaurant.

7 Chinpracha House (98 Th Krabi; 200B; ⏱9am-4.30pm Mon-Sat), built in 1903 on tin-mining wealth, is now a private home/museum.

5 Dating from 1934, the **Phuket Thaihua Museum** (p138) was the oldest Chinese school in Thailand.

Take a Break

Local food at Kopitiam by Wilai (p144).

Th Satun · Th Yaowarat · FINISH · Th Krabi · Fountain Circle

N 0 — 500 m
0 — 0.25 miles

4 Soi Romanee (p138) is home to restored Sino-Portuguese shop-houses turned boutique hotels.

Th Dibuk

Th Thepkasattri

Th Montri

Ao Phuket

Th Thalang

Thai Royal Police

1 START

2

3

Th Rassada

Th Phang-Nga

Th Phuket

Th Takua Pa

3 The **Phuket Philatelic Museum** (158 Th Montri; ⏱9am-5.30pm Tue-Sat) is a magnificent (if flaking) example of Sino-Portuguese architecture.

Classic Photo: Grab a selfie in front of the sun-yellow Thai Police Building (pictured; p140).

1 Phuket's first hotel, **Memory at On On** (www.thememoryhotel.com; 19 Th Phang-Nga), sprawls behind its gleaming-white Sino-Portuguese facade.

2 The former home of the **Standard Chartered Bank** (p140) is now a museum showcasing Phuket's Baba history.

◉ SIGHTS

◉ Phuket Town

Soi Romanee   Street

(ถนนรมณีย์; Map p139) Branching off Th
Thalang, in the heart of the Old Town,
this small, vibrant street flaunts some
of Phuket's most gorgeously revamped
Sino-Portuguese architecture. Once home
to brothels and gambling and opium dens,
it now hosts a smattering of boutique cafes
and guesthouses, and is a favourite photo
spot. It's particularly beautiful at night,
when Chinese lanterns cast a soft glow.

Khao Rang   Viewpoint

(เขารัง, Phuket Hill; Map p139; P) For a bird's-
eye view of the city, climb (or drive) up
Khao Rang, 2.5km northwest of Phuket
Town's centre. An overhanging viewing
platform opens up 270-degree panoramas
across the town to Chalong Bay, Laem
Phanwa and Big Buddha. It's at its most
peaceful during the week. There are a few
restaurants and cafes up here, as well as
monkeys. **Wat Khao Rang** is worth a look
along the way. It's about an hour's walk.

Phuket Thaihua Museum   Museum

(พิพิธภัณฑ์ภูเก็ตไทยหัว; Map p139; ☑076 211224;
28 Th Krabi; 200B; ⊙9am-5pm) Founded in
1934 and formerly a Chinese-language
school, this flashy museum is filled with
photos, videos and English-language
exhibits on Phuket's history, from the
Chinese migration (many influential
Phuketian families are of Chinese origin),
the tin-mining era and the Vegetarian
Festival (p145) to local cuisine, fashion and
literature. The building itself is a stunning
combination of Chinese and European
architectural styles, including art deco,
Palladianism and a Chinese gable roof and
stucco, plus a British-iron gate.

Shrine of the Serene Light   Shrine

(ศาลเจ้าแสงธรรม, Map p139; Saan Jao Sang
Tham; Th Phang-Nga; ⊙8.30am-noon & 1.30-
5.30pm) FREE A handful of Chinese temples
pump colour into Phuket Town, but this
restored shrine, tucked away up a 50m
alley now adorned with modern murals,
is particularly atmospheric, with its Taoist
etchings on the walls and the vaulted ceil-
ing stained from incense plumes. The altar

Shrine of the Serene Light

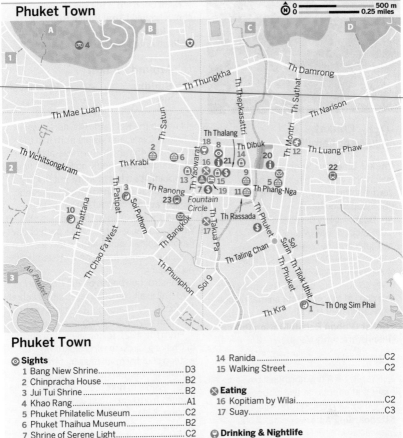

Phuket Town

500 m
0.25 miles

Phuket Town

is always fresh with flowers and burning candles, and the surrounding Sino-Portuguese buildings have been beautifully repainted. The shrine is said to have been built by a local family in 1889.

Standard Chartered Bank
Historic Building

(ธนาคารสแตนดาร์ดชาร์เตอร์ด; Map p139; Th Phang-Nga; ⊙museum 9am-4.30pm Tue-Sun) Thailand's sun-yellow oldest foreign bank

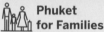

Phuket for Families

Phuket Elephant Sanctuary Feed, watch and walk with rescued pachyderms at this responsible sanctuary in the island's northeast.

Soi Dog (Gill Daley Foundation; Map p142; ☎076 681029; www.soidog.org; 167/9 Mu 4, Soi Mai Khao 10; by donation; ⊙9am-noon & 1-3.30pm Mon-Fri, 9am-noon Sat, tours 9.30am, 11am, 1.30pm & 2.30pm Mon-Fri, 9.30am & 11am Sat) ✏ Meet Thailand's cats and dogs at this nonprofit animal-rescue foundation near Hat Mai Khao.

Phuket Gibbon Rehabilitation Project (โครงการคืนชะนีสู่ป่า; Map p142; ☎076 260492; www.gibbonproject.org; off Rte 4027; by donation; ⊙9am-4.30pm Sun-Fri, to 3pm Sat; P) ✏ A tiny northeastern sanctuary that adopts captive gibbons in the hope they can re-enter the wild.

Kiteboarding Asia (Map p142; ☎081 591 4594; www.kiteboardingasia.com; 26/4 Th Viset; 1-/3-day course 4000/11,000B; ⊙9am-6pm Nov-Apr) Adrenaline-addled older kids can kitesurf the Andaman's waves in Rawai and Hat Nai Yang.

Gibbon
GWENGOAT/GETTY IMAGES ©

is a fine example of Phuket Town's historic Sino-Portuguese architecture. Though you can admire the restored century-old exterior at any time, inside is a small, modest **museum** devoted to Phuket's Baba (Peranakan) culture, which was born in the 19th century as the Phuketian and Chinese populations mixed.

Right opposite is the yellow-walled, similarly styled **Thai Police Building** (Th Phang-Nga; ⊙9am-4.30pm Tue-Sun), with its distinctive four-tiered clock tower.

◎ Around Phuket

Big Buddha
Buddhist Site

(พระใหญ่; Map p142; www.mingmongkolphuket. com; off Rte 4021; ⊙6am-7pm; P) FREE High atop the Nakkerd Hills, northwest of Chalong Circle, and visible from half the island, the 45m-high, Burmese-alabaster Big Buddha sits grandly on Phuket's finest viewpoint. It's a tad touristy, but tinkling bells and flags mean there's an energetic pulse. Pay your respects at the golden shrine, then step up to the glorious plateau, where you can glimpse Kata's perfect bay, Karon's golden sands and, to the southeast, the pebble-sized channel islands of Ao Chalong.

Construction began on Big Buddha in 2007; all in all, the price tag, funded entirely by donations, is around 100 million baht (not that anybody minds).

From Rte 4021, follow signs 1km north of Chalong Circle to wind 5.5km west up a steep country road, passing terraces of banana groves and tangles of jungle. It's also possible to **hike** (Soi Patak 14) up to Big Buddha from Karon: a splendid, challenging, 2.5km climb through the jungle, starting from Soi Patak 14 and taking an hour or so. You'll need plenty of water and an early start.

Laem Phromthep
Viewpoint

(แหลมพรหมเทพ; Map p142; Rte 4233) Come here to the island's southernmost point to see the glittering Andaman Sea wrapped around Phuket. The cape is crowned by a mod lighthouse shaped like a concrete crab, and an evocative, flower-garlanded elephant shrine, so you'll want to stay a while. At sunset the tour buses descend; if you're craving privacy, arrive by 4pm, or follow the faint fisherfolk's trail downhill to watch the sun drop in peace from the rocky peninsula that reaches into the ocean.

Big Buddha

Phuket Aquarium · Aquarium

(สถานแสดงพันธุ์สัตว์น้ำภูเก็ต; Map p142; ☎076 391406; www.phuketaquarium.org; 51 Th Sakdidej; adult/child 180/100B; ⊗8.30am-4.30pm; P) Get a glimpse of Thailand's wondrous underwater world at Phuket's popular aquarium, by the harbour on the tip of Laem Phanwa (12km south of Phuket Town). It's not the largest collection of marine life, but there are useful English-language displays and captions. Check out the blacktip reef shark, the tiger-striped catfish (resembling a marine zebra), the electric eel with a shock of up to 600V, and the 80-million-baht multimedia Aqua Dome, launched in 2018.

⊕ ACTIVITIES

Phuket Thai Cookery School · Cooking

(Map p142; ☎082 474 6592; www.phuketthai cookery.com; Hat Pleum Suk; 1-day course 2900B; ⊗8am-3pm Thu-Tue) Get intimate with aromatic Thai spices at this terrific cooking school on a quiet seafront plot on Ko Sireh's east coast, 7km east of Phuket Town. Courses take in a market tour and last up to six hours, with different menus on different days (veggie options are available). Included is round-trip transport from/to most of Phuket.

Phuket Elephant Sanctuary · Wildlife, Volunteering

(Map p142; ☎088 752 3853; www.phuket elephantsanctuary.org; 100 Mu 2, Paklok, Rte 4027; adult/child 3000/1500B; ⊗9.30am-1pm & 2-5.30pm; 🚹) ✎ Phuket's only genuine elephant sanctuary is a refuge for aged pachyderms who were mistreated for decades while working in logging and tourism. During the morning tour, you get to feed them, before tagging along a few metres away as they wander the forest, chomp on watermelons, bathe and hang out. It's a rare, environmentally responsible opportunity that visitors rave about.

John Gray's Seacanoe · Kayaking

(Map p142; ☎076 254505; www.johngray-sea canoe.com; 86 Soi 2/3, Th Yaowarat; adult/child from 3950/1975B) ✎ John Gray's is the original, the most reputable and by far the most

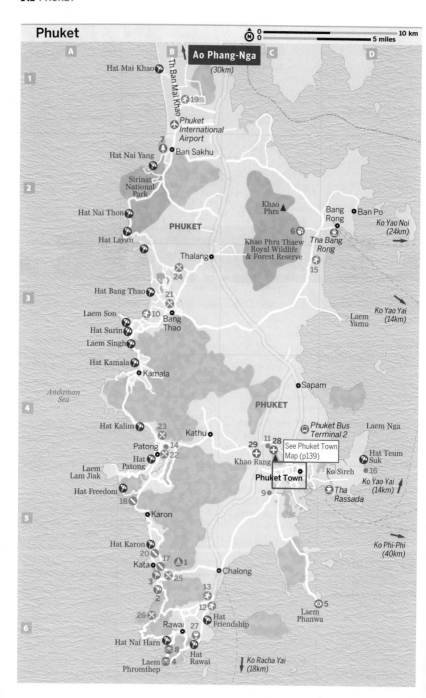

Phuket

Ao Phang-Nga
(30km)

0 ___ 10 km
0 ___ 5 miles

Hat Mai Khao

19

Th Ban Mai Khao

Phuket
International
Airport

7
Ban Sakhu

Hat Nai Yang

Sirinat
National
Park

Hat Nai Thon

PHUKET

Khao
Phra

Bang
Rong
Ban Po

Ko Yao Noi
(24km)

6
Tha Bang
Rong

15

Hat Layan

Khao Phra Thaew
Royal Wildlife
& Forest Reserve

Thalang

24

Laem
Yamu

Ko Yao Yai
(14km)

Hat Bang Thao

21

Laem Son

10

Bang
Thao

Hat Surin

Laem Singh

Hat Kamala

Kamala

Andaman
Sea

Sapam

PHUKET

Laem Nga

Hat Kalim

23

Phuket Bus
Terminal 2

Kathu

Patong

14

29

11 28

See Phuket Town
Map (p139)

Hat Teum
Suk

Hat
Patong

22

Khao Rang

Ko Sireh

16

Laem
Lam Jiak

Phuket Town

Ko Yao Yai
(14km)

Hat Freedom

18

9

Tha
Rassada

Karon

Ko Phi-Phi
(40km)

Hat Karon

20

17   1

Kata

3
25

Chalong

13

2

12

Laem
Phanwa

5

26

Rawai

27

Hat
Friendship

Hat Nai Harn

8

Hat
Rawai

Laem
Phromthep

4

Ko Racha Yai
(18km)

Phuket

ecologically sensitive kayaking company on Phuket. The 'Hong by Starlight' trip dodges the crowds, involves a sunset dinner and will introduce you to Ao Phang-Nga's famed after-dark bioluminescence. Like any good brand in Thailand, John Gray's 'Seacanoe' name and itineraries have been frequently copied. Located 3.5km northwest of Phuket Town.

Raintree Spa   Spa

(Map p139; ☏081 892 1001; www.theraintreespa. com; Sino House, 1 Th Montri; massage/treatment 500-1500B; ☉10am-9.30pm) Amid tranquil tropical grounds, Raintree is a step up in price, quality and atmosphere from Phuket Town's storefront spas. Skilled therapists don't just go through the motions here. Get silky-smooth with an aloe-cucumber body wrap or a 'fruit salad' scrub (pineapple, papaya, mango), or keep it classic with an ever-reliable Thai massage.

🔒 SHOPPING

Walking Street   Market

(Map p139; Th Thalang; ☉4-10pm Sun) Th Thalang morphs into a busy Sunday afternoon/evening market where local creatives sell vintage clothing and quirky homemade goods (leather purses, artisan soaps and candles, wood carvings) alongside sizzling southern Thai food carts and tropical juice stalls.

Ranida   Antiques, Fashion

(Map p139; 119 Th Thalang; ☉10am-8pm Mon-Sat) An elegant antiques gallery and boutique featuring antiquated Buddha statues and sculptures, organic textiles, and ambitious, exquisite high-fashion women's clothing inspired by vintage Thai garments and fabrics.

Pink Flamingo   Fashion & Accessories

(Map p139; 39/12 Th Yaowarat; ☉10am-8pm) In a chicly restored old building with arches over the front door, this self-styled 'tropical concept store' is all about floaty fabrics, bold colours and embroidered handmade dresses, kaftans and accessories from Bali. The upstairs bar-restaurant serves tapas, salads and pastas (105B to 345B) amid gorgeous hand-painted flamingo mural walls.

Pad Thai Shop (p145)

Ban Boran Textiles   Textiles

(Map p139; 51 Th Yaowarat; ⏱10.30am-6.30pm Mon-Sat) Shelves at this hole-in-the-wall fashion shop are stocked with quality silk scarves, lacquerware from Myanmar, sarongs, linen shirts, colourful bags and cotton textiles from Chiang Mai, and fabrics sourced from Southeast Asia's tribal communities.

EATING

Phuket Town

Kopitiam by Wilai   Thai $

(Map p139; ☎083 606 9776; www.facebook.com/kopitiambywilai; 14 & 18 Th Thalang; mains 95-180B; ⏱11am-5pm & 6.30-9pm Mon-Sat; 🛜👶) Family-owned Kopitiam serves fabulous Phuket soul food in an atmospheric old shophouse: Phuketian *pàt tai* (fried noodles) with a kick, *chai chae* (chilli-dressed noodle salad) and fantastic *mee sua* (noodles sautéed with egg, greens, prawns, sea bass and squid). Wash it all down with fresh chrysanthemum or passion-fruit juice. There are two branches (one air-con),

either side of the **Oldest Herbs Shop** (Map p139; Th Thalang; ⏱8am-6pm).

Special kids menus are available.

Suay   Fusion $$$

(Map p139; ☎087 888 6990; www.suayrestaurant.com; 50/2 Th Takua Pa; mains 400-1000B; ⏱5-11pm) Fabulous fusion and fine wines, courtesy of top Phuket chef-owner Noi Tammasak, are the draw at this converted house just south of the Old Town. Spicy eggplant salads, sweet-basil Shanghai noodles, braised-beef-cheek massaman and grilled-lemongrass lamb chops with papaya salsa are just some of the highlights. A new cocktail bar and Thai-tapas menu were in the works at the time of research.

Tables are sprinkled across the romantically lit house, garden and wraparound porch. Don't miss the flamed mango with sticky rice and black-sesame ice cream.

Ao Bang Thao

Bampot   International $$$

(Map p142; ☎093 586 9828; www.bampot.co; 19/1 Mu 1, Th Laguna; mains 550-1200B; ⏱6pm-midnight, closed Mon May-Nov; 🛜✏️)

Cool-blue booths, an open-plan kitchen and white-brick walls plastered with artwork set the scene for chef Jamie Wakeford's ambitious, contemporary European-inspired cooking – cashew-pesto risotto, crispy-skinned salmon with braised fennel, cauliflower tempura drizzled with truffle mayo. Throw in expertly crafted cocktails (try a gin-based BGT), excellent wines and cheerfully professional service, and Bampot delivers as one of Phuket's top international restaurants.

Project Artisan · Multicuisine $$$

(Map p142; ☎093 790 9911; www.theproject artisan.com; 53/17 Mu 6, Rte 4018; meals 200-600B; ⏰8.30am-11pm; 🛜🚲👶) Peachy-pink and pineapple-yellow woodcarved doors frame a lantern-lit garden adorned with dreamcatchers at this boho-chic, Bali-inspired, multipurpose creative venue in northern Cherngtalay. Locally sourced breakfasts of just-baked pastries, tropical smoothie bowls, artisan sliders and organic Phang-Nga eggs are followed by live-music sessions, massages at Saparod Spa (900B to 1800B), and cocktails or Thai craft beers at street-food-stall-style Tipsy Bar.

It's popular with well-heeled local expats and, thanks to its kids menus and massages, families. It also has a takeaway bakery. Find directions on the website.

😑 Karon

Pad Thai Shop · Thai $

(Map p142; Th Patak East; mains 50-80B; ⏰8am-6pm Sat-Thu) This glorified roadside food shack makes absurdly good *kôw pàt boo* (fried rice with crab), *pàt see-éw* (fried noodles), chicken stew and noodle soup. It also serves up some of the best *pàt tai* we've tasted: spicy and sweet, packed with tofu, egg and peanuts, and plated with spring onions, bean sprouts and lime. Don't miss the house-made chilli sauces.

Eat Bar & Grill · Grill $$$

(Map p142; ☎085 292 5652; www.eatbargrill. com; 250/1 Th Patak East; mains 200-900B; ⏰11am-10pm Mon-Sat; 🛜) Expect awesome

🍽️ Vegetarian Festival

The **Vegetarian Festival** (⏰late Sep-Oct), one of Phuket's most important celebrations, takes place during the first nine days of the ninth lunar month of the Chinese calendar, when devout Chinese abstain from meat, dairy and alcohol. Shop owners set up altars offering nine tiny cups of tea, incense, fruit, firecrackers, candles and flowers to the nine emperor gods invoked by the festival. The festival focuses on five Chinese temples. **Jui Tui Shrine** (ศาลเจ้าจุ้ยตุ่ยเต้าโบ้เก๊ง; Map p139; Soi Puthorn; ⏰8am-8.30pm) **FREE**, off Th Ranong, is the most important, followed by **Bang Niew** (ศาลเจ้าบางเหนียว; Map p139; Th Phuket; ⏰8.30am-10pm) **FREE** and **Sui Boon Tong** (ศาลเจ้าซุ่ยบุ่นต๋อง; Map p139; Soi Lorong; ⏰daylight hours) **FREE** shrines. Ceremonies include processions, firewalking and knife-ladder climbing. At the temples, everyone wears white. Fabulous cheap vegetarian food stalls line the side streets; many restaurants turn veg-only for the festival.

Vegetarian Festival
OMMLETT/SHUTTERSTOCK ©

burgers and superb steaks, perhaps the best on Phuket, at this laid-back, busy grill specialist with a wooden bar, concrete walls and limited space (book ahead). The menu includes other dishes (pasta, lamb shank), but beef is the thing: prepared to your taste, stylishly presented and fairly priced, given the quality. There are proper cocktails and coffee.

Kata

Red Duck — Thai $$

(Map p142; ☎084 850 2929; www.facebook.com/redduckrestaurant; 88/3 Th Koktanod; mains 240-380B; ⊗noon-11pm, closed Mon May-Sep; 🛜🌿)
Dishes at this hidden-away eatery with a tiny terrace are more expensive than at Kata's other Thai restaurants, but they're delicious, MSG-free and prepared with the freshest of ingredients. The seafood curries and soups are especially fine. Many of the Thai classics can be done in vegan versions, such as beautifully spiced veggie-packed massaman or vegetable *lâhp*. The service is excellent.

It's 600m inland from the southern end of Hat Kata Yai.

Patong

No 9 2nd Restaurant — International $$

(Map p142; ☎076 624445; 143 Th Phra Barami; mains 165-800B; ⊗11.30am-11.30pm; 🌿)
Deceptively simple, with wooden tables and photo-strewn walls, this is one of the best and busiest restaurants in Patong, thanks to its inventive and delicious mix of Thai,

Japanese and Western dishes. It's a rare feat for a kitchen to serve real-deal sushi, vegetarian Thai curries and meats such as lamb shank without any dip in quality.

Naughty Nuri's in the Forest — Ribs $$$

(Map p142; ☎061 173 0011; www.facebook.com/nnphuket; 112 Th Rat Uthit; mains 250-2000B; ⊗noon-midnight) Meat lovers crowd out an enormous, semi-open, multiroom space with swaying rattan lamps at the hugely popular Phuket outpost of this Bali-born, Australian-Indonesian-owned ribs specialist. Make sure you order the signature barbecue spare ribs (1995B), though the spiced suckling pig is also a huge hit, and the Indonesian-international menu tempts with vegetarian nasi goreng and more.

DRINKING & NIGHTLIFE

Kata

Art Space Cafe & Gallery — Bar

(Map p142; ☎090 156 0677; Th Kade Kwan; ⊗noon-midnight) The most fabulously quirky bar in Phuket, this trippy, multiuse space

From left: Thai green curry; Tropical cocktail; Soi Romanee (p138)

bursts with colour and is smothered in uniquely brushed canvases and sculptures celebrating, especially, the feminine form. It's the work of the creative Mr Pan and his tattoo-artist wife, who whip up both cocktails and veggie meals (160B to 400B). There's normally live music at around 8pm.

Ska Bar   Bar
(Map p142; www.skabar-phuket.com; 186/12 Th Koktanod; ☺1pm-2am) Tucked into the rocks on the southernmost curl of Hat Kata Yai and seemingly intertwined with the trunk of a grand old banyan tree, laid-back, Rasta-vibe Ska is our choice for seaside sundowners, served by welcoming Thai bartenders. Buoys, paper lanterns and flags dangle from the canopy, and there are often fire shows.

🍺 Patong

Nicky's Handlebar   Bar
(Map p142; ☏084 824 7777; www.nickyhandle bars.com; 41 Th Rat Uthit; ☺7am-1am; 🛜) This fun biker bar welcomes all, wheels or not. Once a bit of a dive, Nicky's has never looked better. There's a good selection of beers and the menu encompasses Western

and Thai cooking, including what the team claims is Thailand's spiciest burger. You can go for a ride here by asking about **Harley tours and hire** (Map p142; 1-/2-day tour incl bike hire from 9000/21,000B).

🍺 Phuket Town

Dibuk House   Cocktail Bar
(Map p139; ☏086 796 4646; www.facebook. com/dibukhouse; 39/2 Th Dibuk; ☺7pm-2am) The tiled floors and flickering candles of a restyled Sino-Portuguese shophouse mark out Phuket Town's most talked-about cocktail bar. Upping the ante for the local artisan-cocktail scene, it's a sultry, moody place, where waistcoat-clad mixologists artfully prepare potent, avant-garde cocktails (250B to 350B) at the mir-ror-backed bar. The delicate Wynn de Fleur features gin-infused red-berry tea with aloe, lemon and jasmine.

ℹ️ INFORMATION

Tourism Authority of Thailand (TAT; Map p139; ☏076 211036; www.tourismthailand.org/ Phuket; 191 Th Thalang; ☺8.30am-4.30pm) Has

LOVESEEN/SHUTTERSTOCK ©

Laem Phromthep (p140)

maps, brochures and info on boat trips to nearby islands, as well as handy island-wide transport listings.

❶ GETTING THERE & AWAY

AIR

Phuket International Airport (p306) is 30km northwest of Phuket Town, and has flights to/from Bangkok, as well as other national and international destinations.

BUS & MINIVAN

Phuket Bus Terminal 1 (Map p139; Th Phang-Nga) is used by minivans and the official, bright-orange **airport bus** (www.airportbus phuket.com), which runs 12 times daily to/from the airport (100B, one hour). Interstate buses

depart from **Phuket Bus Terminal 2** (Map p142; Th Thepkrasattri), 4km north of Phuket Town.

BOAT

Phuket's **Tha Rassada** (Map p142), 3km southeast of Phuket Town, is the main pier for boats to/from Ko Phi-Phi, Krabi, Ao Nang, Ko Lanta, the Trang Islands, Ko Lipe and even as far as Pulau Langkawi in Malaysia.

❶ GETTING AROUND

Sŏrng·tăa·ou (passenger pick-up minivans) run between Phuket Town and the west-coast beaches. **Phuket Smart Bus** (086 306 1257; www.phuketsmartbus.com) allows direct beach-to-beach travel. Taxis and túk-túk (pronounced *đúk đúk*) are overpriced.

DOCTOREGG/GETTY IMAGES ©

Where to Stay

The beaches at the southern and northern ends of the west coast feel like escapes from the real world. Patong and Karon are very hyperactive.

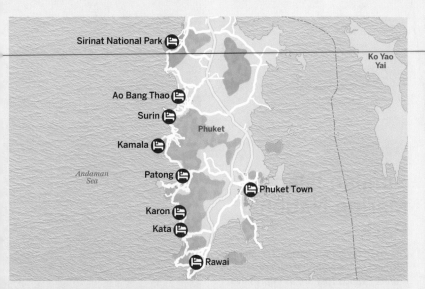

Area	Atmosphere
Phuket Town	Quirky, affordable lodging; commute to the beach.
Patong	Lots of nightlife and dining; noisy, crowded and seedy.
Karon	Lively beach, mix of budget lodging; slightly seedy.
Kata	Lively beach, mainly high-end resorts.
Rawai	Quiet beach, high-end resorts, local eats.
Kamala	Relaxed beach, boutique resorts.
Surin	Low-key beach, classy resorts.
Ao Bang Thao	Luxury resort complex.
Sirinat National Park	Natural beach, a mix of accommodation; far from dining and nightlife.

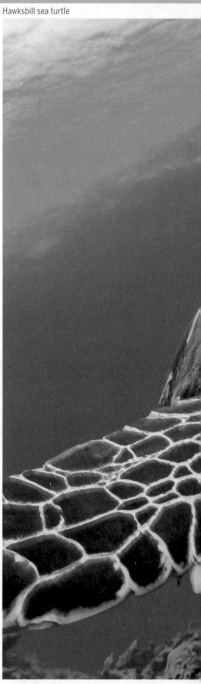
Hawksbill sea turtle

Similan Islands Marine National Park

Known to divers worldwide, the Similan Islands Marine National Park has granite islands that are as impressive above the bright-aqua water as below — topped with rainforest, edged with white beaches and fringed by coral reefs.

Great For...

Similan Islands

Khao Lak

Phang-Nga

Andaman Sea

Phuket

Krabi

Phuket Town

❶ Need to Know

The **park headquarters** (☎076 453272; www.dnp.go.th; 93 Mu 5, Thap Lamu; ☺8am-5pm) is 12km south of Khao Lak on the mainland.

★ **Top Tip**

The Similans close from mid-May to mid-October.

BLUE PLANET ARCHIVE/ALAMY STOCK PHOTO ©

Located 70km offshore from Phang-Nga Province and 90km northwest of Phuket, the granite islands of the Similans amaze with their turquoise water and kaleidoscopic corals. Coral bleaching has killed many hard corals and overtourism is a serious concern, but the soft corals and wildlife remain. The Similans are now on the tourist trail and many beaches and snorkel sites get packed with day trippers. The islands close in monsoon season to allow natural rejuvenation of the environment.

You can stay on Ko Miang (Island 4) and Ko Similan (Island 8). The **park visitors centre** (Ko Miang/Island 4; ☺7.30am-8pm mid-Oct–mid-May) and most facilities are on Ko Miang. Hat Khao Lak is the park's jumping-off point. The pier and mainland park headquarters (p150) are at Thap Lamu, 12km south (take Hwy 4, then Rte 4147).

The only accommodation on the Similans are 20 simple (and overpriced) bungalows on Ko Miang, a neighbouring campsite (with tents provided) and another campsite on Ko Similan. You will need to book at least two to three months ahead to guarantee a bed or a tent. A **restaurant** (Ko Miang/Island 4; mains 120-150B, lunch buffet 230B; ☺7.30am-8.30pm mid-Oct–mid-May) beside the park office on Ko Miang serves simple Thai food. There's another one on Ko Similan for those staying the night. Bring snacks from Khao Lak for the day trip.

Diving

With dramatic underwater gorges and boulder swim-throughs, the Similans cater to all diving levels, at depths of 2m to 30m. You'll find dive sites at the islands north of **Ko Miang**; the park's southern

Ko Similan

section (Islands 1, 2 and 3) is an off limits turtle-nesting ground.

Ko Hin Pousar (เกาะหินพู่ซ่า, Island 7) has rock reefs and there are dive-throughs at **Hin Pousar** (หินพู่ซ่า, Elephant Head Rock); plume worms, soft corals, schooling fish, manta rays and rare whale sharks are among the local marine life. **Ko Bon** (เกาะบอน), largely unscathed by coral bleaching, is Thailand's prime manta-ray dive site. **Ko Tachai** (เกาะตาชัย), home to some of the Similans' best diving, is periodically closed to day trippers due to environmental concerns, though dive boats can still do dives here.

No facilities for divers exist in the national park, so you'll be taking a dive tour. Dive schools in Hat Khao Lak book various trips – day trips (two dives 5000B) and liveaboards (three-/six-day trips from around 19,000/35,000B) – as do Phuket dive centres (two-dive day trips from 5600B, three-day liveaboards from 18,900B). Multiday trips will typically include park transport, food and lodging, which cost little more than what you'd pay getting to and staying on the islands independently.

Hiking

The forest around the park visitors centre on Ko Miang has some walking trails and great wildlife, starting with a small 400m beach track leading east to a little snorkelling bay. If you detour from this track, the **Viewpoint Trail** (Ko Miang/Island 4) unveils panoramic vistas after 500m (30 minutes) of steep scrambling. A 500m (20-minute) forest walk west from the visitors centre leads to a smooth west-facing granite platform, **Sunset Point** (แหลมชันเช็ท; Ko Miang/Island 4).

On **Ko Similan** (เกาะสิมิลัน, Island 8), you can hike 2.5km through the forest to a **viewpoint** (จุดชมวิวเกาะสิมิลัน), and scramble up from the north-coast beach to **Sail Rock** (หินเรือใบ, Balance Rock); during the day it's clogged with visitors.

Wildlife

The Nicobar pigeon, with its wild mane of grey-green feathers, is endemic to the islands and is one of the park's 39 bird species. Hairy-legged land crabs, flying squirrels and fruit bats (flying foxes) are relatively easy to spot amid the forest.

TUPIKOV/GETTY IMAGES ©

KO SAMUI

Ko Samui at a Glance...

Ko Samui is a small city by the sea, adorned by white sand and modern conveniences. Curvaceous beaches, fast flights to Bangkok, high-end hotels, all-night parties and luxury spas cement Samui's reputation as Phuket's little sister. In places it is glitzy, brash and even slapdash, yet sleepy villages can still be found. Samui is everyone's version of an island idyll; you just have to know where to look.

Two Days in Ko Samui

Laze around the beaches, eat, sleep, drink, repeat. Supplement this itinerary with a spa treatment at **Tamarind Springs** (p162). Have dinner at a local seafood spot, such as **Bang Po Seafood** (p162). Party with the pros in Chaweng's beach bars and nightclubs.

Four Days in Ko Samui

Join a tour to **Ang Thong Marine National Park** (p160). Rent a motorcycle and tour the southern part of the island with a stop at **Ban Hua Thanon** (p159). Enjoy a splash-out dinner at **Dining on the Rocks** (p164).

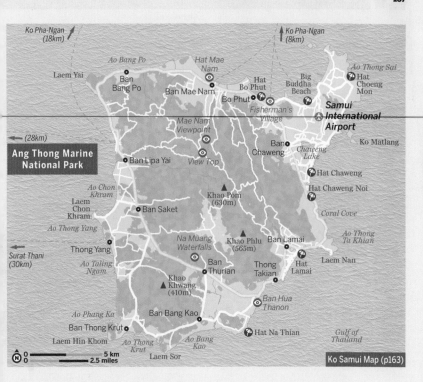

Ko Pha-Ngan (18km)

Ko Pha-Ngan (8km)

Ao Bang Po

Hat Mae Nam

Laem Yai

Ban Bang Po

Ban Mae Nam

Hat Bo Phut

Bo Phut

Fisherman's Village

Big Buddha Beach

Ao Thong Sai

Hat Choeng Mon

Samui International Airport

(28km)

Mae Nam Viewpoint

Ban Chaweng

Ko Matlang

Ang Thong Marine National Park

Ban Lipa Yai

View Top

Chaweng Lake

Hat Chaweng

Hat Chaweng Noi

Ao Chon Khram

Laem Chon Khram

Ban Saket

Khao Pom (630m)

Coral Cove

Ao Thong Yang

Na Muang Waterfalls

Khao Phlu (565m)

Ban Lamai

Ao Thong Tu Khian

Surat Thani (30km)

Thong Yang

Ao Taling Ngam

Ban Thurian

Thong Takian

Hat Lamai

Laem Nan

Khao Khwang (410m)

Ao Phang Ka

Ban Bang Kao

Ban Hua Thanon

Ban Thong Krut

Laem Hin Khom

Ao Thong Krut

Ao Bang Kao

Hat Na Thian

Gulf of Thailand

Laem Sor

5 km
2.5 miles

Ko Samui Map (p163)

Arriving in Ko Samui

Samui International Airport Located in the northeast of the island near Big Buddha Beach.

Boats Boats to nearby islands depart from various piers around Samui.

Where to Stay

Busy Chaweng and Lamai have the largest range of accommodation. The north coast is quieter with pretty Choeng Mon, featuring high-end hotels; Bo Phut, with artsy flash-pads; and low-key Mae Nam, which retains some backpacker spots.

Chaweng beach

OTTO STADLER/GETTY IMAGES ©

Ko Samui Beaches

East-coast beaches are leggy and legendary, famed for their looks and their parties. The north coast is quieter and more family-friendly. And the southwestern beaches are perfect for a sundowner.

Great For...

☑ **Don't Miss**

Doing an around-the-island tour to discover your favourite stretch of sand.

Every beach on Samui has a different personality, ranging from uber-social to quiet recluse.

East Coast

Most of the beach development on Samui is on the east coast. **Chaweng** has the beach version of an hourglass figure: soft white sand that gently curves from Ko Matlang in the north to Chaweng Noi in the south. The wide centre swath is crowded. Music blares from the beach bars and vendors tirelessly trudge through the sand to deliver amusements.

Lamai is just as pretty but not as famous as flamboyant Chaweng. It is the birthplace of Samui's fasting culture thanks to Spa Samui's two Lamai branches, but visitors looking for enlightenment will find hedonism in Lamai's commercial strip of girly

ⓘ Need to Know

Ko Samui's monsoon season runs from October to December; June to August is peak tourist season.

✕ Take a Break

Roadside curry shops along the ring road serve tasty southern-style curries.

★ Top Tip

At 229 sq km, Ko Samui is pretty large – the island's main ring road is more than 50km total.

of white sand (though it's uncomfortably close to the main road). **Bo Phut** and its **Fisherman's Village** (p162) represent the new generation of Thai beaches. The village retains the ambience of an old fishing town now occupied by design-minded restaurants and hotels. **Mae Nam** offers the right balance of beach distractions with enough Thai necessities to give it a sense of place. The northwestern peninsula is carved into a few stunning bays for luxury resorts, but you can spend the day soaking up the views on **Ao Thong Sai**.

South & West Coasts

The south coast is good for exploring: cruising through little village lanes, checking out different spits of land, nodding to a forlorn water buffalo. The coast is spotted with rocky headlands and smaller coves of pebble sand, used more as parking lots for Thai fishing boats than for lounge chairs. En route, a pit stop at **Ban Hua Thanon** allows a glimpse into the bucolic local matrix of life. The west coast also has views out to the **Five Islands** and the shadowy greens of the mainland are beguiling.

bars. The southern end of the beach has a more old-fashioned, castaway feel.

North Coast

Samui's alternative coast, the north coast, is more subdued. Near the northeastern tip, **Choeng Mon** is a scenic bay with shallow waters and a low-key bar scene that is popular with families. Locals consider Choeng Mon's crescent-shaped beach to be the best on the island. Next in line is **Big Buddha Beach** (Bang Rak), named after the huge golden Buddha. The beach's western half is by far the best, with an empty stretch

Ang Thong Marine National Park

Ang Thong Marine National Park

The 40-something jagged jungle islands of Ang Thong Marine National Park stretch across the cerulean sea like a shattered emerald necklace. This virgin territory is best explored on a guided tour from Samui.

Great For...

☑ Don't Miss

The islands' full-time residents are monkeys, birds, bats and crustaceans.

After an hour's boat journey from Samui, you start to see a looming landmass on the horizon. Slipping closer, the jumbled shadow separates into distinct islands, seemingly moored together. Limestone outcroppings jut skyward like ship masts creating the illusion of anchored shapes in the sapphire-coloured water. Closer still and an internal geometry is revealed: primordial figures woven together by a watery maze. The powerful ocean has whittled dramatic arches and hidden caves into the malleable rock.

Birth of a Park

Designated a park in 1980, Ang Thong (Golden Bowl) is 35km west of Samui. The park covers a total area of 102 sq km with land comprising only 18 sq km. It used to be a training ground for the Royal Thai

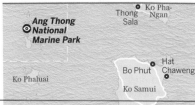

ⓘ Need to Know

อุทยานแห่งชาติหมู่เกาะอ่างทอง, Mu Ko Ang Thong Marine National Park; ☏077 280222; www.nps.dnp.go.th; adult/child 300/150B

✕ Take a Break

Lunch is provided by most tour companies, eg Blue Stars (p162).

★ Top Tip

February, March and April are the best months to visit. The park is often closed during the monsoon months of November and December.

Navy. The rugged islands are devoid of human inhabitants except day trippers. This dynamic landscape hosted the fictionalised commune in the other backpacker bible, *The Beach,* by Alex Garland.

Ko Mae

The myth-maker is Ko Mae (Mother Island) and its inner lagoon. The exterior of the island is a jagged shell of limestone and grizzled vegetation, but a steep climb up to the top reveals a sinkhole with a gleaming gem-coloured lake filled with underwater channels. You can look, but you can't touch: the lagoon is strictly off limits to the unclean human body.

Ko Wua Talap

Ko Wua Talap (Sleeping Cow Island) is the largest island in the chain and hosts the national park office and visitor bungalows. The island has a stunning mountaintop viewpoint, a necessary reward after clawing your way to the summit of the 450m trail, booby-trapped with sharp jagged rocks. A second trail leads to Tham Bua Bok, a cavern with lotus-shaped stalagmites and stalactites. There is a small sandy beach on the sunrise side of the island and a castaway's tranquillity.

Other Islands

The naturally occurring stone arches on **Ko Samsao** and **Ko Tai Plo** are visible during seasonal tides and certain weather conditions. There is also some diving, though the park is not as spectacular as other nearby spots. Soft powder beaches line **Ko Tai Plao**, **Ko Wuakantang** and **Ko Hintap**.

SIGHTS

Fisherman's Village   Village

(หมู่บ้านชาวประมงบ่อผุด; Bo Phut) This concentration of narrow Chinese shophouses in Bo Phut has been transformed into cool boutique hotels, restaurants, cafes and bars. The accompanying beach, particularly the eastern part, is slim and coarse but becomes whiter and lusher further west. The combination of pretty sands and gussied-up old village is a winner, but it can get busy during peak season. In the low season, it's lovely, quiet and elbow free.

> *...combination of pretty sands and old village*

Hat Mae Nam   Beach

(หาดแม่น้ำ; Mae Nam) This 5km stretch of sand sees relatively low visitor numbers, making it easy to find somewhere to sunbathe or go swimming. It's a standout beach, with pretty, white stretches of sand along a sleepy length of coast with a range of accommodation options and restaurants backing onto it from the nearby village.

ACTIVITIES

100 Degrees East   Diving

(☏077 423936; www.100degreeseast.com; Hat Bang Rak; ☺9am-6.30pm Dec-Oct) Highly professional and recommended, with a dedicated team, for excellent diving and snorkelling expeditions to Ang Thong Marine National Park, Ko Tao, Sail Rock and other sites.

Tamarind Springs   Massage

(☏085 926 4626; www.tamarindsprings.com; 205/7 Th Takian, off Rte 4169; spa packages from 1500B; ☺9am-8pm) Tucked away from the bustle of the beach, within a silent coconut-palm plantation, Tamarind's collection of villas and massage studios appear to have organically evolved from their jungle surrounds: some have granite boulders built into walls and floors, while others offer private ponds or creative outdoor baths. There's also a superb, healthy restaurant on-site and residential packages for stays.

Blue Stars   Kayaking

(☏081 894 5032; www.bluestars.info; 82/33 Mu 2, Chaweng Lake Rd; tours adult/child 2600/1700B; ☺10.30am-9pm) There are many choices for snorkelling and kayak tours to Ang Thong Marine National Park all over Ko Samui, but Blue Stars has the best reputation and the coolest boat in Chaweng. It also hse a super-friendly team that will do its utmost to give you the best deal.

EATING

Chaweng Night Food Market   Market $

(Chaweng Beach Rd; mains from 60B; ☺5-11pm) It's a little bit pricier than other food markets on the island, but there's always a great buzz here in the evenings as groups of revellers sit together clinking beer bottles and tucking into one of the many local or Western dishes on offer before hitting Chaweng's lively strip for the night.

Bang Po Seafood   Seafood $$

(☏077 602208; Rte 4169, Bang Po; mains 200B; ☺10am-10pm) A meal at Bang Po Seafood is a test for the taste buds. It's one of the only restaurants that serves traditional Ko Samui fare: recipes call for ingredients such as raw sea urchin roe, baby octopus, sea water, coconut and local turmeric, and they are served in a delightfully local setting that spills onto the beach.

Hemingway's on the Beach   Thai $$

(☏088 452 4433; www.hemingwaysonthebeach. com; off Rte 4170, Ao Thong Krut; mains 225B; ☺10am-8pm Mon-Sat; ☏) With appetising Thai dishes, this beachside choice on Rte 4170 – home to Jaa's Cooking School (1500B per person) – is an excellent reason to escape to the southwest corner of Ko Samui. Tuck into fresh seafood and bask in the views, especially come sundown. Hemingway's also arranges long-tail and

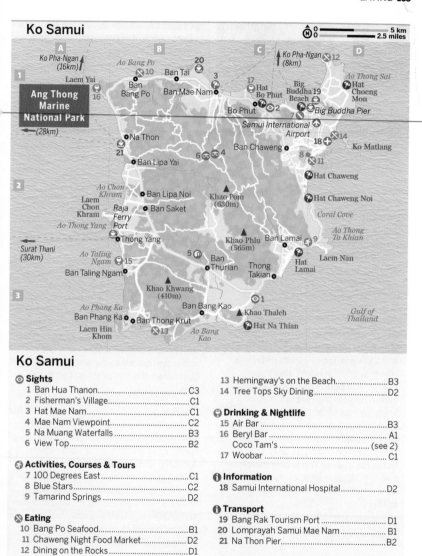

Ko Samui

speedboat island tours, while massage is at hand for post-meal relaxation.

Tree Tops Sky Dining   Fusion $$$
(☏077 960333; www.anantara.com; 92/1 Mu 2, Chaweng Choengmon Rd; mains 1000B, set menu from 4550B; ◷6-11pm Sun-Fri, from noon Sat) The most romantic spot in Chaweng.

This series of beautiful, interconnected, treetop platforms in the trees at the back of the Anantara resort compete with each other to offer the best views towards the sea (that would be table 7). The menu is so modern dishes have no names, only ingredients, and it's ideal for a special occasion.

 ### Ko Samui's Best Hikes

Ko Samui is blessed with a series of treks that explore the uninhabited jungle heart, climbing up to glorious viewpoints for long views over the island. An undemanding but intriguing hike runs from **Beryl Bar** (Hat Laem Yai; ⊘6pm-late; 🐾), near the northwest tip of the island, north along the rocky shoreline to a Buddhist statue that sits gazing out to sea. The hike is only a few hundred metres, though you'll be picking your way over the rocks. The trek up to the **Mae Nam Viewpoint** (จุดชมวิว; entry 50B) and the **View Top** is a more ambitious hike that takes you into the jungle interior and puts the hilly topography of the island in clearer perspective. Many visitors undertake this journey by scooter, but it can be done on foot; the very adventurous can continue down to Na Thon on the west coast. The trek to the **Na Muang Waterfalls** (น้ำตกหน้า เมือง 1; Ⓟ) FREE is another doable hike, best undertaken when the falls are in full flow.

Na Muang Waterfalls

Dining on the Rocks — Fusion $$$

(☎077 245678; www.sixsenses.com/resorts/ samui/dining; Choeng Mon; set menu from 2800B; ⊘6pm-midnight; 🐾🖊) At the isolated Six Senses Samui, the island's ultimate fusion dining experience takes place on nine cantilevered verandas yawning over the gulf. After sunset (and wine), guests feel like they're dining on a barge set adrift on a starlit sea. Each dish on the set menu is the brainchild of cooks experimenting with taste, texture and temperature.

🍷 DRINKING & NIGHTLIFE

Woobar — Bar

(☎077 915999; www.wkohsamui.com; Bo Phut; ⊘11am-11pm; 🐾) With serious wow factor and spectacular panoramas, the W Retreat's signature bar is the best place for sunset cocktails. Get there early to bag the cushion-clad seating pods inside the mesmerising infinity pool that stretches out to an azure horizon, and as the nightly live DJ plays, try to determine where the water ends and the sky begins.

Coco Tam's — Bar

(Th Hat Bo Phut, Fisherman's Village; ⊘1pm-1am) Grab a swing at the bar or plop yourself on a beanbag on the sand, order a giant cocktail or a to-die-for coconut milkshake served in a jar, and take a toke on a shisha (water pipe). It's a bit pricey, but this boho, beach-bum-chic spot oozes relaxation and is particularly lovely when the sun goes down and fire dancers start their performances.

Air Bar — Bar

(☎077 429100; www.samui.intercontinental. com/air-bar; Intercontinental Samui Baan Taling Ngam Resort, Taling Ngam; ⊘5pm-midnight; 🐾) Toast the setting sun as it sinks into the golden gulf from the magnificent outside bar perched above a cliff at a swanky resort. There's an excellent menu of tapas and snacks if you simply can't pull yourself away and want to make a meal of it. This is pretty much the top romantic choice in Na Thon.

ℹ️ INFORMATION

Samui International Hospital (☎077 300394; www.sih.co.th; 90/2 Mu 2, Chaweng Beach Rd; ⊘24hr) Emergency ambulance service is available 24hr and credit cards are accepted.

Kayaking, Ang Thong Marine National Park (p160)

ℹ GETTING THERE & AWAY

Bangkok Airways (www.bangkokair.com) operates flights roughly every 30 minutes between Ko Samui's airport (p306) Bangkok (Suvarnabhumi). It also flies direct from Samui to Phuket, and Chiang Mai. During the high season, buy tickets well in advance. If the Samui flights are full, try flying into Surat Thani from Bangkok and taking the ferry ride to Samui instead.

ℹ GETTING AROUND

Scooter Rentals are widely available and reasonably priced. As well as local taxis there is the Grab (www.grab.com) option. Cars can be hired all over the island.

Beautiful beach in Ko Lipe

Ko Lipe

Ko Lipe is blessed with two wide, beautiful white-sand beaches, separated by forested hills and close to protected coral reefs. Once a serene paradise, it's now a poster child for development.

Great For...

Phuket Town · · Krabi
THAILAND
· · Phatthalung
Trang

Hat Yai ·

Satun ·
Ko Lipe ⊚
MALAYSIA

❶ Need to Know

Do not try to swim the narrow strait between Lipe and Adang at any time of year; currents are swift and can be deadly.

★ **Top Tip**

The best way to see the archipelago is to hire a taxi boat from the stand on **Hat Sunrise** (หาดพระอาทิตย์ขึ้น).

JUREERAT GEAWADUANG / SHUTTERSTOCK ©

Ko Lipe's centre has transformed into an ever-expanding maze of hotels, restaurants, travel agencies and shops. Tourist-inspired growth has led to issues with waste management, noise pollution and energy supplies. The biggest losers have been the 700-strong community of *chow lair* (sea gypsies, also spelt *chao leh*), whose ancestors were gifted Lipe as a home by Rama V (King Chulalongkorn; r 1868–1910) in 1909, but then sold it in the 1970s.

Despite all the development, Lipe's stunning beauty shines through: gorgeous beaches, sensational dive sites, a jungle interior, a contagiously friendly vibe and a good few inhabitants keen to minimise their environmental impact. It's more chill than party, but it's not the remote castaway island it once was.

Diving

While it would be a stretch to call the diving here world-class most of the year, it's outstanding when the visibility clarifies, somewhat counterintuitively in the early part of the wet season (mid-April to mid-June). There are some fun drift dives and two rock-star dive sites.

Eight Mile Rock is a deep pinnacle that attracts devil rays and (very) rare whale sharks. It's the only site in the area to see pelagics. **Stonehenge** is popular because of its beautiful soft corals, resident seahorses, rare leopard sharks and the reef-top boulders behind its inspired name. **Ko Sarang** is another stunner, with gorgeous soft corals, a ripping current and solar flares of fish that make it many people's favourite Lipe dive spot.

Hat Sunrise

Snorkelling

There's good coral along the southern coast and around **Ko Kra** and **Ko Usen**, the islets opposite Hat Sunrise (watch out for oncoming long-tails). Most resorts rent out mask-and-snorkel sets and fins (100B to 200B). Travel agents and some dive operators arrange four-point snorkel trips to Ko Adang, Ko Rawi and other coral-fringed islands from 450B per person.

Beaches & Islands

The most popular among Ko Lipe's beaches is **Hat Sunrise**, a sublime long stretch of powder-fine sand that runs along the island's east coast. It is clearly also the best beach on the island. From its northernmost point, you'll have spectacular views of **Ko Adang**. The southern end is home to upmarket resorts. During low season (May to October) the line-up of boats and long-tails along the beachfront crowds out swimmers.

With its slender strip of golden sand, gentle jungle-covered hills and serene bay that spills into the Adang Strait on the western side of the island, **Hat Sunset** has a different feel to Lipe's other beaches. During high season (November to April), it's something of a retreat from the more crowded beaches. In low season (May to October) it's very quiet. In stark contrast, busy **Hat Pattaya** on Lipe's southern coast has beach bars, seafood and a party vibe during the high season, though long-tails often crowd out swimmers.

Among nearby islands, there are good coral formations to be found around **Ko Kra**, one of the little islands opposite Hat Sunrise. If you enter the water, be aware of, and take care around, oncoming long-tail boats. Most resorts rent out mask-and-snorkel sets and fins for 100B to 200B. **Ko Usen**, one of the little islands opposite Hat Sunrise, has some good coral. Most resorts rent out mask-and-snorkel sets and fins (100B to 200B).

> **✕ Take a Break**
> Find cheap eats at the *roti* stands and small Thai cafes along Walking Street.

JON ARNOLD IMAGES LTD/ALAMY STOCK PHOTO ©

> **☑ Don't Miss**
> There's some great seafood here. The best places are mostly inland.

SUKHOTHAI

In this Chapter

Sukhothai at a Glance...

Sukhothai is widely regarded as the first capital of Siam. After breaking away from the Khmer kingdom in 1238, beautiful temples mixing Khmer and unique Sukhothai styles were built to honour the newly adopted Theravada Buddhism and the new Thai dynasty. Today the old city is sheltered in a quiet park-like setting that creates a meditative calm, perfect for enjoying the gravity of the majestic monuments.

Two Days in Sukhothai

Explore **Sukhothai Historical Park** (p174). The central and northern zones are easily visited by bicycle. The next day hire a motorcycle to explore the western and southern zones.

Four Days in Sukhothai

Spend day three at **Si Satchanalai-Chaliang Historical Park** (p178). On your last day sign up for a **cycling tour** (p182) of Sukhothai, a guided adventure to unexplored corners of the park and environs.

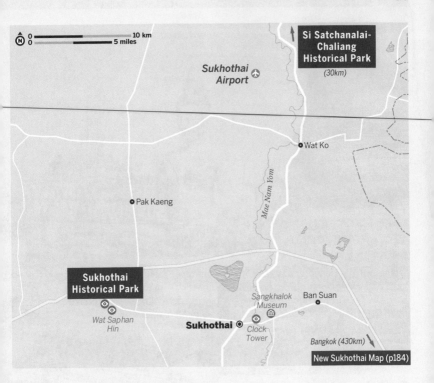

Sukhothai Airport

Si Satchanalai-
Chaliang
Historical Park
(30km)

Wat Ko

Pak Kaeng

Mae Nam Yom

Sukhothai
Historical Park

Sangkhalok
Museum

Ban Suan

Wat Saphan
Hin

Sukhothai

Clock
Tower

Bangkok (430km)

New Sukhothai Map (p184)

Arriving in Sukhothai

Sukhothai Airport Located 27km north of town, and has two daily flights to/from Bangkok.

Bus station Located 1km northwest of New Sukhothai. *Sŏrng·tăa·ou* (pick-up minibuses) leave for Sukhothai Historical Park from here.

Where to Stay

Most lodging is in New Sukhothai, home to some of the best-value budget places in northern Thailand. Clean, cheerful hotels and guesthouses abound, many offering free pick-up from the bus station and free use of bicycles.

Wat Mahathat

MINKO PEEV/SHUTTERSTOCK ©

Sukhothai Historical Park

Crumbling temple ruins and serene Buddha statues provide a meditative journey through this Unesco World Heritage Site. The park includes the remains of 21 sites and four large ponds within the old walls, and 70 other sites within a 5km radius. The ruins are divided into five zones.

Great For...

☑ **Don't Miss**

Hiring a bicycle and cycling around the ruins is the best way to explore the central zone.

The Sukhothai kingdom (*sukhothai* means 'rising happiness') flourished from the mid-13th century to the late 14th century, as the imperial Angkor kingdom in Cambodia was losing its grip on its western frontier. This period is often viewed as the golden age of Thai civilisation. Sukhothai's dynasty lasted 200 years and spanned nine kings. By 1438 Sukhothai was absorbed by Ayuthaya.

Central Zone

The pockmarked ruins of the kingdom, believed to be the administrative centre, are concentrated in the **central zone** (อุทยานประวัติศาสตร์สุโขทัย โซนกลาง; 100B, plus bicycle 10B; ⏱6.30am-7.30pm Sun-Fri, to 9pm Sat), in an area known as *meu·ang gòw* (old city), a 45-sq-km compound.

Banyan tree at Wat Si Sawai

NEELSKY/SHUTTERSTOCK ©

Wat Si Chum

Sukhothai Historical Park

Wat Sa Si

Wat Mahathat

Wat Si Sawai

Wat Trapang Thong

ℹ️ Need to Know

อุทยานประวัติศาสตร์สุโขทัย; 📞055 697527; central, northern & western zones 100B, plus bicycle 10B; 🕐central zone 6.30am-7.30pm Sun-Fri, to 9pm Sat, northern & western zones 6.30am-7.30pm

✗ Take a Break

Coffee Corner (Rte 12; mains 60-350B; 🕐7am-4pm; 📶) serves fresh breads, drinks and other cafe fare.

★ Top Tip

The central, northern and western zones each have a separate 100B admission fee.

Ramkhamhaeng National Museum

A good starting point for exploring the historical park is this **museum** (พิพิธภัณฑสถานแห่งชาติรามคำแหง; 150B; 🕐9am-4pm), named for the third Sukhothai king. King Ramkhamhaeng is considered to be the founding father of the nation. He is credited with creating the Thai script and establishing Theravada Buddhism as the kingdom's primary religion. A replica of the famous Ramkhamhaeng inscription, said to be the earliest example of Thai writing, is kept here among an impressive collection of Sukhothai artefacts. Admission to the museum is not included in the ticket to the central zone.

Wat Mahathat

The largest temple in the historic park, **Wat Mahathat** (วัดมหาธาตุ) was completed in the 13th century and is considered to be the former spiritual and administrative centre of the old capital. It is a hybrid of Khmer and Sukhothai artistic styles. The temple is surrounded by brick walls (206m long and 200m wide) and a moat that is believed to represent the outer wall of the universe and the cosmic ocean, a common theme in Khmer architecture. Multiple *chedi* feature the famous lotus-bud motif, considered a distinctive Sukhothai artistic feature adapted from the Sri Lankan bell-shaped *chedi*. Some of the original stately Buddha figures still sit among the ruined columns of the old *wí·hǎhn* (sanctuary). There are 198 *chedi* within the monastery walls and many photogenic specimens.

Wat Si Sawai

Just south of Wat Mahathat, this Buddhist **shrine** (วัดศรีสวาย) dating from the 12th and 13th centuries features three Khmer-style towers and a picturesque moat. It was originally built by the Khmers as a Hindu temple. Sukhothai craftspeople added stucco reliefs depicting mythical creatures, such as *apsara* (heavenly maidens) and *naga* (serpents).

Wat Sa Si

Wat Sa Si (วัดสระศรี, Sacred Pond Monastery) sits on an island west of the bronze monument of King Ramkhamhaeng. It's a simple, classic Sukhothai-style *wát* containing a large Buddha, one bell-shaped *chedi* and the columns of the ruined *wí·hǎhn*. Bell-shaped *chedi*, an artistic inheritance from Sri Lanka, migrated to Sukhothai thanks to the adoption of Buddhism.

Wat Trapang Thong

Next to the Ramkhamhaeng National Museum, this small, still-inhabited **wát** (วัดตระพัง ทอง; off Rte 12; ⊘daylight hours) with fine stuc-

co reliefs is reached by a footbridge across the large lotus-filled pond that surrounds it. This reservoir, the original site of Thailand's Loi Krathong festival, supplies the Sukhothai community with most of its water.

Northern Zone

The **northern zone** (อุทยานประวัติศาสตร์ สุโขทัย โซนเหนือ; 100B, plus bicycle 10B; ⊘6.30am-7.30pm) is 500m north of the old city walls and is easily reached by bicycle. It rivals the central zone with important architectural ruins.

Wat Si Chum

Beloved by shutterbugs, this **temple** (วัด ศรีชุม) is northwest of the old city and contains an impressive *mon·dòp* (a *chedi*-like spire) with a 15m, brick-and-stucco seated Buddha. The Buddha's elegant, tapered

Wat Sa Si

fingers are much photographed and larger than life. Archaeologists theorise that this image is the 'Phra Atchana' mentioned in the famous Ramkhamhaeng inscription.

Wat Phra Phai Luang

Often viewed as an architectural companion to Wat Si Sawai in the central zone, this somewhat isolated **temple** (วัดพระพายหลวง) featured three 12th-century Khmer-style towers. All but one tower has collapsed and the remaining structure is decorated with time-worn stucco relief indicative of Sukhothai style. This may have been the

centre of Sukhothai when it was ruled by the Khmers of Angkor prior to the 13th century.

Western Zone

The **western zone** (อุทยานประวัติศาสตร์สุโขทัย โซนตะวันตก; 100B, plus bicycle 10B; ⊙6.30am-7.30pm) is about 2km from the old city and is rarely crowded. The road here leads past scenic countryside.

Wat Saphan Hin

Located on the crest of a hill that rises about 200m above the plain, the name of the **wát** (วัดสะพานหิน), which means 'stone bridge', is a reference to the slate path and staircase that leads up to the temple, which are still in place. All that remains of the original temple are a few *chedi* and the ruined *wí·hǎhn,* consisting of two rows of laterite columns flanking a 12.5m-high standing Buddha image on a brick terrace. The site is 3km west of the former city wall and gives a good view of the Sukhothai ruins to the southeast and the mountains to the north and south.

☑ **Don't Miss**

A few worthwhile destinations lie in other sites outside the more popular paid zones.

BOONSOM/GETTY IMAGES ©

★ **Did You Know?**

Sukhothai is often described as the first Thai kingdom. But the kingdom of Chiang Saen had been established 500 years earlier, so this is technically incorrect.

Wat Phra Si Ratana Mahathat

NONOZ/SHUTTERSTOCK ©

Si Satchanalai-Chaliang Historical Park

Pretty countryside and forests frame the ruins of this satellite city of the Sukhothai kingdom, dating to the 13th to 15th centuries. You'll meet fewer visitors here.

Great For...

☑ Don't Miss

Climbing the stairs to the hilltop temple of Wat Khao Phanom Phloeng is a sightseeing workout.

As Sukhothai's influence grew, it expanded to this strategic position on the banks of Mae Nam Yom between two lookout hills. Si Satchanalai hosted many of the Sukhothai kingdom's monasteries and temples as well as ceramics factories that exported to neighbouring countries. After the fall of Sukhothai, this area continued to be used by the rival forces of Lanna and Ayuthaya. Si Satchanalai, along with Sukhothai, is recognised as a Unesco World Heritage Site. The park covers roughly 720 hectares and is surrounded by a 12m-wide moat.

Wat Phra Si Ratana Mahathat

Si Satchanalai's main attraction, **Wat Phra Si Ratana Mahathat** (วัดพระศรีรัตน มหาธาตุ; 20B) sits outside the entrance to the historical park on the banks of Mae Nam Yom. The impressive central tower

Ancient pagoda

SOMRAK JENDEE/SHUTTERSTOCK ©

Wat Khao Phanom Phloeng
Wat Chang Lom
Wat Chedi Jet Thaew
Wat Phra Si Ratana Mahathat
Moe Nam Yom
Wat Nang Phaya
Wat Chao Chan

Si Satchanalai-Chaliang Historical Park

ℹ️ Need to Know

อุทยานประวัติศาสตร์ศรีสัชนาลัย-เชลียง; off Rte 101; 100B, combined ticket with Wat Chao Chan & Si Satchanalai Centre for Study & Preservation of Sangkalok Kilns 250B; ⏰8.30am-4.30pm

✕ Take a Break

Roadside vendors line the main road and sell simple meals and drinks.

★ Top Tip

Be sure to stock up on water because the sites are far-flung without the usual conveniences in between.

poses peacefully among the surrounding greenery and is framed by a large seated Sukhothai Buddha and pillars. Nearby is a smaller standing image and a bas-relief of the famous walking Buddha, exemplary of the flowing, boneless Sukhothai style. The tower is a corn-cob shape, suggestive of Khmer style, but it is actually an Ayuthaya style because it has a smooth curvature rather than the Khmer 'steps'. Near the main entrance, look for a pillar topped by a Khmer-style four-faced figure, evocative of temples in Angkor. The figure depicts the Hindu god Brahma.

Wat Chang Lom

This fine **temple** (วัดช้างล้อม), marking the centre of the old city of Si Satchanalai, is encircled by elephant statues and a towering bell-shaped *chedi* that is somewhat better preserved than its counterpart in Sukhothai. The elephants' entire bodies are intact giving the visual appearance of the structure being carried on the backs of the elephants. In Buddhist iconography, elephants are often regarded as guardians and were a common motif in Sukhothai temples. An inscription states that the temple was built by King Ramkhamhaeng between 1285 and 1291.

Wat Khao Phanom Phloeng

On the hill overlooking Wat Chang Lom are the remains of **Wat Khao Phanom Phloeng** (วัดเขาพนมเพลิง), meaning Holy Fire Mountain Temple. The forest closes in among a *chedi,* a large seated Buddha and stone columns that once supported the roof of the *wí·hǎhn.* From here you can make out the general design of the once great city. It is a sweaty walk up the 44 steps made of laterite blocks to the top, but the surrounding forest adds a mystique of adventure. A small shrine to a local goddess receives supplications of dresses from devotees. The hilltop is also a nesting site for waterbirds, including egrets and cranes; locals often carry umbrellas to protect themselves from bird droppings.

Wat Chedi Jet Thaew

A strong contender for Si Satchanalai's best, **Wat Chedi Jet Thaew** (วัดเจดีย์เจ็ด แถว), next to Wat Chang Lom, is so named because of its seven rows of *chedi,* the largest of which is a copy of one at Wat Mahathat in Sukhothai. An interesting brick-and-plaster *wí·hǎhn* features barred windows designed to look like lathed wood (an ancient Indian technique used all over Southeast Asia). The temple dates back to the 14th century and contains a mix of styles: Khmer, Lanna and Sukhothai.

Wat Nang Phaya

One of the youngest temples in the collection, **Wat Nang Phaya** (วัดนางพญา), south of Wat Chedi Jet Thaew, has a bell-shaped Sinhalese *chedi* and was built in the 15th or 16th century. Stucco reliefs on the large laterite *wí·hǎhn* in front of the *chedi* – now sheltered by a tin roof – date from the Ayuthaya period when Si Satchanalai was known as Sawankhalok. Goldsmiths in the district still craft a design known as *nahng pá·yah,* modelled after these reliefs.

Wat Chao Chan

Sheltered by woods, **Wat Chao Chan** (วัดเจ้า จันทร์) is a large Khmer-style tower similar to later towers built in Lopburi and probably constructed during the reign of Khmer king Jayavarman VII (1181–1217). The tower has

Wat Nang Phaya

been restored and is in fairly good shape. The roofless *wí·hǎhn* on the right contains the laterite outlines of a large standing Buddha that has all but melted away from exposure and weathering.

Si Satchanalai Centre for Study & Preservation of Sangkalok Kilns

At one time, more than 200 huge pottery kilns lined the banks of Mae Nam Yom in the area around Si Satchanalai. The kilns produced glazed ceramics that were exported to other Asian countries. In China – the biggest importer of Thai

pottery during the Sukhothai and Ayuthaya periods – the pieces produced here came to be called Sangkalok, a mispronunciation of Sawankhalok, the original name of the region.

Excavated kilns can be visited at the **Si Satchanalai Centre for Study & Preservation of Sangkalok Kilns** (ศูนย์ศึกษาและ อนุรักษ์เตาสังคโลก), located 5km northwest of the Si Satchanalai ruins. There are also many intact pottery samples and interesting displays despite the lack of English labels. Ceramics are still made in the area, and a local ceramic artist even continues to fire his pieces in an underground wood-burning oven.

> ☑ **Don't Miss**
>
> When visiting the park, make sure to check out the excavated kilns along Mae Nam Yom.

KWANCHAI/SHUTTERSTOCK ©

> ★ **Did You Know?**
>
> Wat Phra Si Ratana Mahathat is one of the largest, oldest and most historically important *wát* in the park and received the status of royal property after a visit by the previous king.

◎ SIGHTS

Sangkhalok Museum
Museum

(พิพิธภัณฑ์สังคโลก; Rte 1293; adult/child 100/50B; ☺8am-5pm) This small but comprehensive museum is an excellent introduction to ancient Sukhothai's most famous product and export, its ceramics. The ground-floor displays offer an impressive collection of original Thai pottery found in the area, plus some pieces traded from Vietnam, Myanmar and China. The 2nd floor features examples of nonutilitarian pottery made as art, including some beautiful and rare ceramic Buddha statues. The museum is about 2.5km east of the centre of New Sukhothai; a túk-túk (pronounced *dúk dúk*) here is about 100B.

✪ ACTIVITIES

Cycling Sukhothai
Cycling

(☏055 612519, 085 083 1864; www.cycling-sukhothai.com; off Th Jarodvithithong; half-/full day 800/990B, sunset tour 450B; ⧫) A resident of Sukhothai for 20-odd years, Belgian cycling enthusiast Ronny Hanquart offers themed bike tours, such as the Historical Park Tour, that also includes stops at lesser-seen wát and villages. The office is about 1.2km west of the Mae Nam Yom, off Th Jarodvithi-thong in New Sukhothai; free transport can be arranged. There are trailers and special seats for kids.

> *bike tours that include lesser-seen wát and villages*

Organic Agriculture Project
Cooking

(☏055 647290; off Rte 1195; half-day incl lunch 900B; ☺8am-5pm Thu-Tue) ⚑ Sukhothai's Organic Agriculture Project allows visitors to take part in traditional Thai farm activities. The compound is also home to a restaurant serving dishes made from the farm's organic produce (mains 50B to 120B, open 8am to 5pm Thursday to Tuesday).

Sukhothai Historical Park (p174)

PIMSARA CHUPROM/SHUTTERSTOCK ©

😋 EATING

Poo Restaurant Multicuisine $

(24/3 Th Jarodvithithong; mains 50-250B; ☺9am-11pm; 🛜) Named after its original owner (if you were wondering), Poo is a traveller-friendly spot that serves everything from tasty Sukhothai noodles to Thai and Western classics. Portions are big. It's also fine for an evening drink: they do cocktails and have a small selection of Belgian beers.

Fueang Fah Thai $$

(107/2 Th Kuhasuwan; dishes 60-350B; ☺10am-10pm; 🛜) Pretend you're a local in the know and have a meal at this long-standing riverside restaurant. The speciality here is freshwater fish dishes, such as the tasty 'fried fish', the first item on the barely comprehensible English-language menu. There's no Roman-script sign; it's just after the bridge on Th Kuhasuwan.

Sukhothai Kitchen Thai $$

(Rte 1272; mains 95-280B; ☺10am-10pm; 🛜) This big and breeezy place is set around a garden with the inevitable lotus pond. The menu spans Thai and Northern Thai dishes, with a few Western options. It's more upmarket than the restaurants close to the Sukhothai Historical Park.

🍷 DRINKING & NIGHTLIFE

Sukhothai's guesthouses, especially those on and around Th Prawet Nakhon, function as the town's low-key bar scene.

Chopper Bar Bar

(Th Prawet Nakhon; ☺5pm-midnight; 🛜) Travellers and locals congregate at this 2nd-floor bar with a vague cowboy theme for drinks, food (the menu is thoughtfully divided into spicy and nonspicy sections) and live music. Take advantage of Sukhothai's cool evenings on the rooftop terrace. The bar is owned by Sukhothai's finest locksmith, just in case you get locked out.

🍽️ Sukhothai Noodles

Sukhothai's signature dish is *gŏo·ay dĕe·o sù·kŏh·tai* (Sukhothai-style noodles), which features a slightly sweet broth with different preparations of pork, ground peanuts and thinly sliced green beans. The best places in town to get the dish are:

Jayhae (off Th Jarodvithithong; dishes 40-120B; ☺7am-4pm; 🛜) An extremely popular restaurant that serves Sukhothai-style noodles, *pàt tai* and tasty coffee drinks. It's located about 1.3km west of Mae Nam Yom.

Tapui (off Th Jarodvithithong; dishes 40-80B; ☺7.30am-4pm) Claims to be the first shop in Sukhothai to have sold the dish. It's also about 1.3km west of Mae Nam Yom.

Sukhothai-style noodles
SUTTISAK_INP/SHUTTERSTOCK ©

ℹ️ INFORMATION

Tourism Authority of Thailand (TAT; 📞055 616228, nationwide 1672; www.tourismthailand.org; Th Jarodvithithong; ☺8.30am-4.30pm) About 750m west of the bridge in New Sukhothai, this office has a pretty good selection of maps and brochures and a few English-speaking staff.

ℹ️ GETTING THERE & AWAY

AIR

Sukhothai Airport (off Rte 1195) is located 27km north of town. **Bangkok Airways** (📞055 647224, nationwide 1771; www.bangkokair.com; Sukhothai

New Sukhothai

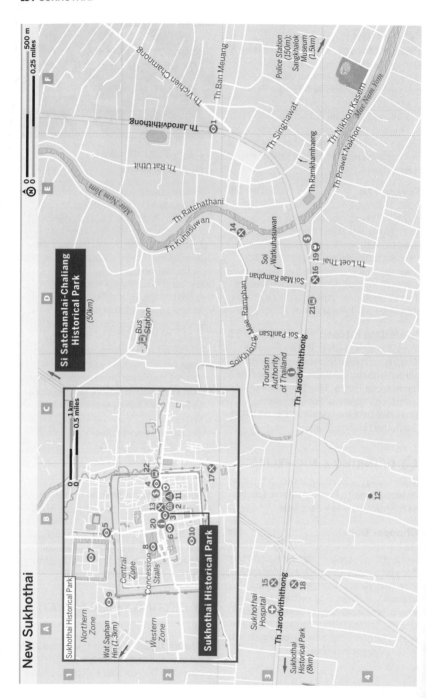

Si Satchanalai-Chaliang
Historical Park
(50km)

Sukhothai Historical Park

New Sukhothai

Airport; ⊗7am-6pm) has two daily flights to/ from Bangkok.

BUS & MINIVAN

Sukhothai's **bus station** (⊡055 614529; Rte 101) is almost 1km northwest of the centre of New Sukhothai. *Sŏrng·tăa·ou* (passenger pick-up minivans) bound for Sukhothai Historical Park stop at the bus station. **Win Tour** (⊡099 135 5645; Rte 12; ⊗6am-9.50pm) has an office where you can board buses to Bangkok (six

hours, three daily) and Chiang Mai (five hours, four daily).

GETTING AROUND

A sǎhm·lór (three-wheeled pedicab) ride within New Sukhothai should cost no more than 40B to 50B. The best way to get around the historical park is by bicycle. Motorbikes (from 200B for 24 hours) can be hired at many guesthouses.

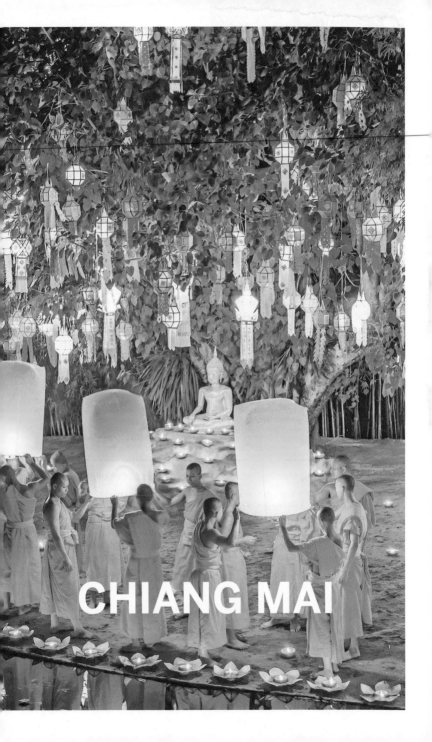

CHIANG MAI

In this Chapter

Chiang Mai at a Glance...

The cultural capital of the north, Chiang Mai is beloved by temple-spotters, culture vultures and adventure-loving families. The narrow streets steeped in history provide an atmosphere that's more like a country town than a modern city. Great escapes from the city lie just an hour away and tours shuttle visitors to jungle treks and minority villages.

Two Days in Chiang Mai

Visit the temples and museums of the old city. Have either lunch or dinner at **Kao Soi Fueng Fah** (p212). Spend your second day doing a Thai cooking course, then visit the **Saturday Walking Street** (p196) or **Sunday Walking Street** (p197).

Four Days in Chiang Mai

On your third day join a full-day **outdoor activity** (p198), such as trekking, ziplining or mountain biking. The next day, tour the shops and restaurants of Th Nimmanhaemin – try **Tong Tem Toh** (p211) for northern Thai cuisine – and stay for the nightlife.

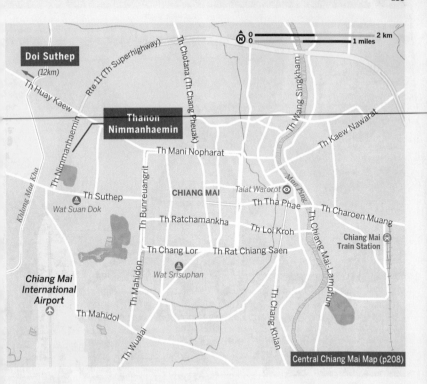

Central Chiang Mai Map (p208)

Arriving in Chiang Mai

Chiang Mai International Airport
About 3km southwest of the old city.
Has plenty of domestic and international connections.

Arcade Bus Terminal About 3km
northeast of the city centre. Handles
long-distance services to major Thai
cities.

Chiang Mai Train Station About 2.5km
east of the old city, with connections to
Bangkok.

Where to Stay

Accommodation prices in the city are
slowly creeping up, but you can still find
a respectable air-con room from 650B.
Make reservations far in advance if visiting during Chinese New Year, Songkran
and other holiday periods.

Wat Phra Singh

SAMO3P/SHUTTERSTOCK ©

Old City Temples

Chiang Mai's temples showcase traditional Lanna art and architecture, using teak harvested in the once-dense frontiers and demonstrating traditions inherited from Myanmar and China.

Great For...

☑ **Don't Miss**

Learn about Buddhism and being a monk at Wat Chedi Luang's Monk Chat.

The temples featured here are all located in the old city, but other beautiful temples lie outside of the city walls.

Wat Phra Singh

Chiang Mai's most revered temple, **Wat Phra Singh** (วัดพระสิงห์; Th Singharat; ⊘5am-8.30pm) sits regally at the end of Th Ratchadamnoen. Behind its whitewashed walls are lavish monastic buildings and immaculately trimmed grounds, dotted with coffee stands and massage pavilions. Pilgrims flock here to venerate the famous Buddha image known as Phra Singh (Lion Buddha), housed in Wihan Lai Kham, a small chapel immediately south of the *chedi* (stupa) to the rear of the temple grounds.

This elegant idol is said to have come to Thailand from Sri Lanka and was enshrined

Wat Chedi Luang

Akha Ama Cafe (p213), near Wat Phra Singh

❶ Need to Know

Temples are open during daylight hours and donations are appreciated.

✗ Take a Break

Akha Ama Cafe (p213), near Wat Phra Singh, is a cute cafe with a development mission for Akha hill tribes.

★ Top Tip

Dress modestly and remove your shoes before entering a temple building.

Trai, decorated with bas-relief angels. The temple's main *chedi*, rising over a classic Lanna-style octagonal base, was constructed by King Pa Yo in 1345; it's often wrapped in bolts of orange cloth by devotees.

Wat Chedi Luang

Wat Chedi Luang (วัดเจดีย์หลวง; Th Phra Pokklao; adult/child 40/20B; ⊙5am-10.30pm) is not quite as grand as Wat Phra Singh, but its towering, ruined Lanna-style *chedi* (built in 1441) is much taller and the sprawling compound is powerfully atmospheric. The famed Phra Kaew (Emerald Buddha), now held in Bangkok's Wat Phra Kaew, resided in the eastern niche of the *chedi* until 1475; today you can view a jade replica, given as a gift from the Thai king in 1995 to celebrate the 600th anniversary of the *chedi*.

In the main *wí·hǎhn* (sanctuary) is a revered standing Buddha statue, known as Phra Chao Attarot, flanked by two disciples. There are more chapels and statues in teak pavilions at the rear of the compound, including a huge reclining Buddha and a handsome Chinese-influenced seated Buddha barely contained by his

in 1367. The chapel is similarly striking, with gilded *naga* (mythical serpent) gables and sumptuous *lai·krahm* (gold-pattern stencilling) inside.

Despite Phra Singh's exalted status, very little is actually known about the image, which has more in common with images from northern Thailand than with Buddha statues from Sri Lanka. Adding to the mystery, there are two nearly identical images elsewhere in Thailand, one in the Bangkok National Museum and one in Nakhon Si Thammarat. Regardless of its provenance, the statue has become a focal point for religious celebrations during the Songkran festival, when it is ceremoniously paraded for worshippers to bathe.

As you wander the monastery grounds, note the raised temple library, housed in a dainty teak and stucco pavilion known as Ho

robes. The daily Monk Chat under a tree in the grounds always draws a crowd of interested travellers.

Next to the main entrance on Th Phra Pokklao, you'll pass Wat Chedi Luang's other claim to fame: the *làk meu·ang* (city pillar), allegedly raised by King Mengrai himself when Chiang Mai was founded in 1296. Buddhist rules dictate that only men can enter the pavilion to view the pillar. The gateway to the shrine on Th Phra Pakklao is flanked by *yaksha* (guardian demons) and Lanna warriors are depicted in bas-relief on the gates.

Wat Phan Tao

Without doubt the most atmospheric *wát* in the old city is **Wat Phan Tao** (วัดพันเตา; Th Phra Pokklao; donations appreciated; ☺daylight hours). This teak marvel sits in the shadow of Wat Chedi Luang. Set in a compound full of fluttering orange flags, the monastery is a monument to the teak trade, with an enormous prayer hall supported by 28 gargantuan teak pillars and lined with dark teak panels, enshrining a particularly graceful gold Buddha image. The juxtaposition of the orange monks' robes against this dark backdrop during evening prayers is particularly sublime.

Above the facade is a striking image of a peacock over a dog, representing the astrological year of the former royal resident's birth. The monastery is one of the focal points for celebrations during the Visakha Bucha festival in May or June, when monks light hundreds of butter lamps around the pond in the grounds.

Wat Chiang Man

Wat Chiang Man

Chiang Mai's oldest temple, **Wat Chiang Man** (วัดเชียงมั่น; Th Ratchaphakhinai; donations appreciated; ☺daylight hours), was established by the city's founder, Phaya Mengrai, sometime around 1296. In front of the *ubosot* (ordination hall), a stone slab, engraved in 1581, bears the earliest known reference to the city's founding. The main *wí·hǎhn* also contains the oldest known Buddha image created by the Lanna kingdom, cast in 1465.

A smaller second *wí·hǎhn* enshrines the city's guardian images; the bas-relief marble Phra Sila Buddha, believed to have been carved in Sri Lanka more than 1000 years ago; and the tiny crystal Phra Sae Tang Khamani Buddha, reportedly crafted for the king of Lopburi in around AD 200.

The sacred images are housed inside a handsome, *mon·dòp*−like altar known as a *khong phra chao*, a distinctive feature of ancient Lanna temples. The monastery has a glorious *chedi*, with an elephant-flanked stucco base and a gilded upper level.

Wat Inthakhin Saduemuang

Tucked to the side of the Chiang Mai City Arts & Cultural Centre, **Wat Inthakhin Saduemuang** (วัดอินทขิลสะดือเมือง; Th Inthawarorot; donations accepted; ☺5am-9pm) was the original location of the *làk meu·ang*; part of its name refers to the 'city navel', or geographic centre, which was chosen some 700 years ago. The city pillar was moved to Wat Chedi Luang in 1800 after this temple fell into disrepair. It has since been given an intense makeover, making it one of the old city's most glittering temples. Marooned in the middle of Th Inthawarorot, its gilded teak *wí·hǎhn* is one of the most perfectly proportioned monuments in the city.

Chiang Mai City Arts & Cultural Centre

SIMON POON/SHUTTERSTOCK ©

Old City Museums

Chiang Mai's museums are modern and provide an excellent introduction to the former Lanna kingdom's culture and history. These historical showcases are conveniently clustered near each other in renovated colonial-style government buildings.

Great For...

☑ **Don't Miss**

A string of shops on Th Inthawarorot sells Thai sweets and other local dishes.

Just when you think you've got this country figured out, you land in a place like Chiang Mai and discover a whole new regional identity. Thankfully these museums explain the unique aspects of the Lanna kingdom, a closer cousin to southern China and Myanmar than Bangkok.

Chiang Mai City Arts & Cultural Centre

The **Chiang Mai City Arts & Cultural Centre** (หอศิลปวัฒนธรรมเชียงใหม่; ☎053 217793; www.cmocity.com; Th Phra Pokklao; adult/child 90/40B, combo ticket adult/child 180/80B; ⏰8.30am-5pm Tue-Sun) provides an excellent primer on Chiang Mai history. Dioramas, photos, artefacts and audiovisual displays walk visitors through the key battles and victories in the Chiang Mai story, from the first settlements to wars

Lanna Folklife Museum

TAKE PHOTO/SHUTTERSTOCK ©

Th Ratwithi — *Lanna*
Folklife Museum
Chiang Mai 🏛 🏛 🏛
Historical Centre

Th Phra Pokklao

Chiang Mai City Arts
& Cultural Centre

ℹ️ Need to Know

The museums are closed on Mondays.

🍴 Take a Break

Get a massage and help inmates learn work skills at the Vocational Training Centre of the Chiang Mai Women's Correctional Institution (p211).

★ **Top Tip**

Combination tickets (180B) allow entry to all three museums.

lai·krahm stencilling and *fon lep* (traditional Lanna dance) to the intricate symbolism of different elements of Lanna-style temples. Each room is designed like an art installation with engaging lessons on cultural titbits. You'll leave knowing a little more Lanna than before.

Chiang Mai Historical Centre

Housed in an airy building, this **museum** (หอประวัติศาสตร์เมืองเชียงใหม่; ☎053 217793; www.cmocity.com; Th Ratwithi; adult/child 90/40B, combo ticket adult/child 180/80B; ⏰8.30am-5pm Tue-Sun) covers the history of Chiang Mai Province, with displays on the founding of the capital, the Burmese occupation and the modern era of trade and unification with Bangkok. Downstairs is an archaeological dig of an ancient temple wall. There is a bit of overlap between the Chiang Mai City Arts & Culture Centre, but sometimes an air-conditioned building is all one really needs.

with Myanmar and to the arrival of the railroad. Upstairs is a charming recreation of a wooden Lanna village. The building previously housed the provincial hall and is a handsomely restored Thai-colonial-style building dating from 1927. Restoration of the building was recognised by the Royal Society of Siamese Architects in 1999.

Lanna Folklife Museum

A real gem, the **Lanna Folklife Museum** (พิพิธภัณฑ์พื้นถิ่นล้านนา; ☎053 217793; www.cmocity.com; Th Phra Pokklao; adult/child 90/40B, combo ticket adult/child 180/80B; ⏰8.30am-5pm Tue-Sun) is set inside the former 1935 provincial court and recreates Lanna village life in a series of life-sized dioramas that explain everything from

Saturday Walking Street

Evening Shopping

The evening market is a popular fixture across Thailand but Chiang Mai invented the 'walking street', which transforms streets into a pedestrian zone for itinerant vendors, a tradition that dates back to the Silk Road days.

Great For...

☑ Don't Miss

Local vendors selling refreshing ice cream, advertised as 'ancient' ice cream, at the walking streets.

Saturday Walking Street

The **Saturday Walking Street** (ถนนเดิน วันเสาร์; Th Wualai; ⊘4-11pm Sat) takes over Th Wualai, running southwest from Pratu Chiang Mai at the southern entrance to the old city. There is barely space to move as locals and tourists haggle for carved soaps, novelty dog collars, woodcarvings, Buddha paintings, hill-tribe trinkets and more.

The market unfolds along the city's historic silversmithing neighbourhood. Come early enough and you can see the craftspeople tapping out a rhythm as they impress decorative patterns into bowls, jewellery boxes and plaques made from silver or, more often, aluminium.

Candles at Chiang Mai Night Bazaar

ARUNPOTARA/GETTY IMAGES ©

Sunday
Walking Street

Th Moon Muang

Th Loi Kroh

Chiang
Mai Night
Bazaar

Th Rat Chiang Saen

Saturday Walking Street

ℹ Need to Know

The walking streets and the night market start in the late afternoon and continue to midnight.

✕ Take a Break

Grab dinner at Talat Pratu Chiang Mai (p212) before hitting the Saturday Walking Street.

★ Top Tip

Remember to stand respectfully when the national anthem is played at 6pm.

Sunday Walking Street

Th Ratchadamnoen is taken over by the boisterous **Sunday Walking Street** (ถนน เดินวันอาทิตย์; Th Ratchadamnoen; ⊘6-11pm Sun), which feels even more animated than the Saturday Walking Street because of the energetic food markets that open up temple courtyards along the route. There's not a lot of breathing room as crowds slowly pass stalls selling woodcarvings, Buddha paintings, hill-tribe trinkets, Thai musical instruments, T-shirts, paper lanterns and umbrellas, silver jewellery and herbal remedies.

The market is a major source of income for local families and many traders spend the whole week hand-making merchandise to sell on Saturday and Sunday.

Chiang Mai Night Bazaar

You don't have to wait for a weekend to scratch your shopping itch. The **Chiang Mai Night Bazaar** (Th Chang Khlan; ⊘6pm-midnight) is one of the city's main night-time attractions and is the modern legacy of the original Yunnanese trading caravans that stopped here along the ancient trade route between China and Myanmar's Gulf of Martaban coast.

The night bazaar sells the usual tourist souvenirs. In true market fashion, vendors form a gauntlet along the footpath of Th Chang Khlan from Th Tha Phae to Th Loi Kroh. In between are dedicated shopping buildings: the Chiang Mai Night Bazaar Building is filled mainly with antique and handicraft stores. Across the street is the Kalare Night Bazaar selling upmarket clothes and home decor.

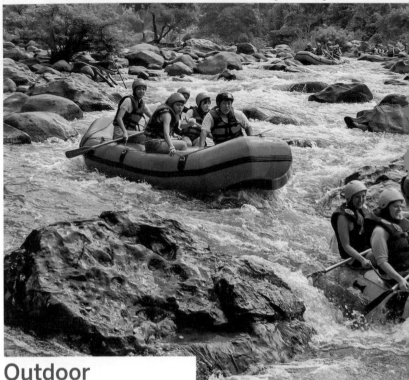

White-water rafting on Mae Taeng river

THRUS PANYAWACHIROPAS/SHUTTERSTOCK ©

Outdoor Activities

Outdoor escapes are easy in Chiang Mai thanks to nearby looming mountains, rushing rivers, hill-tribe villages and elephant sanctuaries and camps. Dozens of operators offer adventure tours on foot, bike, raft and zipline.

Great For...

☑ Don't Miss

Mae Taeng is the closest rushing river for white-water rafting and kayaking.

Trekking & Outdoor Adventuring

Thousands of visitors trek into the hills of northern Thailand hoping for adventure. Recommended companies include **Green Trails** (☎053 141356; www.green-trails.com; 111/70 Th Mahidol; treks for 2 people from 2900B) 🍃, which has a strong environmental ethos, and **Peak Adventure Tour** (☎053 800567; www.thepeakadventure.com; 302/4 Th Chiang Mai-Lamphun; tours 600-3200B), for soft-adventure. Everyone loves Flight of the Gibbon (p210), a nearly 2km zipline course through the forest.

Elephant Parks

Elephant camps can look a lot like a prison but Chiang Mai has many humane alternatives.

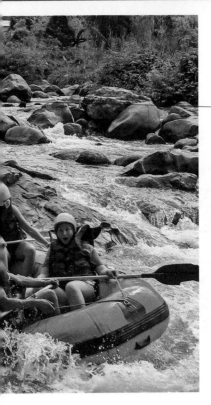

❶ Need to Know

Most day tours involve an hour's travel out of the city, and include hotel transfer and lunch.

✗ Take a Break

After a sweaty adventure, reward yourself with a massage at **Lila Thai Massage** (📞053 327243; Th Ratchadamnoen; standard/oil massage from 250/550B; ⏱10am-10pm).

★ Top Tip

Book your tickets directly with the tour operator to cut out agent commission charges.

Bicycling

The city's closest green space, Doi Suthep, has mountain-biking trails traversed by **Chiang Mai Mountain Biking & Kayaking** (📞081 024 7046; www.mountainbikethailand. com; 92/1-2 Th Si Donchai; tours 1250-2700B; ⏱7am-10pm). **Click and Travel** (📞053 281553; www.chiangmaicycling.com; 158/40-41 Soi Mu Ban Wiang Phing 5; half-/full-/multiday tours from 990/1500/5350B; ⏱9am-6pm; 👪) cycles through cultural sights outside the city centre.

Water Sports

White-water rafting takes on the wild and frothy part of Mae Taeng (best from July to March). **Siam River Adventures** (📞089 515 1917; www.siamrivers.com; 17 Th Ratwithi; per day from 1800B; ⏱8.30am-8pm) has well-regarded safety standards for the 10km stretch. Chiang Mai Mountain Biking & Kayaking paddles down a remote part of Mae Ping.

Elephant Nature Park (📞053 272850, 053 818754; www.elephantnaturepark.org; 1 Th Ratchamankha; 1-/2-day tours 2500/5800B) 🐘 provides a semi-wild state where visitors observe the natural interactions of elephants, while **Thai Elephant Care Center** (📞053 206247; www.thaielephantcarecenter. com; Mae Sa; entrance 250B, half-/full-day program 2000/3000B) was set up to provide care for elderly elephants retired from logging camps and elephant shows; there are no rides and visitors feed the old-timers and help out at bath time.

BLUR LIFE 1975/SHUTTERSTOCK ©

Thanon Nimmanhaemin

The epicentre of 'new' Chiang Mai, Th Nimmanhaemin is the place to wine, dine and stay up all night (or at least until closing time). The main road and its tributary soi are frequented by hip uni students and NGO expats.

Great For...

☑ Don't Miss

The food stalls near Soi 10 sell fried chicken, cut fruit and noodle dishes.

Dining

There is a bewildering array of food to be found on Nimmanhaemin.

Tong Tem Toh (p211) is set in an old teak house and serves northern Thai cuisine, such as *nám prík òng* (a chilli dip with vegetables for dipping) and *gaang hang·lair* (Burmese-style pork curry with peanut and tamarind).

Need a break from Thai? **Tengoku** (☏087 725 9888; Soi 5, Th Nimmanhaemin; mains 200-1650B; ⏱11am-2pm & 5.30-10pm Tue-Sun, 5.30-10pm Mon; 🛜) serves superior sushi, yakitori, spectacular sukiyaki and wonderful wagyu steaks, plus cheaper bento boxes. The farm-to-table dishes at **Rustic & Blue** (☏053 216420; www.rusticandblue. com; Soi 7, Th Nimmanhaemin; mains 185-720B; ⏱8.30am-9.30pm; ❄🛜) are in perfect

Th Huay Kaew

Chiang Mai University

Thanon Nimmanhaemin

Th Suthep

ℹ️ Need to Know

Th Nimmanhaemin is accessible by *rót daang* (trucks operating as shared taxis) travelling along Th Huay Kaew.

✕ Take a Break

Ristr8to (p213) treats coffee like wine, complete with tasting notes.

★ Top Tip

The soi branching off Th Nimmanhaemin don't have sidewalks so be careful as a pedestrian.

Drinking & Nightlife

Nimman draws in an eclectic crowd of night owls, from rowdy uni students to Thai yuppies and in-the-know foreigners. Check out the urban tribe at **Sangdee Gallery** (📞 053 894955; www.sangdeeart.com; 5 Soi 5, Th Sirimungklajarn; ⊙2pm-midnight Tue-Sat), part gallery, music club, bar and cafe.

harmony with the decor. And **Italics** (📞 053 216219; www.theakyra.com/chiang-mai; 22/2 Soi 9, Th Nimmanhaemin; pizzas 260-550B; ⊙7am-11pm; ❄️ 🛜) does some of the best pizzas in town.

Ice cream with star power, **iberry Garden** (📞 053 895171; www.facebook.com/pg/iberrygardenchiangmai; 13 Soi 17, Th Nimmanhaemin; ice cream from 90B; ⊙10am-9pm; ❄️ 🛜) is owned by Thai comedian Udom Taepanich (nicknamed 'Nose' for his signature feature). This kitschy shop in a leafy garden is mobbed day and night.

The trendy spots change but the formula stays the same: beer garden venues with brews, food and friends. The more people who can pack in, the merrier. Come to **Namton's House** (Th Chiang Mai-Lamphun; ⊙3-11.30pm Thu-Tue) for the biggest selection of Thai craft beers in town.

Warmup Cafe (📞 053 400677; www.facebook.com/warmupcafe1999; 40 Th Nimmanhaemin; ⊙7pm-1am) is a Nimman club survivor, rocking out since 1999. Each room does a different music genre: hip-hop, electronica and rock.

Wat Phra That Doi Suthep

Doi Suthep

Ascending Doi Suthep is something of a spiritual experience: switchback roads leave behind the lowland plains and ascend into the cool cloud belt filled with mosses and ferns. The mountain shelters a national park, holy temple, royal palace and hill-tribe villages.

Great For...

☑ Don't Miss

The spectacular views of Chiang Mai from Wat Phra That Doi Suthep.

Wat Phra That Doi Suthep

Overlooking the city from its mountain throne, **Wat Phra That Doi Suthep** (วัดพระ ธาตุดอยสุเทพ; Th Huay Kaew; 30B; ⏱5am-9pm) is one of northern Thailand's most sacred temples, and its founding legend is learned by every school kid in Chiang Mai. The wát itself is a beautiful example of northern Thai architecture, reached via a strenuous, 306-step stair-case flanked by mosaic *naga;* the climb is intended to help devotees accrue Buddhist merit, but less energetic pilgrims can take a funicular lift (20B).

The monastery was established in 1383 by King Keu Naone to enshrine a piece of bone, said to be from the shoulder of the historical Buddha. The bone shard was brought to Lanna by a wandering monk from Sukhothai and it broke into two pieces

Doi Suthep-Pui
National Park

⊙
Doi Suthep

⊙
**Chiang
Mai**

Bo Sang

ⓘ Need to Know

Rót daang go from the zoo for Wat Phra
That Doi Suthep (50B per person, half-
day charter 600B).

✕ Take a Break

Ban Khun Chang Kian village has a coffee shop overlooking its coffee plants.

★ Top Tip

Bring a long-sleeved shirt, because it
can be cool on the mountain.

city's independence from Myanmar and
its union with Thailand. Pilgrims queue to
leave lotus blossoms and other offerings at
the shrines surrounding the *chedi*.

Bhubing Palace

Above Wat Phra That Doi Suthep, the
grounds of the royal family's **winter palace**
(พระตำหนักภูพิงค์, Phra Tamnak Bhu Bing; ☏053
223065; www.bhubingpalace.org; Th Huay Kaew,
Doi Suthep; 50B; ⏱8.30-11.30am & 1-3.30pm)
are open to the public. Thanks to the mountain's cool climate, the royal gardeners are
able to raise 'exotic' species such as roses.
More interesting is the reservoir, brought
to life by fountains that dance to the king's
own musical compositions.

Ban Kun Chang Kian

Ban Kun Chang Kian is a Hmong coffee-
producing village about 500m down a dirt
track just past the Doi Pui campground.
You'll need private transport to reach the
village.

at the base of the mountain, with one piece
being enshrined at **Wat Suan Dok** (วัด
สวนดอก; Th Suthep; donations accepted, hall
admission 20B; ⏱daylight hours). The second
fragment was mounted onto a sacred white
elephant who wandered the jungle until
it died, in the process selecting the spot
where the monastery was later founded.

The terrace at the top of the steps is
dotted with small shrines, rock gardens and
a statue of the white elephant that carried
the Buddha relic. Before entering the inner
courtyard, children pay their respects to a
lizard-like guardian statue known as 'Mom'.

Steps lead up to the inner terrace, where
a walkway circumnavigates the gleaming
golden *chedi* enshrining the relic. The
crowning five-tiered umbrella marks the

Walking Tour: Chiang Mai

Chiang Mai's famous temples reside in the historic old city. Start in the morning hours, dress modestly (covering shoulders and knees), and remove your shoes before entering and sit in the 'mermaid' position inside the sanctuary halls.

Start Wat Phra Singh
Distance 1km
Duration Four hours

7 Get a massage at the **Vocational Training Centre of the Chiang Mai Women's Correctional Institution** (p211).

Th Ratwithi

7

FINISH

Th Inthawarorot

Th Singharat

START

1

Th Ratchadamnoen

Th Jhaban

1 Start at **Wat Phra Singh** (p190), a textbook example of Lanna architecture.

2 Before condo towers, the now ruined **Wat Chedi Luang** (p191) was Chiang Mai's tallest structure.

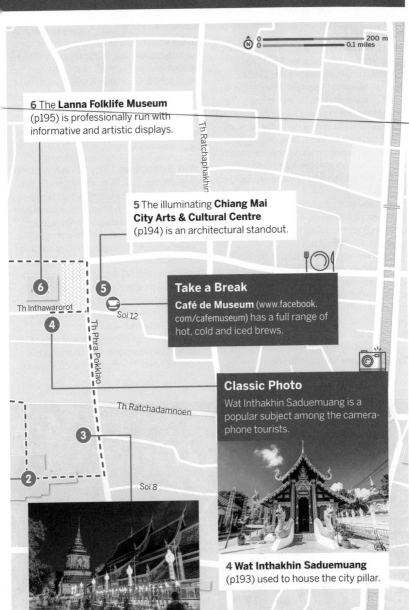

6 The **Lanna Folklife Museum** (p195) is professionally run with informative and artistic displays.

5 The illuminating **Chiang Mai City Arts & Cultural Centre** (p194) is an architectural standout.

Th Ratchaphakhin

Th Inthawararot

Th Phra Pokklao

Soi 12

Take a Break

Café de Museum (www.facebook. com/cafemuseum) has a full range of hot, cold and iced brews.

Th Ratchadamnoen

Classic Photo

Wat Inthakhin Saduemuang is a popular subject among the camera-phone tourists.

Soi 8

4 Wat Inthakhin Saduemuang (p193) used to house the city pillar.

3 Next door is **Wat Phan Tao** (p192), a teak temple that is more photogenic than venerated.

1 BUSHTON2/GETTY IMAGES © 2 SEAN PAVONE/GETTY IMAGES © 3 ALEXANDER MAZURKEVICH/SHUTTERSTOCK © 4 APIGUIDE/SHUTTERSTOCK ©

◉ SIGHTS

Talat Warorot   Market

(ตลาดวโรรส; cnr Th Chang Moi & Th Praisani;
⊙6am-5pm) Chiang Mai's oldest public
market, Warorot (also spelt Waroros) is a
great place to connect with the city's Thai
soul. Alongside souvenir vendors you'll find
numerous stalls selling items for ordinary
Thai households: woks, toys, fishing nets,
pickled tea leaves, wigs, sticky-rice steam-
ers, Thai-style sausages, *kâab mŏo* (pork
rinds), live catfish and tiny statues for spirit
houses.

It's easy to spend half a day wandering
the covered walkways, watching locals
browsing, and haggling for goods that actually have a practical use back home.

You'll know you've arrived at the market
when traffic comes to a standstill and carts
laden with merchandise weave between
the cars. The location by the river is no
coincidence; historically, most of the farm
produce sold in Chiang Mai was delivered
here by boat along Mae Ping.

Immediately adjacent to Talat Warorot is
Talat Ton Lam Yai (ตลาดต้นลำไย; Th Praisani;

⊙24hr), the city's main flower market, and
to the south are more bazaars, full of 'wet
and dry' foodstuffs, fabric vendors, Chinese
goldsmiths and apparel stalls. The northern
end of the bazaar area is thronged by fruit
vendors selling bushels of lychees, longans,
mangosteens and rambutans. *Săhm·lór*
(three-wheel pedicabs, now rarely seen in
the city) wait to shuttle shoppers home
with their produce.

Wat Srisuphan   Buddhist Temple

(วัดศรีสุพรรณ; Soi 2, Th Wualai; ⊙6am-6pm) It
should come as no surprise that the sil-
versmiths along Th Wualai have decorated
their patron monastery with the same
fine artisanship shown in their shops. The
'silver' *ubosot* (ordination hall) is covered
with silver, nickel and aluminium panels,
embossed with elaborate repoussé-work
designs. The effect is like a giant jewellery
box, particularly after dark, when the monastery is illuminated by coloured lights.

Wat Srisuphan was founded in 1502, but
little remains of the original *wát* except for
some teak pillars and roof beams in the
main *wí·hăhn*. The murals inside show an

Wat Pha Lat

EDENEXPOSED/GETTY IMAGES ©

interesting mix of Taoist, Zen and Theravada Buddhist elements. Note the gold and silver Ganesha statue beneath a silver *chatra* (umbrella) by the *ubosot,* a sign of the crossover between Hinduism and Buddhism in Thailand.

Because this is an active ordination hall, only men may enter the *ubosot.*

While guests can enter the main temple building free of charge, there is a 50B fee to enter the area near the *ubosot* to see it up close.

Lanna Architecture Center
Museum

(ศูนย์สถาปัตยกรรมล้านนา; www.lanna-arch.net; 117 Th Ratchadamnoen; ☺9am-5pm Tue-Sat, 1-8pm Sun) FREE Formerly owned by prince Jao Maha In, this handsome mansion built in a hybrid Lanna and European style between 1889 and 1893 houses a small education centre with some interesting models showing the changing face of Lanna architecture through the centuries.

Wat Pha Lat
Buddhist Temple

(วัดผาลาด) A hidden jungle temple tucked into the mountain along the way to Wat Phra That Doi Suthep (p202). Old stone structures, intricate carvings, *naga*-flanked stairways and Buddhist statues dot the serene grounds, and a walkway over a sheetrock waterfall affords postcard-pretty views of Chiang Mai. The temple was seldom visited before 2018, but word of its beauty spread among travellers and expats, and the Monk's Trail (a jungle path from the city to the temple) is now an open secret.

As the story of the temple goes, in 1355 a white elephant belonging to King Kuena took a break to rest on the future site of Wat Pha Lat before dying at the future site of Wat Phra That Doi Suthep. The king ordered temples constructed on both sites, and the hidden jungle temple became a rest stop for monks making the pilgrimage to the larger, more opulent temple. After the road was constructed in 1935, Wat Pha Lat became a monks' residence and meditation site.

River Cruises

Few vessels ply the waters of the Mae Ping River with the exception of tour boats, which provide an excellent vantage point from which to view the city. **Mae Ping River Cruise** (☑053 274822; www.maepingrivercruise.com; Wat Chaimongkhon, 133 Th Charoen Prathet; 2hr cruise from 550B; ☺9am-5pm) offers trips starting from Wat Chaimongkhon, south of the centre on Th Charoen Prathet, as well as longer cruises to **Wiang Kum Kam** (เวียงกุมกาม; Rte 3029; tours by horse cart/tram 300/400B; ☺8am-5pm) and dinner cruises. Riverside Bar & Restaurant (p212) also runs popular, nightly dinner cruises. If you don't mind paddling yourself, Chiang Mai Mountain Biking & Kayaking (p199) offers guided kayak tours along Mae Ping, visiting forested stretches north of the city.

Mae Ping River cruise
PICKUAUNG/SHUTTERSTOCK ©

Note that there are no food stalls or shops here, which for many visitors is preferable.

Weave Artisan Society
Cultural Centre

(สานสังคมช่างฝีมือ; ☑080 071 3218; https://weaveartisansociety.com; 12/8 Soi 3, Th Wualai; ☺9am-6pm) A brand-new culture centre, gallery, coffee shop, bookstore and immersive theatre space south of the old city, where you can attend a performance or just sip on some local coffee and admire the displayed local artworks. Check the website for upcoming events, which include things

Central Chiang Mai

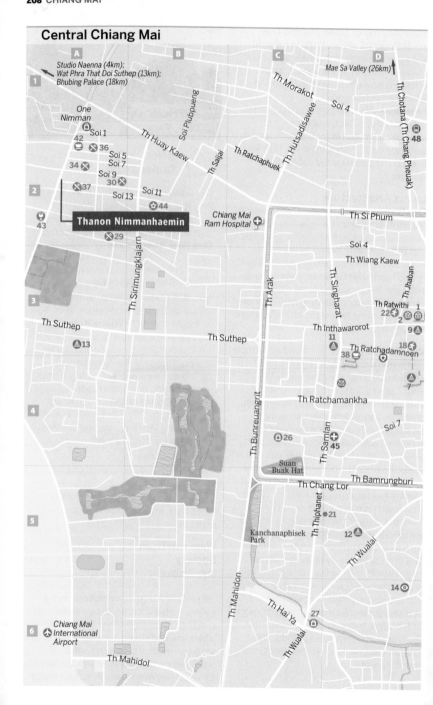

A

B

C

D

1

Studio Naenna (4km);
Wat Phra That Doi Suthep (13km);
Bhubing Palace (18km)

Th Morakot

Mae Sa Valley (26km)

Soi 4

Th Chotana (Th Chang Pheuak)

One
Nimman

Soi 1

42

36

Th Huay Kaew

Soi Plubpueng

Th Saijai

Th Ratchaphuek

Th Hutsadisawee

48

Soi 5

Soi 7

34

Soi 9

30

Soi 11

37

Soi 13

44

Thanon Nimmanhaemin

Chiang Mai
Ram Hospital

Th Si Phum

2

43

29

Th Sirimungklajarn

Soi 4

Th Wiang Kaew

Th Arak

Th Singharat

Th Jhaban

Th Ratwithi

22

1

2

Th Suthep

13

Th Suthep

Th Inthawarorot

11

9

38

Th Ratchadamnoen

18

3

7

Th Ratchamankha

4

Th Bunreuangrit

26

Th Samlan

45

Soi 7

Suan
Buak Hat

Th Bamrungburi

Th Chang Lor

5

Kanchanaphisek
Park

Th Thiphanet

21

12

Th Wualai

14

Th Mahidon

Th Hai Ya

27

Chiang Mai
International
Airport

6

Th Wualai

Th Mahidol

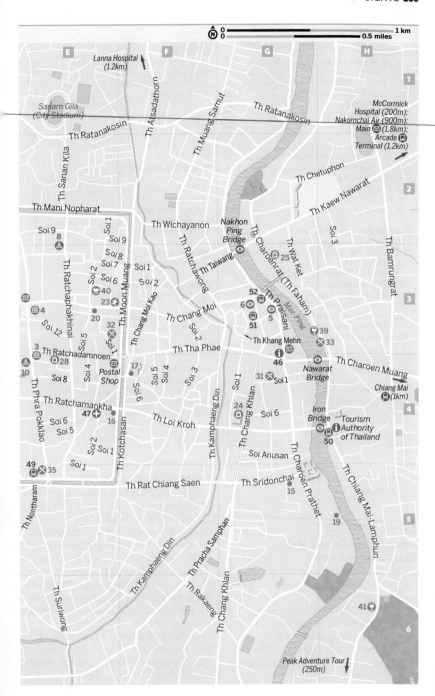

0 — 1 km
0 — 0.5 miles

E
F
G
H

1

Lanna Hospital
(1.2km)

Th Alsadathorn

Th Muang Samut

Th Ratanakosin

McCormick
Hospital (200m);
Nakornchai Air (900m);
Main ✉ (1.8km);
Arcade 🚌
Terminal (1.2km)

Sanam Gila
(City Stadium)

Th Ratanakosin

Th Chetuphon

Th Kaew Nawarat

2

Th Sanan Kila

Th Mani Nopharat

Th Wichayanon

Nakhon
Ping
Bridge

Th Charoenrat (Th Faham)

Th Wat Ket

Soi 3

Th Bamrungrat

Soi 9
8

Th Ratchaphakhinai

Soi 1
Soi 9

Soi 8
Soi 7

Th Ratchawong

Th Taiwang

25

52

Mae Ping

Soi 2
Soi 6

Th Moon Muang

Soi 1
Soi 2

Th Prai sani

3

40

23

Th Chang Moi Kao

Th Chang Moi

6

51

5

4

20

32

Soi 2

39

33

3

Soi 12

Soi 5

Th Chang Moi

Th Khang Mehn

Th Charoen Muang

Th Ratchadamnoen
28

Th Tha Phae

46

Nawarat
Bridge

Chiang
Mai
🚉 (1km)

10

17

Postal
Shop

Soi 5
Soi 4

Soi 3

Soi 1

31

Soi 1

Iron
Bridge

Tourism
Authority
of Thailand

Soi 8

Th Phra Pokklao

Th Ratchamankha
47

16

Th Loi Kroh

Th Kamphaeng Din

24

Soi 6

50

4

Soi 6
Soi 5

Th Kotchasan

Soi 2
Soi 1

Soi 1

Th Chang Khlan

Soi Anusan

Th Charoen Prathet

Th Chiang Mai-Lamphun

49

35

Soi 1

Th Nontharam

Th Rat Chiang Saen

Th Sridonchai

15

19

5

Th Suriwong

Th Kamphaeng Din

Th Pracha Samphan

Th Rakaeng

Th Chang Khlan

41

6

Peak Adventure Tour
(250m)

Central Chiang Mai

like bamboo building, weaving and natural dye workshops.

⊕ ACTIVITIES

Small House Chiang Mai Thai Cooking School Cooking

(📞095 674 4550; www.chiangmaithaicooking. com; 19/14 Th Thiphanet; group classes per person 1500B, day-long private classes from 3500B) Arm offers delightful and intimate Thai cooking classes in a dwelling outside Chiang Mai. Courses include transport and a visit to a local market, and they span northern Thai dishes. The small two- to four-person classes feel more local than touristy.

Flight of the Gibbon Ziplining

(📞053 010660; www.flightofthegibbon.com; 29/4-5 Th Kotchasan; day tours 4199B; ⊙8am-5.30pm) This adventure outfit started the zipline craze, with nearly 5km of wire strung up like spiderwebs in the gibbon-populated forest canopy near Ban Mae Kampong, an hour's drive east from Chiang Mai. The day tour includes an optional village visit, waterfall walk and lunch cooked by the community. There are also multiday, multiactivity tours that can include a night at a village homestay.

In 2019 a 25-year-old tourist plunged from the zipline to his death. The operation closed temporarily for an investigation, after which no information was released. The tours later resumed, but were temporarily suspended at the time of research due to the COVID-19 pandemic.

Zira Spa
Spa

(053 222288; www.ziraspa.com; 8/1 Th Ratwithi; treatments 700-6200B; 10am-10pm) In the centre of Chiang Mai, Zira Spa offers some of the best spa treatments and massages in the region, all for a decent price. You need to book in advance for the larger spa packages, but same-day service is available for one or two of the 30-, 60- or 90-minute treatments.

Vocational Training Centre of the Chiang Mai Women's Correctional Institution
Massage

(053 122340; 100 Th Ratwithi; foot or traditional massage from 200B; 8am-4.30pm Mon-Fri, from 9am Sat & Sun) Offers fantastic massages performed by female inmates participating in the prison's job-training rehabilitation program. The cafe next door is a nice spot for a post-massage brew.

SHOPPING

Studio Naenna
Clothing

(www.studio-naenna.com; 138/8 Soi Chang Khian; 9am-5pm Mon-Fri) The colours of the mountains have been woven into the naturally dyed silks and cottons here, part of a project to preserve traditional weaving and embroidery. You can see the whole production process at this workshop. The goods are also available for purchase at the Nimmanhaemin store, **Adorn with Studio Naenna** (open 10am to 7pm).

Mengrai Kilns
Ceramics

(www.mengraikilns.com; 79/2 Th Arak; 8am-5pm) In the southwestern corner of the old city, Mengrai Kilns keeps the tradition of Thai handmade pottery alive, with cookware, dining sets, ornaments and Western-style nativity scenes.

Baan Kang Wat
Arts & Crafts

(www.facebook.com/Baankangwat; 123/1 Mu 5 Muang, Th Baan Ram Poeng, Suthep; 10am-6pm Tue-Sat, from 7am Sun) Though a little out of the way, Baan Kang Wat is worth the trip simply to coo over the cute architecture and picturesque ambience. The open-air artist's enclave is home to several small art and handicraft shops and studios, intimate cafes, a community garden and plenty of potted succulents.

Along the same road as Baan Kang Wat you'll find several other clusters of shops and cafe hubs to check out – bring your camera!

Elephant Parade
Arts & Crafts

(053 111849; www.elephantparade.com; Th Charoenrat/Th Faham; 10am-8pm;) In venues around Chiang Mai, you may notice life-sized, decorated baby elephant sculptures created by artists and celebrities through the social enterprise Elephant Parade. The organisation runs this store to educate visitors about the plight of elephants, with large and small statues available for purchase. Children and artsy adults will appreciate the station for painting your own.

EATING

Tong Tem Toh
Thai $

(053 894701; www.facebook.com/TongTemToh; 11 Soi 13, Th Nimmanhaemin; mains 57-177B; 7am-9pm) Set in an unpretentious garden of a teak house, this highly popular restaurant serves deliciously authentic northern Thai cuisine. The menu roams beyond the usual to specialities such as *nám prík òng, gaang hang·lair* plus a few more adventurous dishes using snake-head fish and ant eggs.

The grilled fermented pork, known as *naem,* with egg in banana leaf is divine. Due to its popularity with both Thai and foreign tourists, expect a wait, morning, noon or night.

Kao Soi Fueng Fah
Thai $

(Soi 1, Th Charoen Phrathet; mains 40-60B; 7.30am-9pm) The most flavourful of the Muslim-run *kôw soy* (wheat-and-egg noodles in a curry broth) joints along Halal

St, with the choice of beef or chicken with your noodles.

Lert Ros   Thai $

(Soi 1, Th Ratchadamnoen; mains 30-160B; ⏲noon-9pm) As you enter this local-style hole-in-the-wall, you'll pass the main course: delicious whole tilapia fish, grilled on coals and served with a fiery Isan-style dipping sauce. Eaten with sticky rice, this is one of the great meals of Chiang Mai. The menu also includes fermented pork grilled in banana leaves, curries and *sôm·dam* (spicy green papaya salad).

> *This is one of the great meals of Chiang Mai.*

Talat Pratu Chiang Mai   Market $

(Th Bamrungburi; mains from 40B; ⏲4am-noon & 6pm-midnight) In the early morning, this market is Chiang Mai's larder, selling foodstuffs and ready-made dishes. If you want to make merit to the monks, come early and find the woman who sells pre-assembled food donations (20B); she'll explain the ritual to you. Things quiet down by lunchtime, but the burners are reignited for a popular night market that sets up along the road.

Riverside Bar & Restaurant   International $$

(☎053 243239; www.theriversidechiangmai. com; Th Charoenrat/Th Faham; mains 100-370B, dinner cruise adult/child 180/90B; ⏲10am-1am) Almost everyone ends up at Riverside at some point in their Chiang Mai stay. Set in an old teak house, it feels like a countryside reimagining of a Hard Rock Cafe, and bands play nightly until late. Stake out a claim on the riverside terrace or the upstairs balcony to catch the evening breeze on Mae Ping.

The restaurant also runs a popular dinner cruise along Mae Ping that leaves the dock at 8pm each night. Over an enchanting, 75-minute ride, the boat drifts past ancient temples and centuries-old homes along the riverbank. Reserve well in advance.

From left: Ziplining; Riverside Bar & Restaurant; Food stall, Talat Pratu Chiang Mai

🍷 DRINKING & NIGHTLIFE

Good View
Bar

(www.goodview.co.th; 13 Th Charoenrat/Th Fa-ham; ⏰10am-1am) Good View attracts plenty of locals, with a big menu of Thai standards, Japanese dishes and Western options (mains 100B to 400B), and a nightly program of house bands with rotating line-ups (meaning the drummer starts playing guitar and the bass player moves behind the piano).

Graph
Coffee

(📞086 567 3330; www.graphdream.com; 25/1 Soi 1, Th Ratwithi; coffee 80-220B; ⏰9am-5pm; 📶) A tiny cafe with enormously good coffee. Only about 10 people fit inside, and the line often snakes down the old city block. Favourites include the Nitro cold-brew coffee with orange and lime, and the 'boy with girlfriend', which comes with lime, raw sugar, soda and espresso.

Graph employees are involved in every step from 'tree to cup', as its owners spent years choosing where to get beans and learn the process. The incredible results are also available at its sister cafe in One Nimman.

Akha Ama Cafe
Cafe

(www.akhaama.com; 175/1 Th Ratchadamnoen; ⏰8am-5.30pm; 📶) 🍃 Akha Ama serves locally harvested, sustainable, direct-trade beans from the jungles north of Chiang Mai, but – perhaps most importantly to some – the coffee's just plain good. Come also for tasty baked snacks and the wi-fi.

Ristr8to
Coffee

(📞053 215278; www.ristr8to.com; Th Nimman-haemin; espresso drinks from 88B; ⏰7am-6pm) Inspired by Australian coffee culture and using roasting skills learned in the US, this place takes your cup of Joe to the highest heights, from flat whites and marocchinos to the hyper-caffeinated doppio ristret-to that uses 18g of ground coffee and award-winning latte art. The small brick-walled cafe is well-loved and often packed. There's also a Ristr8to Lab near Soi 3.

Lanna-style food

 INFORMATION

Tourism Authority of Thailand (TAT; ☏053 248604; www.tourismthailand.org; Th Chiang Mai-Lamphun; ◷8am-5pm) English-speaking staff provide maps and advice on travel across Thailand.

ⓘ GETTING THERE & AWAY

AIR

Domestic and international flights arrive and depart from Chiang Mai International Airport (p306), 3km southwest of the old city.

Schedules vary with the seasons and tourist demand. Tickets to Bangkok start at around 540B. Heading south, expect to pay from 2160B to Phuket and 1080B to Surat Thani.

Direct flights linking Chiang Mai to neighbouring nations are also expanding fast, with regular flights to Kuala Lumpur (Malaysia), Yangon (Myanmar), Hanoi (Vietnam) and destinations around China.

BUS

Arcade Bus Terminal (Th Kaew Nawarat) is the point to connect to Bangkok or any other major city in Thailand. It's located about 3km northeast of the city centre, near the junction of Th Kaew Nawarat and Rte 11.

TRAIN

Chiang Mai Train Station (☏053 245363, nationwide 1690; Th Charoen Muang) is about 2.5km east of the old city. Trains run five times daily on the main line between Bangkok and Chiang Mai.

ⓘ GETTING AROUND

Cycling is a good way to get around Chiang Mai. Bikes can be rented for around 50B a day or 300B. Grab Car and Uber taxis are also available.

Launched in 2018, the **RTC City Bus** (☏052 060001; http://rtccitybus.com; per ride 20B; ◷6am-late) is the most affordable and convenient way to get around the city of Chiang Mai. The spacious, air-conditioned buses transport passengers along nine routes, which can be monitored in real time via a mobile app, CM Transit. Be sure to raise your arm as the bus approaches so that the driver knows to stop.

At the time of research, the service had been temporarily put on hold due to the COVID-19 pandemic.

Where to Stay

Make reservations far in advance if visiting during Chinese New Year, Songkran and other holiday periods.

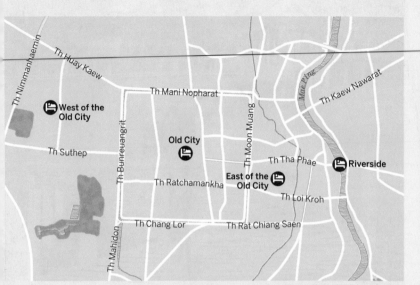

Neighbourhood	Atmosphere
Old City	Close to sights, old-school Chiang Mai feel, international dining and bars; lots of touts and tourists.
East of the Old City	Lots of budget and midrange options, easy access to markets; noisy and hectic, sexpat hang-outs.
West of the Old City	Less touristy, easy access to dining and nightlife; far from sights.
Riverside	Lots of midrange and top-end options; lack of dining and entertainment, far from sights.

Pai at a Glance...

First-time visitors to Pai might wonder if they've strayed into a northern version of a Thai island getaway, only without the beaches. The town has a picture-perfect setting in a mountain valley, and the temples and fun afternoon market are a reminder that Pai has not forgotten its ethnic roots. There's heaps of quiet accommodation, lots of activities and a relaxed vibe that makes some people consider never leaving.

Two Days in Pai

Visit Pai's picturesque **waterfalls** (p227), then go caving in the hills around **Soppong** (p220), visiting the crypts in Tham Lot. Do some casual shopping along **Walking Street** (p224), before filing in for a **thermal spa session** (p222) to soothe your limbs.

Four Days in Pai

Spend a night at the legendary **Cave Lodge** (p221) guesthouse. Go river rafting on **Mae Nam Pai** (p224) or trekking through the villages. Tuck into an authentic Thai meal at **Larp Khom Huay Poo** (p225), and end the night with a drink at **Don't Cry** (p227).

Previous page: Bamboo bridge over rice paddies

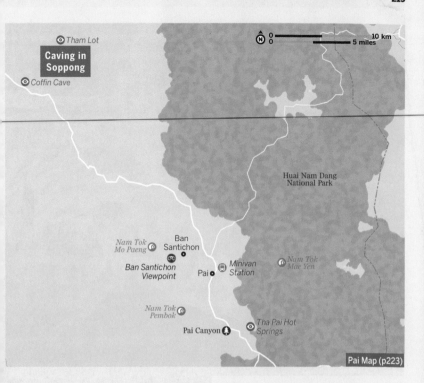

Arriving in Pai

Minivan Pai's minivan station handles all public transport to and from town. If possible, book tickets a day in advance.

Where to Stay

Pai is reportedly home to more than 500 hotels, hostels, guesthouses and resorts, and new places continue to spring up.

Tham Lot

EUGENE GA/SHUTTERSTOCK ©

Caving in Soppong

Located one hour northwest from Pai, Soppong is a serious backpacker destination defined by dense forests, rushing rivers and dramatic limestone outcrops. It is also the place in northern Thailand for caving.

Great For...

☑ **Don't Miss**

Tham Lot, a limestone cave with grand stalagmites, is 1600m in length.

The most accessible cave in the area is **Tham Lot**, but many others are also waiting to be explored. There are several Shan, Lisu, Karen and Lahu villages in the area that can be visited on hikes.

The Caves

The 900-sq-km area of Pangmapha district is famous for its high concentration of cave systems, where more than 200 have been found. Apart from Tham Lot, one of its most famous is **Tham Nam Lang**, which is 20km northwest of Soppong near Ban Nam Khong. It's 8.5km long and thought to be one of the largest caves in the world in terms of volume.

Many of the caves are essentially underground river systems, some of which boast waterfalls, lakes and sandy 'beaches'.

VIKTORIYA KRAYN/SHUTTERSTOCK ©

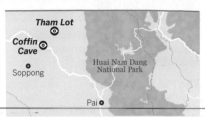

ⓘ Need to Know

Cave Lodge (☎053 617203; www. cavelodge.com; Tham Lot Village; r & bungalows 300-2000B; 🛜) has the best information on caving and trekking in the area.

✕ Take a Break

Outdoor stalls outside Tham Lot park entrance offer simple rice and noodle dishes.

★ Top Tip

Wild Times, by John Spies, is a great informal guide to the area's caves.

Cryptotora thamicola, an eyeless, waterfall-climbing troglobitic fish that forms its own genus, is found in only two caves in the world, both of which are in Pangmapha. Other caves contain little or no life, due to an abundance of noxious gases or very little oxygen.

More than 85 of the district's 200 limestone caverns are known to contain ancient teak coffins carved from solid teak logs. Up to 9m long, the coffins are typically suspended on wooden scaffolds inside the caves. The coffins have been carbon-dated and shown to be between 1200 and 2200 years old. The ends are usually carved

and Thai archaeologists have identified at least 50 different design schemes. The local Shans know these burial caves as *tâm pĕe* (spirit caves) or *tâm pĕe maan* (coffin caves). It is not known who made them or why they were placed in the caves, but as most caves have fewer than 10 coffins it's thought that only select individuals were accorded such an elaborate burial. Similar coffins have been found in karst areas west of Bangkok and also in Borneo, China and the Philippines, but the highest concentration of coffin caves from this period is in Pangmapha.

The easiest coffins to visit are in **Tham Lot** (ถ้ำลอด; from 150B; ⊙8am-5.30pm), 9km northeast of Soppong. Several caves that scientists are currently investigating are off limits to the public.

⊙ SIGHTS

Most of Pai's sights are found outside the city centre, making hiring a motorcycle a necessity.

Tha Pai Hot Springs
Hot Springs

(บ่อน้ำร้อนท่าปาย; adult/child 300/150B; ⊙7am-6pm) Across Mae Nam Pai and 7km southeast of town via a paved road is this well-kept local park. Through it flows a scenic stream, which mixes with the hot springs in places to make pleasant bathing areas. The water is also diverted to a couple of nearby spas.

Pai Canyon
Nature Reserve

(กองแลนปาย; Rte 1095; ⊙daylight hours) Pai Canyon is located 8km from Pai along the road to Chiang Mai. A paved stairway here culminates in an elevated lookout over high rock cliffs and the Pai valley. It is best climbed in the early morning when it's not too hot, or at sunset for the views.

Wat Phra That Mae Yen
Buddhist Temple

(วัดพระธาตุแม่เย็น; ⊙daylight hours) This temple sits atop a hill and has terrific views overlooking the valley. To get here, walk 1km east from the main intersection in town to get to the stairs that lead to the top (there are 353 steps). Or, if you've got your own wheels, take the 400m sealed road that follows a different route.

Ban Santichon Viewpoint
Viewpoint

(จุดชมวิว บ้านสันติชล; Ban Santichon; 20B; ⊙4.30am-6pm) A viewpoint at the Chinese village of Ban Santichon (บ้านสันติชล) that offers decent views over the surrounding area.

Wat Nam Hoo
Buddhist Temple

(วัดน้ำฮู; Ban Nam Hoo; ⊙daylight hours) FREE Wat Nam Hoo is about 2km west of Pai and houses a sacred Buddha image said to have once emitted holy water from its head. The place is popular with visiting Thais and there's a small market on the grounds.

Wat Klang
Buddhist Temple

(วัดกลาง; Th Chaisongkhram; ⊙daylight hours) A Burmese-inspired Buddhist temple in Pai.

Pai Canyon

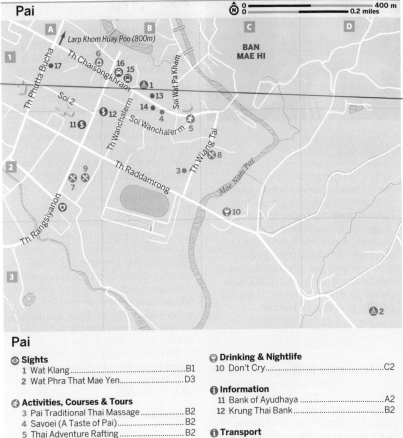

Pai

◎ Sights
1 Wat Klang	B1
2 Wat Phra That Mae Yen	D3

◈ Activities, Courses & Tours
3 Pai Traditional Thai Massage	B2
4 Savoei (A Taste of Pai)	B2
5 Thai Adventure Rafting	B2

🛍 Shopping
6 Walking Street	A1

✗ Eating
7 Charlie & Lek Restaurant	A2
8 Maya Burger Queen	C2
9 Om Garden Cafe	A2

◐ Drinking & Nightlife
10 Don't Cry	C2

ⓘ Information
11 Bank of Ayudhaya	A2
12 Krung Thai Bank	B2

ⓘ Transport
13 Aya Service	B1
14 Duan-Den	B1
15 Minivan Station	B1
16 Motorcycle-Taxi Stand	B1
17 North Wheels	A1

✈ ACTIVITIES

Pai Hotsprings Spa Resort — Spa

(☏053 065748; www.paihotspringsparesort.com; 84-84/1 Mu 2, Ban Mae Hi; thermal water soak 100B, 1hr massage 350B) A resort-style hotel that also offers massage (from 8am to 5pm) and thermal water soaks (from 7am to 7pm).

Aroma Pai Spa — Spa

(☏053 065745; www.aromapaispa.com; 110 Mu 2, Ban Mae Hi; thermal water soak 100B, spa treatments 850-1500B; ⊗8am-10pm) Aroma Pai Spa offers soaks in private rooms and in a communal pool, as well as a variety of spa treatments.

Rafting & Kayaking

Rafting along Mae Nam Pai during the wet season (approximately June to October) is a popular activity. Trips run from Pai to Mae Hong Son, which, depending on the amount of water, can traverse rapids from Class I to Class V. Rates are all-inclusive (rafting equipment, camping gear, dry bags, insurance and food) and run to around 1800B per person for a one-day trip and to around 3400B per person for two days.

Rafting, Pang Oung Lake
SARAWUT CHAMSAENG/SHUTTERSTOCK ©

Thai Adventure Rafting   Rafting

(☎053 699111; www.thairafting.com; Th Chaisongkhram; ⊙10am-9pm) This experienced, French-run outfit leads one- and two-day rafting excursions. Rafters visit a waterfall, a fossil reef and hot springs en route, with one night spent at the company's permanent riverside camp. It also offers combined rafting/trekking trips.

COURSES

The curriculum of courses available in Pai ranges from circus arts and drumming to yoga in all its forms. Keep an eye on the flyers in every cafe, or check the *Pai Events Planner* (PEP) or the *Pai Explorer* (www.facebook.com/PaiExplorer) to see what's on when you're in town.

Xhale Yoga Pai   Health & Wellbeing

(☎089 758 3635; www.xhaleyogapai.com; 5 days from 14,500B) Need some time out? Sign up for a five-night yoga retreat (Monday to Saturday) in the foothills outside Pai. Courses suit beginners to intermediates and include accommodation, standout meals, yoga and meditation classes, plus an excursion to a nearby hot spring. Instructor Bhud is all smiles, laughter and sunshine, and the vibe is welcoming and noncompetitive.

No drop-ins. Pick-up from Pai's minivan station is provided.

**Pai Traditional
Thai Massage**   Health & Wellbeing

(PTTM; ☎083 577 0498; 68/3 Soi 1, Th Wiang Tai; massage per 1/1½/2hr 200/300/400B, sauna per visit 100B, 3-day massage course 3500B; ⊙9am-9pm) This long-standing, locally owned outfit offers very good northern Thai massage, as well as a sauna (November to February only) where you can steam yourself in medicinal herbs. Three-day massage courses begin every Monday and Friday and run three hours per day.

The friendly couple that do the massages and teach the courses are accredited and are graduates of Chiang Mai's Old Medicine Hospital.

Savoei (A Taste of Pai)   Cooking

(☎085 620 9918; Th Chaisongkhram; lessons 700-750B; ⊙lessons 9.30am-1.30pm & 4-8pm) The half-day classes here involve a visit to the fresh market and instruction in four dishes.

🔒 SHOPPING

Walking Street   Market

(Th Chaisongkhram & Th Rangsiyanon; ⊙6-10pm) Every evening, a walking street forms in the centre of town, with vendors selling food, clothes, souvenirs and knick-knacks. It's far busier during high season (November to February).

Night market street-food stall

EATING

Pai has an impressive number of restaurants, but many places appear to just be duplicates of their neighbours. Nevertheless, there's some good food to be found, including a notable increase in the number of quality vegetarian/vegan eateries.

Vendors set up along Th Chaisongkhram and Th Rangsiyanon every evening, selling all manner of food from stalls and refurbished VW vans. There are more during high season.

Larp Khom Huay Poo Thai $

(Ban Huay Pu; mains 50-100B; ☺8am-8pm; 🛜)
Escape the wheatgrass-and-tofu crowd at this unabashedly carnivorous local eatery. The house special is *'larp moo kua'*, northern-style *lâhp* (minced pork fried with herbs and spices). Accompanied by sticky rice, bitter herbs and an ice-cold beer, it's one of the best meals in Pai. Their soups and bamboo worms are fine, too. Located 1km north of town, on the road to Mae Hong Son.

They'll adjust the spice levels on request.

Maya Burger Queen American $

(www.facebook.com/MayaBurgerQueen; Th Wiang Tai; mains 80-165B; ☺1-10pm; 🛜🖋)
Burgers are a big deal in Pai and our arduous research has concluded that Maya does the best job. Everything is homemade, from the soft, slightly sweet buns to the rich garlic mayo that accompanies the thick-cut fries. There are no less than six veggie burger options, too.

Om Garden Cafe International $

(off Th Raddamrong; mains 60-140B; ☺8.30am-5pm Wed-Mon; 🛜🖋) Meat-free takes on international dishes, fresh-pressed juices, a pleasant shaded garden, a noticeboard advertising yoga classes, the odd hippy: basically everything you'd expect at a place called Om Garden, except that the food is actually good. It's not exclusively veggie: dishes range from Middle Eastern *meze* to breakfast burritos, salads and pasta. There are also pastries and fine coffee.

Baan Benjarong Thai $

(179 Th Rangsiyanon; dishes 90-170B; ☺11am-1pm & 5-8pm) Emulate local families and come to this classy home-based restaurant

Entrance to Wat Phra That Mae Yen (p222)

at the southern end of town on the edge of the fields. Dishes such as stewed salted crabs in coconut milk and a salad of banana flower, shrimp and chicken are some of the better Thai food offerings in town.

Charlie & Lek Restaurant Thai $
(Th Rangsiyanon; mains 55-125B; ⊙11am-9.30pm; 🛜🎤) Foreigner-friendly, and none the worse for it, Charlie & Lek serves Thai classics as well as a few northern Thai specialities in a no-fuss atmosphere that draws the crowds. There are veggie options, too.

🍷 DRINKING & NIGHTLIFE

Don't Cry Bar
(Th Raddamrong; ⊙4pm-late) Located just across the river from central Pai, Don't Cry touts itself as the kind of reggae bar you used to get on Ko Pha-Ngan. In fact, when it's swinging (don't bother showing up till after 11pm), it's more like a grungy semi-open-air club. Packed most nights with a young backpacker crowd, it stays open until the last punter staggers home.

ℹ️ INFORMATION

Police Station (📞053 699191, 24hr emergency 191; Th Rangsiyanon; ⊙24hr) Pai's principal police station.

ℹ️ GETTING THERE & AWAY

Pai's **minivan station** (Th Chaisongkhram) handles all public transport to and from town. It is wise to book tickets a day in advance.
Aya Service (📞053 699888; www.ayaservice.com; 22/1 Th Chaisongkhram; motorcycles per 24hr 140-200B; ⊙7am-10pm) also runs air-con minivan buses to Chiang Mai (150B, three hours, hourly 7am to 5.30pm).

🔭 Pai's Waterfalls

There are a few waterfalls around Pai that are worth visiting, particularly after the rainy season (October to early December). The closest and the most popular, **Nam Tok Mo Paeng** (น้ำตก หมอแปง), has a couple of pools that are suitable for swimming. The waterfall is about 8km from Pai along the road that also leads to Wat Nam Hoo – a long walk indeed, but suitable for a bike ride or a short motorcycle trip. Roughly the same distance in the opposite direction is **Nam Tok Pembok** (น้ำตกแพมบก), just off the road to Chiang Mai. The most remote is **Nam Tok Mae Yen** (น้ำตกแม่ เย็น), a couple of hours' walk down the rough road east of Pai.

Nam Tok Mo Paeng
YUTTANA JOE / SHUTTERSTOCK ©

ℹ️ GETTING AROUND

Most of Pai is accessible on foot. Motorcycle taxis wait at the **stand** (Th Chaisongkhram) next to the minivan station. It costs 50B to Ban Santichon village and 100B to Nam Tok Mo Paeng waterfall.

There are many places around town that rent out motorbikes (from 100B per day), including **Duan-Den** (📞053 699966; 20/1 Th Chaisongkhram; motorcycles per 24hr 100-150B; ⊙7.30am-9pm), as well as bicycles (from 50B per day).

CHIANG RAI

In this Chapter

Chiang Rai at a Glance...

Sprawled across a rugged mountain range, Thailand's northernmost province, Chiang Rai, belts the border between Southeast Asia and China. The province is home to many minority hill tribes, Shan and other Tai groups, and Chinese immigrants, all holding on to their cultural identity and traditional lifestyle in the modern age.

Two Days in Chiang Rai

Dip into local culture at **Mae Fah Luang Art & Culture Park** (p238). Devote the evening to shopping at the **Walking Street** (p239). The next day visit **Wat Rong Khun** (p234) and enjoy dinner at **Lung Eed** (p240).

Four Days in Chiang Rai

Head out of town for a **multiday trek** (p233), the proceeds of which go to aid local hill-tribe villages with infrastructure and education projects. Or do an overnight trip to **Doi Mae Salong** (p236), an ethnic Chinese village that balances on a mountain ridge cultivated with tea plantations.

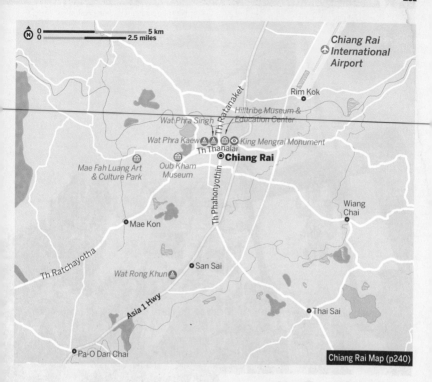

Chiang Rai Map (p240)

Arriving in Chiang Rai

Chiang Rai International Airport
Located approximately 8km north of
the city.

Bus station Located 5km from 'downtown' Chiang Rai. Frequent *sŏrng·tăa·ou*
(pick-up minibus) link it with town.

Interprovincial bus station Located in
the centre of town.

Where to Stay

Chiang Rai has a great selection of places to stay. Most budget places are in the
centre, clustered around Th Jetyod; the
majority of midrange places are a brief
walk from 'downtown'. Upscale country-
style resorts are located out of town.

Akha hill-tribe community, Swing Festival

Minority Cultures

Thailand's ethnic minorities who inhabit the mountainous region of Chiang Rai province are often called 'hill tribes', or in Thai vernacular, chow kŏw (mountain people). *Hill-tribe villages host trekking groups from the provincial capital to showcase their unique culture.*

Great For...

☑ Don't Miss

Sharing a meal with a village family is a treasured cultural exchange.

Hill-Tribe History

Most of the hill-tribe communities are of semi-nomadic origin, having come from Tibet, Myanmar, China and Laos during the past 200 years or so. The Tribal Research Institute in Chiang Mai recognises 10 different hill tribes, but there may be up to 20. Hill tribes are increasingly integrating into the Thai mainstream and many of the old ways and traditional customs are disappearing.

Hilltribe Museum

This **museum** (พิพิธภัณฑ์และศูนย์การศึกษาชาว เขา; www.pdacr.org; 3rd fl, 620/25 Th Thanalai; 50B; ⊘9am-6pm Mon-Fri, 10am-6pm Sat & Sun) and education centre is a good place to visit before undertaking any hill-tribe trek. Run by the nonprofit Population and Community Development Association (PDA),

Wooden dolls made by Karen hill tribe

JACKIE JIAN/GETTY IMAGES

ℹ️ **Need to Know**

Three-night treks start at 3500B per person with meals, lodging and hotel transfer.

✕ **Take a Break**

Upon returning to Chiang Rai, relax at one of the cafes such as BaanChivitMai Bakery (p239).

★ **Top Tip**

Ask your guide about the village's dos and don'ts so that you're a respectful guest.

the displays are a bit dated, but contain a wealth of information.

A visit begins with a 20-minute slide show on Thailand's hill tribes, followed by self-guided exploration through exhibits on traditional clothing, tools and implements, and other anthropological objects. The curator is passionate about his museum and, if present, will talk about the different hill tribes and the community projects that the museum funds. The PDA also runs highly recommended treks.

Trekking

Nearly every guesthouse and hotel in Chiang Rai offers hill-tribe hiking excursions. The following have a grassroots, sustainable or nonprofit emphasis.

Rai Pian Karuna (📱062 246 1897; www.facebook.com/raipiankaruna; treks 2000-5000B) A new, community-based enterprise conducting one- and multiday treks and homestays at Akha, Lahu and Lua villages in Mae Chan, north of Chiang Rai.

PDA Tours & Travel (📱053 740088; Hilltribe Museum & Education Center, 3rd fl, 620/25 Th Thanalai; treks 1200-3900B; ⏰9am-6pm Mon-Fri, 10am-6pm Sat & Sun) A well-established NGO offering one- to three-day treks. Profits go back into community projects such as HIV/AIDS education, mobile health clinics, education scholarships and the establishment of village-owned banks.

Mirror Foundation (📱053 719554; www.thailandecotour.org; 1-/2-/3-day treks from 2800/4300/5650B) Higher rates than most but this NGO helps support the training of its local guides. Treks range from one to three days and traverse the Akha, Karen and Lahu villages of Mae Yao District, north of Chiang Rai. Tours were suspended at the time of research due to government restrictions following the COVID-19 pandemic.

Pha Soet Hot Spring

ROLF 52/ALAMY STOCK PHOTO ©

Day Trips from Chiang Rai

Dabble in the bizarre and the foreign with these day trips. Wat Rong Khun is an elaborate and fantastic hybrid of modern and religious art, while Doi Mae Salong is a sleepy ethnic Chinese village perched on a mountain spine.

Great For...

☑ Don't Miss

Strawberries and other fruits grow in the cool northern climate. Buy from roadside stands.

Wat Rong Khun

Looking like a supersized confection, **Wat Rong Khun** (วัดร่องขุ่น, White Temple; off Rte 1/ AH2; 50B; ☺8am-5.30pm) **FREE** is Thailand's most eclectic and avant-garde temple. It was built in 1997 by noted Thai painter-turned-architect Chalermchai Kositpipat and mixes modern motifs and pop-culture references with traditional religious iconography.

The exterior of the temple is covered in whitewash and clear-mirrored chips. Walk over a bridge and sculpture of reaching arms (symbolising desire) to enter the sanctity of the wát where the artist has painted contemporary scenes representing *samsara* (the realm of rebirth and delusion). Images such as a plane smashing into the Twin Towers and, oddly enough, Keanu Reeves as Neo from *The Matrix*

Baandam

VALOGA/SHUTTERSTOCK ©

dining table and chairs made from deer antlers – a virtual Satan's dining room. Other buildings include white, breast-shaped bedrooms, dark phallus-decked bathrooms, and a bone- and fur-lined 'chapel'.

It's located 13km north of Chiang Rai in Nang Lae; any Mae Sai–bound bus will drop you off here for around 20B.

Ban Ruam Mit & Around

Ruam Mit means 'mixed', an accurate description of this riverside village, a convenient jumping-off point for the surrounding hilly area that's home to ethnic groups including Thai, Karen, Lisu and Akha.

Most visitors come to Ban Ruam Mit to ride elephants (which we don't recommend as it's been proven to be harmful to the animals). But a better, not to mention more sustainable, reason is hiking among the surrounding area's numerous villages, and visiting **Pha Soet Hot Spring** (บ่อน้ำพุร้อนผาเสริฐ; Ban Pha Soet; adult/child 30/10B; ⊘8.30am-6pm) or **Lamnamkok National Park** (อุทยานแห่งชาติลำน้ำกก; ⊘8am-4.30pm).

There are a couple of riverside Thai-style 'resort' hotels in Ban Ruam Mit. Alternatively, both basic hotels and homestay-style accommodation can be found in the surrounding villages. One of the best options is **Bamboo Nest de Chiang Rai** (☑089 953 2330, 095 686 4755; www.bamboonest-chiangrai.com; bungalows incl breakfast & dinner 1100-1400B), which takes the form of simple but spacious bamboo huts perched on a hill

dominate the one wall. If you like what you see, an adjacent gallery sells reproductions of Chalermchai Kositpipat's rather New Age–looking works.

The temple is 13km south of Chiang Rai. Take a regular bus bound for Chiang Mai or Phayao and ask to get off at Wat Rong Khun.

Baandam

The bizarre brainchild of Thai National Artist Thawan Duchanee, and a rather sinister counterpoint to Wat Rong Khun, **Baandam** (บ้านดำ, Black House; off Rte 1/AH2; adult/child 80B/free; ⊘9am-5pm) unites several structures, most of which are stained black and ominously decked out with animal pelts and bones.

The centrepiece is a black, cavernous, temple-like building holding a long wooden overlooking tiered rice fields. There are a few basic eateries in Ban Ruam Mit, and each of the hotels has its own restaurant.

From Chiang Rai, the easiest way to get to Ban Ruam Mit is via boat. A daily passenger boat departs from **CR Pier** (☏053 750009; ⊙7am-4pm), 2km northwest of Chiang Rai, at 10.30am (100B, about one hour); a charter will run about 800B. In the opposite direction, boats stop in Ban Ruam Mit around 2pm.

Doi Mae Salong

Doi Mae Salong was originally settled by the 93rd Regiment of the Kuomintang (KMT), who had fled to Myanmar from China after the establishment of communist rule in 1949. The KMT were forced to leave Myanmar in 1961. Crossing into northern Thailand with their pony caravans, they recreated a society like the one they had left behind in Yunnan. Generations later, this unique community still persists and is a domestic tourist attraction.

A tiny but busy and vibrant **morning market** (ตลาดเช้าดอยแม่สลอง; off Rte 1130; ⊙6-8am) convenes at the T-intersection near Shin Sane Guest House. The market attracts town residents and tribespeople from the surrounding districts and is worth waking up early for.

Shin Sane Guest House (☏053 765026; www.shinsaneguesthouse.com; Rte 1130; r 400B, bungalows 800B; 🛜) and **Little Home Guesthouse** (☏053 765389; www.maesa longlittlehome.com; Rte 1130; r & bungalows 800-1000B; ❄🛜) both have free maps with hiking routes to hill-tribe villages. The best hikes are north of Mae Salong between

Akha woman at a market stall

Ban Thoet Thai and the Myanmar border. Ask first about political conditions before heading off in this direction; Shan and Wa armies competing for control over this section of the Thailand–Myanmar border do occasionally clash in the area.

For a spot of self-pampering, spend a night at the charming **Phu Chaisai Resort & Spa** (☏053 910500; www.phu-chaisai.com; off Rte 1130; bungalows incl breakfast 4200-11,200B; ❄🛜🏊), located on a bamboo-covered hilltop and featuring a host of activities (spa, massage, yoga, hikes, rafting and swimming) to keep you occupied.

★ **Did You Know?**

Gǎm méuang, the northern dialect, has a slower rhythm than Thailand's three other main dialects.

Many Thai tourists come to Doi Mae Salong simply to eat Yunnanese dishes such as *màn·tǒh* (steamed Chinese buns) served with braised pork belly and pickled vegetables, or black chicken braised with Chinese-style herbs. Homemade wheat and egg noodles are another speciality of Doi Mae Salong, and are served with a local broth that combines pork and a spicy chilli paste. Places to dig into the local cuisine include the morning market, **Sue Hai** (Rte 1130; mains 40-300B; ⏱8am-9pm; 🍴) and **Salima Restaurant** (Rte 1130; mains 50-250B; ⏱9am-8pm).

The easiest way to get to Doi Mae Salong from Chiang Rai is to take a bus to Mae Chan, from where *sǒrng·tǎa·ou* run to Doi Mae Salong from the market area when full (50B, one hour). In the reverse direction, you can flag down *sǒrng·tǎa·ou* near Doi Mae Salong's 7-Eleven.

BORRIPATBKN./SHUTTERSTOCK ©

★ **Top Tip**

Tea houses in Doi Mae Salong sell locally grown teas (mostly oolong and jasmine).

⊙ SIGHTS

Mae Fah Luang Art & Culture Park   Museum

(ไร่แม่ฟ้าหลวง; www.maefahluang.org; 313 Mu 7, Ban Pa Ngiw; adult/child 200B/free; ⊙8.30am-5.30pm Tue-Sun) In addition to a museum that houses one of Thailand's biggest collections of Lanna artefacts, this vast, meticulously landscaped compound includes antique and contemporary art, Buddhist temples and other structures. It's located about 4km west of the centre of Chiang Rai; a túk-túk (pronounced *đúk đúk*) or taxi here will run to around 100B.

Wat Phra Kaew   Buddhist Temple

(วัดพระแก้ว; Th Trairat; donations appreciated; ⊙temple 7am-7pm, museum 9am-5pm) Originally called Wat Pa Yia (Bamboo Forest Monastery) in the local dialect, this is the city's most revered Buddhist temple. The main prayer hall is a well-preserved wooden structure. The octagonal *chedi* (stupa) behind it dates from the late 14th century and is in typical Lanna style. The adjacent two-storey teak building is a museum housing various Lanna artefacts.

Wat Phra Singh   Buddhist Temple

(วัดพระสิงห์; Th Singhaclai; donations appreciated; ⊙daylight hours) This temple dates back to the late 14th century, and its oldest surviving original buildings are typical northern Thai–style wooden structures with low, sweeping roofs. The main *wí·hăhn* (sanctuary) houses impressive wooden doors thought to have been carved by local artists, as well as a copy of Chiang Mai's sacred Phra Singh Buddha.

Oub Kham Museum   Museum

(พิพิธภัณฑ์อูบคำ; www.oubkhammuseum.com; Th Nakhai; adult/child incl tour 300/200B; ⊙8am-5pm) This slightly zany private museum houses an impressive collection of paraphernalia from virtually every corner of the former Lanna kingdom. The items, some of which truly are one of a kind, range from a monkey-bone food taster used by Lanna royalty to an impressive carved throne from Chiang Tung, Myanmar. The museum is located 2km west of the town centre and can be a bit tricky to find; túk-túk will go here for about 60B.

Oub Kham Museum

⚙ ACTIVITIES

Chiang Rai Bicycle Tours Cycling
(☎053 774506, 085 662 4347; www.chiangrai
bicycletour.com; half-/full-day tours from
1250/1850B) Recommended two-wheeled
excursions in the area surrounding Chiang
Rai. The office is 7km south of town: call or
email to book a tour.

**Suwannee Thai
Cooking Class** Cooking
(☎084 740 7119; www.thaicookingclasschiangrai.
com; lessons 1250B; ☺courses 9.30am-2pm)
Suwannee's cooking courses involve a visit
to a local market and instruction in cooking
four dishes. Her house is about 3km
outside the city centre, but she can pick
you up at most centrally located hotels and
guesthouses.

Thailand Hilltribe Holidays Trekking
(☎085 548 0884; www.thailandhilltribeholidays.
com; 1-/2-day trek for 4 people 1600/3200B)
This outfit offers sustainably minded
guided tours and homestays in and around
Chiang Rai.

🛍 SHOPPING

Walking Street Market
(Th Thanalai; ☺4-10pm Sat) If you're in town
on a Saturday evening, don't miss the
open-air Walking Street, an expansive
street market focusing on all things Chiang
Rai, from handicrafts to local dishes. The
market spans Th Thanalai from the Hill-
tribe Museum to the main fresh-produce
market.

Thanon Khon Muan Market
(Th Sankhongnoi; ☺6-9pm Sun) Come Sunday
evening, the stretch of Th Sankhongnoi
from Soi 2 heading west is closed to traffic
and in its place are vendors selling clothes,
handicrafts and local food. Th Sankhongnoi is called Th Sathanpayabarn where
it intersects with the southern end of Th
Phahonyothin.

 **Chiang Rai
Cafe Culture**

Chiang Rai has an enviable spread of
high-quality cafes, mainly because
some of Thailand's finest coffee beans
are grown in the province.

BaanChivitMai Bakery (www.bcmthai.
com; Th Prasopsook; ☺8am-6pm Mon-Fri,
8am-5pm Sat & Sun; 🛜) In addition to a
proper cup of coffee made from local
beans, there are surprisingly authentic
Swedish-style sweets and Western-style
meals and sandwiches at this popular
bakery.

Palamer Cafe (881/8 Th Nongsrijang;
☺10am-8pm Tue-Fri, 10am-10pm Sat & Sun;
🛜) A stylish but relaxed place that offers
both local and foreign beans in a refined
atmosphere. There's a good bakery
here, too.

Doi Chaang (Th Thanalai; ☺6.30am-
7.30pm; 🛜) Doi Chaang is the leading
brand among Chiang Rai coffees, and
its beans are now sold as far as Canada
and Europe.

Pangkhon Coffee (Th Sookathit; ☺7am-
6pm; 🛜) Combine coffee brewed from
local beans with views of Chiang Rai's
gilded clock tower.

AMABIRD/SHUTTERSTOCK ©

🍴 EATING

Come dinner time, you'll inevitably be point-
ed in the direction of Chiang Rai's night
bazaar, but the food there is generally average – you've been warned. Instead, if you're
in town on a weekend, hit the vendors at
Chiang Rai's open-air markets, Thanon

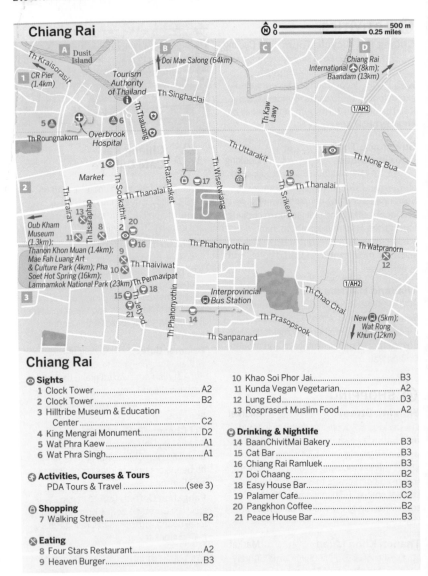

Chiang Rai

0 — 500 m
0 — 0.25 miles

Chiang Rai

Khon Muan and the Walking Street, which feature a good selection of local dishes.

Lung Eed   Thai $

(Th Watpranorn; mains 40-60B; ⏰11am-9pm Mon-Sat) One of Chiang Rai's most delicious dishes is available at this simple, friendly shophouse restaurant. There's an English-language menu on the wall, but don't miss the sublime *làhp gài* (minced chicken fried with local spices and topped with crispy deep-fried chicken skin, shallots and garlic). The restaurant is about 150m east of Rte 1/AH2.

Khao Soi Phor Jai   Thai $

(Th Jetyod; mains 40-50B; ◷8am-4pm) Phor Jai serves mild but delicious bowls of the eponymous curry noodle dish, as well as a few other northern Thai staples. There's no Roman-script sign, but look for the open-air shophouse with the white-and-blue interior.

Heaven Burger   Burgers $

(1025/5 Th Jetyod; mains 99-129B; ◷8am-9pm; 🍴) Owned and run by the whip-smart Jane, a member of the Akha minority, this place has a rustic setting with random garden furniture and sawn-off doors as tables. The food is great – all-day breakfasts and, above all, the superb burgers, including a fine veggie option, which come with self-baked buns and gratinated potato-skin fries.

Rosprasert Muslim Food   Thai $

(Th Itsaraphap; mains 50-100B; ◷7am-8pm) This shophouse restaurant next to the mosque on Th Itsaraphap dishes up tasty Thai-Muslim favourites, including a fine *kôw mòk gài* (the Thai version of chicken *biryani*). It also does a decent beef oxtail soup and *kôw soy* (noodles in a curry broth). The English-language sign says 'Muslim Food'.

Kunda Vegan Vegetarian   Vegetarian $$

(www.kundacafe.com; 372 Trairat Rd; mains 150-360B; ◷9am-5pm; 🍴) There's no tofu, no wi-fi and no reservations at this delightful addition to the Chiang Rai dining scene set over two floors of a former shophouse. Lounge on cushions and enjoy the old-school wood-panelled decor while tucking into vegan or veggie breakfasts, crêpes, salads and super smoothies. Everything – the bread, pesto, yoghurt and hummus – is made fresh daily.

Four Stars Restaurant   Thai $$

(423/3 Th Baanpa Pragarn; mains 45-240B; ◷10am-9pm Sun-Fri; 🍴) Popular with both Thais and foreign tourists thanks to a consistently tasty *kôw soy*, though the *sâi òo·a* (northern Thai sausage with herbs) is equally good. It also does a selection of classic rice and noodle dishes.

🍸 DRINKING & NIGHTLIFE

Th Jetyod is Chiang Rai's rather tacky drinking strip. The streets close to Th Jetyod are also home to a growing number of Thai-style bars, a few with live music.

Chiang Rai Ramluek   Bar

(Th Phahonyothin; ◷4pm-midnight) For a Thai-style night out on the town, consider this lively place. There's no English-language sign, but follow the live music and look for the knot of outdoor tables. Food is also available.

Peace House Bar   Bar

(Th Jetyod; ◷6pm-midnight; 🛜) Flying the Rasta flag in Chiang Rai, the Peace House has a pool table, live music a few nights a week, a mellow vibe and a shady garden that's popular with people who like to roll their own cigarettes.

Easy House Bar   Bar

(cnr Th Jetyod & Th Permavipat; ◷11am-midnight; 🛜) Easy House Bar has a friendly, relaxed, semi-open-air vibe and a dinner menu of Thai and Western classics.

Cat Bar   Bar

(1013/1 Th Jetyod; ◷5pm-1am) Long-standing Cat Bar has a pool table and, on some nights, live music.

ℹ️ INFORMATION

Tourism Authority of Thailand (TAT; 📞053 717433, nationwide 1672; tatchrai@tat.or.th; Th Singhaclai; ◷8.30am-4.30pm) English is limited, but staff here do their best to give advice and can provide a small selection of maps and brochures.

Overbrook Hospital (📞053 711366; www.overbrook-hospital.com; Th Singhaclai) English is spoken at this modern hospital.

ℹ️ GETTING THERE & AWAY

AIR

Chiang Rai International Airport (p306) is approximately 8km north of the city. A new bus

Hill-tribe woman, Doi Mae Salong (p236)

บ้านชนเผ่าอิ้วเมี่ยน

connects the airport with Chiang Rai's two bus stations (6am to 6pm, every 40 minutes, 20B). Taxis run into town from the airport for 160B. From town, a metered trip with Chiang Rai Taxi will cost around 130B. There are 15 daily flights to Bangkok's Don Mueang International Airport, and 14 to Bangkok's Suvarnabhumi International Airport.

BUS & MINIVAN

Buses bound for destinations within Chiang Rai Province, as well as some minivans, depart from the **interprovincial bus station** (053 715952; Th Prasopsook) in the centre of town. If you're heading beyond Chiang Rai, you'll have to go to the **new bus station** (053 773989; Rte 1/AH2), 5km south of town.

Frequent *sŏrng·tăa·ou* linking the new bus station and the interprovincial station run from 6am to 5.30pm (20B, 15 minutes). Or you can catch the purple-coloured bus that links the airport to the bus stations (6am to 6pm, every 40 minutes, 20B).

 GETTING AROUND

Central Chiang Rai is easy enough to tackle on foot or bicycle. Bicycles (from 50B per day) and motorbikes (from 200B per day) can be hired from your accommodation or at travel agencies and shops around town. Otherwise, túk-túk congregate around the interprovincial bus station and charge approximately 30B to 50B per person for destinations in town.

A number of car-rental companies have offices at the airport. **Chiang Rai Taxi** (053 773477) operates inexpensive metered taxis in and around town. Taxis can be found at the bus stations as well.

NONG KHAI

In this Chapter

Nong Khai at a Glance...

Rest and relaxation are Nong Khai's draws. It is a pleasant northeastern town perched on the banks of the muddy Mekong River, just across from Vientiane in Laos. As a border town it enjoys many Lao characteristics, including a friendly and laid-back disposition. Seduced by its dreamy pink sunsets and sluggish pace of life, many visitors who intend staying one night end up bedding down for many more.

Two Days in Nong Khai

Rent a bicycle and tour around the town enjoying the laid-back provincial lifestyle. Visit **Sala Kaew Ku** (p248) and have dinner along the riverside prom- enade. The next day, visit **Tha Sadet Market** (p252), filled with shoppers and diners. Experience the local food scene at **Daeng Namnuang** (p254).

Four Days in Nong Khai

Read a book, get a massage, pick up some handicraft souvenirs. Join the great Thai tradition of near constant eating through the day. If you develop itchy feet through the downtime, dis- appear across the Laotian border for a quick day trip to **Vientiane** (p250).

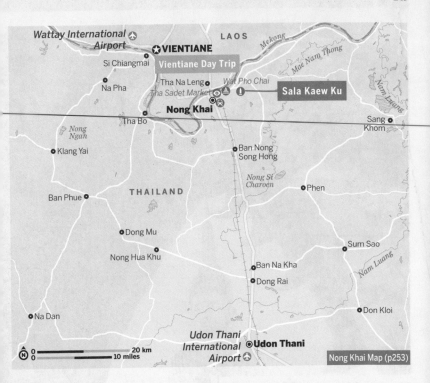

Arriving in Nong Khai

Udon International Thani Airport
Located 55km south of town. Minivans run to/from the airport.

Nong Khai bus terminal Located in town.

Nong Khai train station Located 2km west of the city centre; túk-túks (pronounced đúk đúk) take you downtown.

Where to Stay

Catering to the steady flow of backpackers, Nong Khai's budget lodging is the best in northeastern Thailand. Most guesthouses are centred along the river.

AMNAT30/SHUTTERSTOCK ©

Sala Kaew Ku

Tour the dream-like garden of Sala Kaew Ku, filled with larger-than-life figures from Hindu-Buddhist mythology. It is a surreal combination of art and religion that exemplifies the experimental aspects of Buddhist worship.

Great For...

☑ **Don't Miss**

The mummified body of the park's founder on the 3rd floor of the pavilion.

Built over a period of 20 years, the park features a weird and wonderful array of gigantic sculptures that merge Hindu and Buddhist imagery. The temple is locally known as Wat Kaek.

Mystic Visionary

The park's founder was a mystic shaman named Luang Pu Boun Leua Sourirat. As he tells his own story, Luang Pu tumbled into a hole as a child and met an ascetic named Kaewkoo, who introduced him to the manifold mysteries of the underworld and set him on course to become a Brahmanic-yogi-priest-shaman. Though he attracted followers, he had no formal training as a religious leader.

Shaking up his own unique blend of Hindu and Buddhist philosophy, mythology and iconography, Luang Pu developed a

LAOS

Mekong River

Nong Khai ⊚ Ⓐ Train Station

Nong Khai

❶ Sala Kaew Ku

THAILAND

❶ Need to Know

ศาลาแก้วกู่, Wat Khaek; 40B; ⏱7am-6pm

✕ Take a Break

Stop by Tha Sadet Market (p252) for a pre- or post-outing meal.

★ Top Tip

Mut Mee Garden Guesthouse (☏042 460717; www.mutmee.com; Soi Mutmee; d 220-1200B; ❄ ☎) distributes a map of the site with explanatory text.

large following on both sides of the Mekong in this region. In fact, his original project was on the Lao side of the river where he had been living until the 1975 communist takeover in Laos. He died in 1996.

The main shrine building, almost as strange as the sculptures, is full of images of every description and provenance (guaranteed to throw even an art historian into a state of disorientation). There are also photos of Luang Pu at various ages and Luang Pu's corpse lying under a glass dome ringed by flashing lights.

Life-Sized Parables

The park is a smorgasbord of large and bizarre cement statues of Buddha, Shiva, Vishnu and other celestial deities born of Luang Pu's dreams and cast by workers under his direction. They crowd together like a who's who of religious celebrities. Other pieces depict stories and parables meant to teach the seekers how to gain enlightenment. Touring the grounds is a 3D experience of Hindu-Buddhist symbols and tales.

Some of the sculptures are quite amusing. The serene elephant wading through a pack of anthropomorphic dogs teaches people to not be bothered by gossip.

The tallest sculpture, a Buddha seated on a coiled *naga* (serpent) with a spectacular seven-headed hood, is 25m high. It is a classic Thai Buddhist motif but with Luang Pu's unique twist.

Also of interest is the Wheel of Life (the process of life and rebirth), which you enter through a giant mouth. The final scene is of a young man stepping across the installation to become a Buddha figure.

Patuxai monument

MUELLEK JOSEF/SHUTTERSTOCK ©

Vientiane Day Trip

Being unbelievably close to the Laotian border, Nong Khai provides a great jumping-off point for a quick and fun run to Vientiane, all within a day. If you leave early, you can pack in a few hours of sightseeing in the Laotian capital and be back in Nong Khai by sundown.

Great For...

☑ Don't Miss

The journey by local transport promises pleasant interactions with the friendly country folk.

For most of its modern existence, the Nong Khai territory fell within the boundaries of the Vientiane (Wiang Chan) kingdom, which itself vacillated between independence and tribute to Lan Xang and Siam. When western Laos was partitioned off from Thailand by the French in 1893, the French demanded that Thailand have no soldiers within 25km of the river, and so the soldiers and administrators moved south and created Udon Thani. This means that though separated by an international border, the regions on both sides share plenty of commonalities in terms of culture.

Transport Options

If you already have your Lao visa, the easiest way to Vientiane is the direct bus from Nong Khai's bus terminal (55B, 1½ hours,

Pha That Luang

ⓘ Need to Know

Avoid border-area tùk-tùks as they often charge exorbitant prices.

✕ Take a Break

You'll find street food stalls en route. Save your lunch plans for Vientiane.

★ Top Tip

Having a Laotian visa in advance will save you time at the border.

Visa on Arrival

If you plan to get your visa at the border (6am to 10pm), take a tùk-tùk there – expect to pay 100B from the bus station or 60B from the town centre. Schedule some time for the visa process (getting here early helps). Unless you're travelling in a large group, there's no good reason to use a visa service agency, so don't let a driver take you to one.

Crossing the Border

After getting stamped out of Thailand, you can take the buses (15B to 20B) that carry passengers across the bridge to the hassle-free, but sometimes busy, Lao immigration checkpoint, where 30-day visas are available. It's about 20km to Vientiane. Plenty of buses, tùk-tùk and taxis will be waiting for you, and it's easy to find fellow travellers to share the costs.

six daily 7.30am to 6pm). There's a 5B surcharge for tickets to Laos on weekends, holidays and the 7.30am and 6pm weekday services. You can also go to Laos by train (there are immigration booths at both stations), though it doesn't go through to Vientiane, so this is not recommended. The 15-minute ride (20B to 30B, 7.30am and 2.45pm) drops you in Thanaleng (aka Dongphasay) station just over the bridge, leaving you at the mercy of túk-túk drivers who charge extortionate prices.

SIGHTS

Tha Sadet Market
Market

(ตลาดท่าเสด็จ; Th Rimkhong; ⊘8.30am-6pm)
This is the most popular destination in town. Almost everyone loves a stroll through this covered market despite it being a giant tourist trap. It offers the usual mix of clothes, electronic equipment, food and assorted bric-a-brac, most of it imported from Laos and China, but there are also a few shops selling quirky and quality stuff.

Wat Pho Chai
Buddhist Temple

(วัดโพธิ์ชัย; Th Phochai; ⊘daylight hours, ubosot 6am-6.30pm) FREE Luang Po Phra Sai, a large Lan Xang–era Buddha image awash with gold, bronze and precious stones, sits at the hub of Nong Khai's holiest temple. The head of the image is pure gold, the body is bronze and the ùt·sà·nít (flame-shaped head ornament) is set with rubies. Due to the great number of miracles attributed to it, this royal temple is a mandatory stop for most visiting Thais.

Luang Po Phra Sai was one of three similar statues made for each of the daughters of Lao king Setthathirat, and they were taken as bounty after King Rama I sacked Vientiane in 1778. The awesome murals in the hall housing the Buddha image depict their travels from the interior of Laos to the banks of the Mekong, where they were put on rafts. A storm sent one of the statues to the bottom of the river, where it remains today. It was never recovered because, according to one monk at the temple, the naga (which live in the river) wanted to keep it. The third statue, Phra Soem, is at Wat Pathum Wanaram, next to Siam Paragon in Bangkok. Phra Sai was supposed to accompany it, but, as the murals show, the cart carrying it broke down here and so this was taken as a sign that it wished to remain in Nong Khai.

☻ ACTIVITIES

Pantrix Yoga
Health & Wellbeing

(www.pantrix.net; Soi Mutmee; per week 9900B) Pantrix offers week- and month-long yoga courses (they are not live-in) for serious

Tha Sadet Market

AMNAT30/SHUTTERSTOCK ©

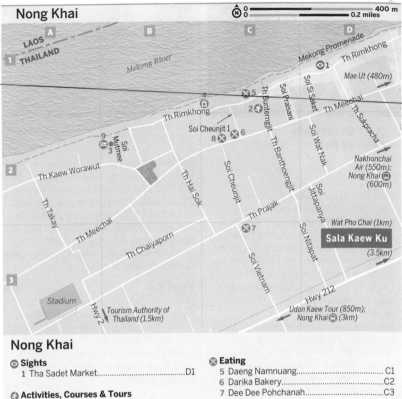

Nong Khai

◎ **Sights**

1 Tha Sadet Market......................D1

◉ **Activities, Courses & Tours**

2 Healthy Garden..........................C1
3 Pantrix Yoga..............................B2

🔒 **Shopping**

4 Nong Khai Walking Street Market.............C1

❌ **Eating**

5 Daeng Namnuang........................C1
6 Darika Bakery.............................C2
7 Dee Dee Pohchanah....................C3
8 Khao Soi....................................C2

🛌 **Sleeping**

9 Mut Mee Garden Guesthouse..................B2

---

students by experienced teachers. There's also a free daily yoga session from 2pm to 3pm. It's in the lane leading to Mut Mee Garden Guesthouse, where staff can point you in the right direction.

Healthy Garden   Massage

(☎042 423323; Th Banthoengjit; Thai/foot massage per hr 170/200B; ⊙8am-8pm) For the most effective treatment in Nong Khai, this place has foot massage and traditional Thai massage in air-conditioned rooms.

🔒 SHOPPING

Nong Khai Walking Street Market   Market

(⊙4-10pm Sat) This weekly street festival featuring music, handmade items and food takes over the promenade every Saturday night. It's smaller, but far more pleasant than the similar Walking Street markets in Chiang Mai.

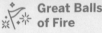

Great Balls of Fire

The sighting of the *bâng fai pá·yah·nâhk* (loosely translated, '*naga* fireballs') is an annual event along the Mekong River. Sometime in the early evening, at the end of the Buddhist Rains Retreat (usually October), small reddish balls of fire shoot from the Mekong River and float 100 or so metres into the air before vanishing without a trace. Most Thai and Lao see the event as a sign that resident *naga* are celebrating the end of the holiday. There are many theories about the fireballs, ranging from methane and phosphane being released from the river bottom, to monks having found a way to make a 'miracle'. The fireballs have become big business in Nong Khai Province, and curious Thais from across the country converge at various spots on the banks of the Mekong for the annual show. Little Phon Phisai, the locus of fireball-watching, hosts around 40,000 guests.

Naga fireball festival
YAMAN MUTART/SHUTTERSTOCK ©

EATING

Dee Dee Pohchanah   Thai $

(1155/9 Th Prajak; mains 50-150B; ⊙11am-1am; 🛜) How good is Dee Dee? Just look at the dinner-time crowds. But don't be put off by them: despite having a full house every night, this open-air place is a well-oiled machine and you won't be waiting long.

Mae Ut   Vietnamese $

(637 Th Meechai; mains 50-100B; ⊙9.30am-4pm) This little place, serving just four items, including fried spring rolls, *khâo gee·ab þahk mŏr* (fresh noodles with pork), and a Vietnamese take on a pancake-pizza, is essentially grandma's kitchen, and it's fascinating to watch the food being made to order on large banana leaves. No English sign, and English is limited, but the welcome is friendly.

Darika Bakery   Thai $

(Sweet Cake & Coffee; Th Meechai; mains 40-150B; ⊙5.30am-3pm) It's hard to categorise this place, run by a sweet old lady who makes standard Thai dishes and also many international favourites such as baked cakes and banana pancakes. Enjoy the homely atmosphere for breakfast or lunch, or just a coffee (instant, brewed or traditional Thai).

Khao Soi   Thai $

(949 Th Meechai; mains 40-50B; ⊙8am-3pm) If you're missing the flavours of northern Thailand, this descriptively named hole-in-the-wall will satisfy your cravings. For the uninitiated, *kôw soy* (curry noodle soup) is northern Thailand's most famous dish. Friendly owner.

Daeng Namnuang   Vietnamese $$

(Th Rimkhong; mains 70-270B; ⊙6am-8.30pm; 🅿🛜) This massive river restaurant has grown into a Nong Khai institution, and hordes of out-of-towners head home with car boots and carry-on bags stuffed with their *nǎam neu·ang* (DIY pork spring rolls).

DRINKING & NIGHTLIFE

There are several small bars along the river between Mut Mee Garden Guesthouse and Tha Sadet Market that cater to travellers and expats. For something truly Thai, follow Mekong-hugging Th Rimkhong east past Tha Sadet Market and you'll pass a bevy of restaurants and bars, some earthy, some fashionable, churning out dinner and drinks. They're less convenient, but much livelier.

Mural in Wat Pho Chai (p252)

ℹ️ INFORMATION

Immigration (📞042 990935; Hwy 2; ⏰8.30am-noon & 1-4.30pm Mon-Fri) One kilometre south of the Friendship Bridge. Offers Thai visa extensions.

ℹ️ GETTING THERE & AWAY

AIR

The nearest airport is 55km south in Udon Thani. **Udon Kaew Tour** (📞042 411530; Th Pranang Cholpratan, Hwy 212; ⏰8.30am-5.30pm) travel agency runs minivans (200B per person) to/from the airport.

BUS & MINIVAN

Nong Khai bus terminal (📞042 421246) is located just off Th Prajak. Vans depart from the border/bridge to Udon Thani (50B, hourly, 7am to 7pm). **Nakhonchai Air** (📞042 420285) has a bus to Bangkok (nine hours, 10am, 7.45pm and 8.30pm).

TRAIN

For Bangkok, four express trains (2nd-/3rd-class 498/253B, 9½ hours to 11½ hours, 7.45am, 6.30pm, 6.50pm and 7.40pm) leave from **Nong Khai train station** (📞042 411637, nationwide 1690).

ℹ️ GETTING AROUND

Nong Khai is a great place for cycling due to the limited traffic and the nearby countryside. Many guesthouses let you use their bikes for free. You can find metered taxis at the bus station and the bridge.

Wat Rong Khun (p234)

In Focus

MATTEO COLOMBO/GETTY IMAGES ©

History

Thai history has all the dramatic elements to inspire the imagination: palace intrigue, wars waged with spears and elephants, popular protest movements and a series of military coups. It began with migrants heading into a frontier land claimed by distant empires for trade, labour and patronage, and evolved through notable social and political events that had indelible effects on the collective national narrative.

1240–1438
Approximate dates of Sukhothai kingdom.

1351
The legendary kingdom of Ayuthaya is founded.

1511
Portuguese mission is founded in Ayuthaya. Other European nations follow.

King Taksin Monument

From the Beginning

Though there is evidence of prehistoric peoples, most scholars start the story of Thai nationhood at the arrival of the 'Tai' people during the first millennium AD. The Tai people migrated from southern China and spoke Tai-Kadai, a family of tonal languages said to be the most significant ethno-linguistic group in Southeast Asia. The language group branched off into Laos (the Lao people) and Myanmar (the Shan).

Most of these new arrivals were farmers and hunters who lived in loosely organised villages, usually near a river source, with no central government or organised military. The indigenous Mon people are often recognised as assembling an early confederation (often referred to as Mon Dvaravati) in central and northeastern Thailand from the 6th to 9th centuries. Little is known about this period, but scholars believe that the Mon Dvaravati had a centre in Nakhon Pathom, outside of Bangkok, with outposts in parts of northern Thailand.

1767	**1768–82**	**1782**
Ayuthaya falls at the hands of the Burmese.	King Taksin rules from the new capital of Thonburi.	Chakri dynasty is founded, and the capital is moved to Bangkok.

Headless Buddha statue, Ayuthaya (p88)

The ancient superpower of the region was the Khmer empire, based in Angkor (in present-day Cambodia), which expanded across the western frontier into present-day northeastern and central Thailand starting in the 11th century. Sukhothai and Phimai were regional administrative centres connected by roads with way-station temples that made travel easier and were a visible symbol of imperial power. The Khmer monuments started out as Hindu but were later converted into Buddhist temples after the regime converted. Though their power would eventually decline, the Khmer imparted to the evolving Thai nation an artistic, bureaucratic and even monarchical legacy.

Thai history is usually told from the perspective of the central region, where the current capital is. But the southern region has a separate historical narrative that didn't merge with the centre until the modern era. Between the 8th and 13th centuries, southern Thailand was controlled by the maritime empire of Srivijaya, based in southern Sumatra (Indonesia), and controlled trade between the Straits of Malacca.

The Rise of the Thai Kingdoms

In the 13th century, the regional empires started to decline and prosperous Tai city-states emerged with localised power and military might. The competing city-states were ultimately united into various kingdoms that began to establish a Thai identity. Scholars recognise Lanna, Sukhothai and Ayuthaya as the unifying kingdoms of the period.

Lanna

In the northern region, the Lanna kingdom, founded by King Mengrai, built Chiang Mai (meaning 'new city') in 1292 and proceeded to unify the northern communities into one cultural identity. For a time Chiang Mai was something of a religious centre for the region. However, Lanna was plagued by dynastic intrigues, fell to the Burmese in 1556 and was later eclipsed by Sukhothai and Ayuthaya as the progenitor of the modern Thai state.

1826
Thailand allies with Britain during the first Anglo-Burmese War.

1868–1910
King Chulalongkorn (Rama V) reigns; it's a time of modernisation and European imperialism.

1932
A bloodless revolution ends absolute monarchy.

Sukhothai

Then just a frontier town on the edge of the ailing Khmer empire, Sukhothai expelled the distant power in the mid-13th century and crowned the local chief as the first king. But it was his son Ramkhamhaeng who led the city-state to become a regional power with dependencies in modern-day Laos and southern Thailand. Sukhothai replaced Chiang Mai as a centre of Theravada Buddhism on mainland Southeast Asia. The monuments built during this era helped define a distinctive architectural style. After his death, Ramkhamhaeng's empire disintegrated. In 1378 Sukhothai became a tributary of Ayuthaya.

Ayuthaya

Close to the Gulf of Thailand, the city-state of Ayuthaya grew rich and powerful from the international sea trade. The legendary founder was King U Thong, one of 36 kings and five dynasties that steered Ayuthaya through a 416-year lifespan. Ayuthaya presided over an age of commerce in Southeast Asia. Its main exports were rice and forest products, and many commercial and diplomatic foreign missions set up headquarters outside the royal city. Ayuthaya adopted Khmer court customs, honorific language and ideas of kingship. The monarch styled himself as a Khmer *devaraja* (divine king) instead of the Sukhothai ideal of *dhammaraja* (righteous king).

Ayuthaya paid tribute to the Chinese emperor, who rewarded this ritualistic submission with generous gifts and commercial privileges. Ayuthaya's reign was constantly under threat from expansionist Burma. The city was occupied in 1569 but later liberated by King Naresuan. In 1767 Burmese troops successfully sacked the capital and dispersed the Thai leadership into the hinterlands. The destruction of Ayuthaya remains a vivid historical event for the nation, and the tales of court life are as evocative as the stories of King Arthur.

The Bangkok Era

The Revival

With Ayuthaya in ruins and the dynasty destroyed, a general named Taksin filled the power vacuum and established a new capital in 1768 in Thonburi, across the river from modern-day Bangkok. King Taksin was deposed and executed in 1782 by subordinate generals. One of the leaders of the coup, Chao Phraya Chakri, was crowned King Buddha Yot Fa (Rama I), the founder of the current Chakri dynasty. He moved the capital across the river to the Ko Ratanakosin district of present-day Bangkok. The new kingdom was viewed as a revival of Ayuthaya and its leaders attempted to replicate the former kingdom's laws, government practices and cultural achievements. They also built a powerful military that avenged Burmese aggression, kicking them out of Chiang Mai. The Bangkok rulers continued courting Chinese commercial trade.

1939	1941	1945
The country's English name is officially changed from Siam to Thailand.	Japanese forces enter Thailand during WWII.	WWII ends; Thailand cedes seized territory from Laos, Cambodia and Malaysia.

Name Change

Phibul Songkhram officially changed the name of the country in 1939 from 'Siam' to 'Prathet Thai' (or 'Thailand' in English); it was considered an overt nationalistic gesture intended to unite all the Tai-speaking people.

The Reform

The Siamese elite had long admired China, but by the 1800s the West dominated international trade and geopolitics.

King Mongkut (Rama IV; r 1851–68), often credited with modernising the kingdom, spent 27 years prior to assuming the crown as a monk in the Thammayut sect, a reform movement he founded to restore scholarship to the faith. During his reign the country was integrated into the prevailing market system that broke up royal monopolies and granted more rights to foreign powers.

Mongkut's son, King Chulalongkorn (Rama V; r 1873–1910) took greater steps in replacing the old political order. He abolished slavery and introduced the creation of a salaried bureaucracy, a police force and a standing army. His reforms brought uniformity to the legal code, law courts and revenue offices. Schools were established along European models. Universal conscription and poll taxes made all men the king's men. Many of the king's advisors were British, and they ushered in a remodelling of the old Ayuthaya-based system. Distant sub-regions were brought under central command and railways were built to link them to population centres. Pressured by French and British colonies on all sides, the modern boundaries of Siam came into shape by ceding territory.

Democracy versus Dictatorship

The 1932 Revolution

During a period of growing independence movements in the region, a group of foreign-educated military officers and bureaucrats led a successful (and bloodless) coup against absolute monarchy in 1932. The pro-democracy party soon splintered and, by 1938, General Phibul Songkhram, one of the original democracy supporters, had seized control of the country. During WWII, Phibul, who was staunchly anti-royalist, strongly nationalistic and pro-Japanese, allowed that country to occupy Thailand as a base for assaults on British colonies in Southeast Asia. In the post-WWII era, Phibul positioned Thailand as an ally of the US in its war on communism.

The Cold War

During the Cold War and the US conflict in Vietnam, the military leaders of Thailand gained legitimacy and economic support from the US in exchange for the use of military installations in Thailand. By the 1970s a new political consciousness bubbled up from the universities. In 1973 more than half a million people – intellectuals, students, peasants and

1946	**1957**	**1973**
King Bhumibol Adulyadej (Rama IX) ascends the throne; Thailand joins the UN.	A successful coup by Sarit Thanarat starts a period of military rule that lasts until 1973.	Civilian demonstrators overthrow the military dictatorship; a democratic government is installed.

workers – demonstrated in Bangkok and major provincial towns, demanding a constitution from the military government. The bloody dispersal of the Bangkok demonstration on 14 October led to the collapse of the regime and the creation of an elected constitutional government. This lasted only three years until another protest movement was brutally squashed and the military returned to restore civil order.

By the 1980s the so-called political soldier General Prem Tinsulanonda forged a period of political and economic stability that led to the 1988 election of a civilian government. Prem is still involved in politics today as the president of the palace's privy council, a powerful position that joins the interests of the monarchy with the military.

The Business Era

The new civilian government was composed of former business executives, many of whom represented provincial commercial interests, instead of Bangkok-based military officials, signalling a shift in the country's political dynamics. Though the country was doing well economically, the government was accused of corruption and vote-buying and the military moved to protect its privileged position with a 1991 coup. Elected leadership was restored shortly after the coup, and the Democrat Party, with the support of business and the urban middle class, dominated the parliament.

The 1997 Asian currency crisis derailed the surging economy and the government was criticised for its ineffective response. That same year, the parliament passed the watershed 'people's constitution', which enshrined human rights and freedom of expression and granted more power to a civil society to counter corruption. (The 1997 constitution was thrown out during the 2006 coup.)

By the turn of the millennium, the economy had recovered and business interests had succeeded the military as the dominant force in politics. The telecommunications billionaire and former police officer Thaksin Shinawatra ushered in the era of the elected CEO. He was a capitalist with a populist message and garnered support from the rural and urban poor and the working class. From 2001 to 2005 Thaksin and his Thai Rak Thai party transformed national politics into one-party rule.

The Thaksin Era

Though Thaksin enjoyed massive popular support, his regime was viewed by urban intellectuals as a kleptocracy, with the most egregious example of corruption being the tax-free sale of his family's Shin Corporation stock to the Singaporean government in 2006, a windfall of 73 billion baht (US$1.88 billion) that was engineered by special legislation. This enraged the upper and middle classes and led to street protests in Bangkok. On 19 September 2006 the military staged a bloodless coup, the first in 15 years, which brought an end to the country's longest stretch of democratic rule. The military dissolved the constitution that had sought to ensure a civilian government and introduced a new constitution that limited the resurgence of one-party rule by interests unsympathetic to the military and the aristocrats.

1997	**2004**	**2006**
The Asian economic crisis hits; 'people's constitution' is passed in parliament.	A tsunami kills 5000 people and damages tourism and fishing on the Andaman Coast.	Prime Minister Thaksin Shinawatra is ousted by a military coup.

The Coup Decade

Following Thaksin's ouster, general elections were held with Thaksin's political allies forming a government led by Samak Sundaravej. This was an unsatisfactory outcome to the military and the anti-Thaksin group known as People's Alliance for Democracy (PAD), comprised of mainly urban elites nicknamed 'Yellow Shirts' because they wore yellow (the colour associated with the king's birthday). It was popularly believed that Thaksin was consolidating power during his tenure so that he could interrupt royal succession.

In September 2008, Samak Sundaravej was unseated by the Constitutional Court on a technicality: while in office, he hosted a TV cooking show deemed to be a conflict of interest. Concerned that another election would result in a Thaksin win, the Yellow Shirts seized control of Thailand's main airports, Suvarnabhumi and Don Mueang, for a week in November 2008, until the military manoeuvred a silent coup and another favourable court ruling that further weakened Thaksin's political proxies. Through last-minute coalition building, Democrat Abhisit Vejjajiva was elected in a parliamentary vote, becoming Thailand's 27th prime minister.

Thaksin supporters organised their own counter-movement as the United Front for Democracy Against Dictatorship (UDD), better known as the 'Red Shirts'. Supporters hail mostly from the north and northeast, and include anti-coup, pro-democracy activists; anti-royalists; and die-hard Thaksin fans. There is a degree of class struggle, with many working-class Red Shirts expressing bombastic animosity towards the aristocrats.

The Red Shirts' most provocative demonstration came in 2010, when Thailand's Supreme Court ordered the seizure of US$46 billion of Thaksin's assets after finding him guilty of abusing his powers as prime minister. The Red Shirts occupied Bangkok's central shopping district for two months and demanded the dissolution of the government and reinstatement of elections. In May 2010 the military used force to evict the protesters, resulting in bloody clashes where 91 people were killed and shopping centres set ablaze (US$1.5 billion of crackdown-related arson damage was estimated).

The next round of the political ping-pong game began in 2011 when Thaksin's politically allied Puea Thai party won a parliamentary majority and Thaksin's sister Yingluck Shinawatra was elected as prime minister. Yingluck Shinawatra became both the first female prime minister of Thailand and the country's youngest-ever premier. The belief that the Yingluck government was a Thaksin administration in all but name ensured she faced bitter opposition.

The most disastrous misstep was a proposed bill granting amnesty for Thaksin, which would have allowed him to return to the country. Street demonstrations began in October 2013 with sporadic violence between Yingluck's supporters and opponents. Yingluck and nine of her ministers stepped down on 7 May of the next year. The military seized control 15 days later.

2011	**2014**	**2015**
Yingluck Shinawatra becomes the first female prime minister; destructive floods hit the country.	Yingluck Shinawatra is found guilty of abuse of power. The Thai military assumes control of the country.	Terrorist bomb explosion at popular Bangkok Erawan shrine kills 20 people.

Return to Military Dictatorship

On 22 May 2014, the Thai military under General Prayut Chan-o-cha overthrew the elected government and brought to an end months of political crisis. Prayut said the coup was necessary to restore stability.

Prayut's military government was known as the National Council for Peace and Order (NCPO). The NCPO set about restoring stability by implementing martial law and silencing critics. All media were under orders to refrain from dissent. Internet providers were ordered to block any content that violated the junta's orders. In March 2015 Prayut jestfully told journalists that he would execute those who did not toe the official line.

The crackdown extended into the civilian sphere as well. More than 1000 people – opposition politicians, academics, journalists, bloggers and students – were detained or tried in military courts. In March 2015, the UN's High Commissioner for Human Rights claimed that the military was using martial law to silence opposition and to call for 'freedom of expression to ensure genuine debate'.

In preparation for the inevitable transfer of the crown, the military also increased prosecution of the country's strict lèse-majesté laws. Yet while the NCPO was busy silencing critics, it failed to address Thailand's slumping economy. Foreign investment, exports and GDP all contracted after the coup. In 2016 a much-needed infrastructure investment plan was announced to help bolster the downturn. Tourism continued to be the bright spot in the economy.

Thai Constitution

Thailand has had 20 constitutions, all rewritten following various miltary coups. A draft version of constitution number 20 was approved by popular referendum in 2016. Each new version redefines how much of the legislature will be popularly elected, who is eligible to be prime minister and how the PM will be selected.

Elections & A New Government

In March 2019, after five years of delays which saw the constitution amended once again, Thailand held its first general election since the 2014 coup. The junta and its leader, former general Prayuth Chan-o-cha, campaigned under the name of the Palang Pracharath party.

Despite attempts to restrict the media coverage of the other parties – and allegations of voting irregularities – Palang Pracharath failed to win a parliamentary majority. Instead, the Pheu Thai party associated with the Shinawatra clan captured the most seats, while the new Future Forward party came third. Under the latest constitution, though, the unelected, 250-member senate (the upper house of parliament) also votes on the appointment of the prime minister, and Prayuth was duly chosen to head a coalition government in June 2019.

2016
King Rama IX dies; his son succeeds the throne. Military-backed constitution wins popular referendum.

2019
First general election is held since the 2014 coup. Former army general Prayuth Chan-o-cha is appointed prime minister.

2019
King Vajiralongkorn (Rama X) is formally crowned in an elaborate three-day ceremony in Bangkok.

Thai wedding items

RABYESANG/GETTY IMAGES ©

Culture & Customs

It is easy to love Thailand: the pace of life is unhurried and the people are friendly and kind-hearted. A smile is a universal key in most social situations, a cheerful disposition will be met in kind, and friendships require little more than curiosity and humour. Thais don't expect foreigners to know much about their country, but they are delighted if they do.

The Monarchy

Thailand expresses deep reverence for its monarchy. Pictures of the king – both present and former – are enshrined in nearly every household and business, and life-size billboards of the monarchs line Th Ratchadamnoen Klang, Bangkok's royal avenue. The previous king's image, which is printed on money, is regarded as sacred, and criticising the king or the monarchy is a criminal offence. The monarchy's relationship to the people is inter-twined with religion; it is deeply spiritual and personal. Most Thais view their king with great reverence, as an exalted father figure (the previous king's birthday is recognised as national Father's Day) and as a protector of the good of the country.

The National Psyche

In most social situations, establishing harmony is often a priority and Thais take personal pride in making others feel at ease.

Sà·nùk

Thais place a high value on having *sà·nùk* (fun). It is the underlying measure of a worthwhile activity and the reason why the country ranks so highly as a tourist destination. Thais are always up for a party, be it of their own invention or an import. Case in point: Thais celebrate three new years – the eve of the resetting of the international calendar, the Chinese lunar New Year and Songkran (the Southeast Asian Buddhist new year).

This doesn't mean that Thais are averse to work. Most offices are typically open six, and sometimes seven, days a week, and most Thais have side jobs to provide extra income. But every chore has a social aspect that lightens the mood and keeps it from being too 'serious' (a grave insult). Whether it's the backbreaking work of rice farming, the tedium of long-distance bus driving or the dangers of a construction site, Thais often mix their work tasks with socialising.

Status

Though Thai culture is famously nonconfrontational and fun-loving, it isn't a social free-for-all. Thais are very conscious of status and the implicit rights and responsibilities. Buddhism defines the social strata, with the heads of the family, religion and monarchy sitting at the top of various tiers. Gauging where you fit into this system is a convenient ice-breaker. Thais will often ask a laundry list of questions: where are you from, how old are you, are you married, do you have children? They are sizing you up in the social strata.

In most cases, you'll get the best of both worlds: Thais will care for you as if you are a child and honour you as if you are a *pôo yài* (literally 'big person', or elder). When sharing a meal, don't be surprised if a Thai host puts the tastiest piece of fish on your plate.

Thais regard each other as part of an extended family and will use familial prefixes such as *pêe* (elder sibling) and *nórng* (younger sibling) when addressing friends as well as blood relations. Rarely do foreigners get embraced in this grand family reunion; *fa·ràng* is the catch-all term for foreigner. It is mostly descriptive but can sometimes express cultural frustrations.

Saving Face

Thais believe strongly in the concept of saving face, or avoiding confrontation and endeavouring not to embarrass themselves or other people (except when it's *sà·nùk* to do so). The ideal face-saver doesn't bring up negative topics in conversation, doesn't express firm convictions or opinions, and doesn't claim to have an expertise. Agreement and harmony are considered to be the most important social graces.

Dos & Don'ts

- Always stand for the royal and national anthems.

- Don't show anger or frustration in public.

- Remove shoes before entering homes or temples; step over the threshold.

- Keep your feet off furniture.

- In temples, sit in the 'mermaid' position (with your feet tucked behind you).

- Pass and receive things with your right hand.

- Use your spoon like a fork and your fork like a knife.

While Westerners might think of heated discussion as social sport, Thais regard any instance where voices are raised as rude and potentially volatile. Losing your temper causes a loss of face for everyone, and Thais who have been crossed may react in extreme ways. Minor embarrassments, such as tripping or falling, might elicit giggles from a crowd of Thais. In this case they aren't taking delight in your mishap, but helping you save face by laughing it off.

Social Conventions & Etiquette

Thais are generally tolerant of most social faux pas as they assume that foreign visitors know very little about their culture. Their graciousness should be returned with a concerted effort of respect.

Greetings

The traditional Thai greeting is with a prayer-like palms-together gesture known as a *wâi*. If someone shows you a *wâi*, you should return the gesture, unless the greeting comes from a child or a service person. A *wâi* can also express gratitude or an apology. The all-purpose greeting is a cheery *'sà·wàt·dee kráp'* if you're male or *'sà·wàt·dee kâ'* if you're female. A smile usually accompanies this and goes a long way to defuse a tense social situation.

Visiting Temples

When visiting a temple, it is important to dress modestly (cover yourself to the elbows and the ankles) and to take your shoes off when you enter any building that contains a Buddha image. Buddha images are sacred objects, so don't pose in front of them for pictures and definitely do not clamber on them. When visiting a religious building, act like a worshipper by finding a discreet place to sit in the 'mermaid' position (with your feet tucked behind you so that they point away from the Buddha images). Temples are maintained from the donations received and contributions from visitors are appreciated.

Touching

In the traditional parts of the country, it is not proper for members of the opposite sex to touch one another. Same-sex touching is quite common and is typically a sign of friendship, not sexual attraction. Older Thai men might grab a younger man's thigh in the same way that buddies slap each other on the back. Thai women are especially affectionate, often sitting close to female friends or linking arms. Women should not touch monks or their belongings; they should not sit next to them on public transport or accidentally brush against them on the street.

Spirit house (p271)

Religion

Religion is a fundamental component of Thai society, and colourful examples of worship can be found on every corner. Walk the streets in the morning and you'll see the solemn progression of Buddhist monks engaged in bin·da·bàht, the daily house-to-house alms gathering. Household shrines decorate the humblest abodes, and protective amulets are common pieces of jewellery.

Buddhism

Approximately 95% of Thai people are Theravada Buddhists. This form of Buddhism is often called the Southern School because it travelled from the Indian subcontinent to Southeast Asia.

Religious Principles

Buddhism was born in India in the 6th century. A prince named Siddhartha Gautama left his life of privilege, seeking religious fulfilment. According to the practices of the time, he became an ascetic before he realised that this was not the way to reach the end of suffering.

★ **Buddhist Festivals**

Makha Bucha (February)

Poy Sang Long (March/April)

Visakha Bucha (May)

Khao Phansaa (July)

Ork Phansaa (October)

Monks during Visakha Bucha (p23)

Adopting a more measured Middle Way, his practice became more balanced until, on the night of the full moon of the fifth month (celebrated as Visakha Bucha), he became enlightened under the Bodhi tree. He became known as Buddha, 'the enlightened' or 'the awakened', and spoke of four noble truths that had the power to liberate any human being who could realise them.

The four noble truths deal with the nature and origin of suffering and the path to the cessation of suffering. Loosely explained, this includes *dukkha* (all forms of existence are subject to suffering, disease, imperfection), *samudaya* (the origin of suffering is desire), *nirodha* (cessation of suffering is giving up desire) and *magga* (the path to cessation of suffering is the eightfold path). The eightfold path is often described as the middle path: a route between extreme asceticism and indulgence. Following the path will lead to *nibbana* ('nirvana' in Sanskrit), which literally means the 'blowing out' or extinction of all grasping and thus all suffering. Effectively, *nibbana* is also an end to the cycle of rebirths (both moment-to-moment and life-to-life) that is existence.

Religious Practices

In reality, most Thai Buddhists aim for rebirth in a 'better' existence rather than the supra-mundane goal of *nibbana*. By feeding monks, giving donations to temples and worshipping regularly at their local temple, they hope to improve their lot, acquiring enough merit (*bun* in Thai) to prevent rebirths (or at least reduce their number). The concept of rebirth is almost universally accepted in Thailand, even by non-Buddhists.

Thai Buddhists look to the Triple Gems for guidance in their faith: the Buddha, the *dhamma* and the *sangha*. The Buddha is usually the centrepiece of devotional activity in-side a temple and many of the most famous Thai Buddha images have supernatural tales associated with them. The *dhamma* (teachings) is chanted morning and evening in every temple and taught to every Thai citizen in primary school. There are two *sangha* (monas-tic) sects in Thailand: the Mahanikai and Thammayut. The former is more mainstream, while the latter is aligned with the monarchy and stricter in its practices.

Hinduism & Animism

There are many enduring legacies of Hinduism and animism in Thai culture and in the practice of Thai Buddhism today. Hinduism was the religious parent of Buddhism, impart-ing lasting components of mythology, cosmology and symbolism.

Thais recognise the contributions of Hinduism and treat its deities with reverence. Bangkok is especially rich in Hindu shrines. Many of the royally associated ceremonies stem from Brahmanism. Spirit worship and Buddhism have commingled to the point that it is difficult to filter the two. Monks often perform obviously animistic rituals, and Thais be-lieve that merit-making (Buddhist religious rituals) benefits deceased relatives. Trees are wrapped in sacred cloth to honour the spirits of the natural world. Altars are erected on the dashboards of taxis to ensure immunity from traffic laws and accidents. Thais often wear amulets embossed with a Buddha figure or containing sacred soil from a revered temple to protect the wearer from misfortune. In fact, many of the religious rituals of Thai Buddhists, apart from meditation, appear to be deeply rooted in the spirit world.

Monks & Monasteries

Every Thai male is expected to become a monk (*prá* or *prá pík·sù* in Thai) for a short period, optimally between the time he finishes school and the time he starts a career or marries. A family earns great merit when one of its sons 'takes robe and bowl' and many young men enter the monastery to make merit for a deceased patriarch or matriarch.

Traditionally, Buddhist Lent (*pan·săh*), which begins in July and coincides with the three-month period of the rainy season, is when most temporary monks enter the monastery. Nowadays, though, men may spend as little as a week there. Historically the temple provided a necessary social safety net for families. The monastery was a de facto orphanage and also acted as a retirement home for older rural men. Though these charitable roles are not as sought after today, the temples still give refuge and sanctuary to all living creatures. This might mean that they help feed families in need, adopt orphaned or injured animals, and give shelter to overnight travellers (usually impoverished Thai university students).

In Thai Buddhism, women who seek a monastic life are given a minor role in the temple that is not equal to full monkhood. A Buddhist nun is known as *mâa chee* (mother priest) and lives as an *atthasila* nun (following eight precepts of Buddhism's code of ethics as opposed to the five for laypeople and 227 for ordained monks), a position traditionally occupied by women who had no other place in society. Thai nuns shave their heads, wear white robes and take care of temple chores. Generally speaking, *mâa chee* aren't considered as prestigious as monks and don't have a function in the merit-making rituals of lay people. An increasing number of foreigners come to Thailand to be ordained as Buddhist monks and nuns.

Temple Visits

Thai Buddhism has no particular sabbath day when the faithful are supposed to congregate weekly. Instead, Thai Buddhists visit most often on *wan prá* (holy days), which occur every seventh or eighth day, depending on phases of the moon. A temple visit is usually a social affair involving groups of friends, families or office workers. Thais will also make special pilgrimages to famous temples in other regions as sightseeing and merit-making outings. Most merit-makers visit the *wí·hăhn* (central sanctuary), which houses the primary Buddha figure. Worshippers will offer lotus buds (a symbol of enlightenment) or flower garlands, light three joss sticks and raise their hands to their forehead in a prayerlike gesture.

Other merit-making activities include offering food to the temple *sangha*, meditating (individually or in groups), listening to monks chanting *suttas* (Buddhist discourse) and attending a *têht* or *dhamma* talk by the abbot or some other respected teacher.

Houses of the Holy

Many dwellings in Thailand have a 'spirit house' for the property's *prá poom* (guardian spirits). Based on pre-Buddhist animistic beliefs, guardian spirits live in rivers, trees and other natural features and need to be honoured (and placated) like a respected but sometimes troublesome family member. Elaborate doll-house-like structures, where the spirits can 'live' comfortably separated from human affairs, are consecrated by a Brahman priest and receive daily offerings of rice, fruit, flowers and water.

Islam

Islam was introduced to Thailand's southern region between AD 1200 and 1500 through the influence of Indian and Arab traders and scholars. About 5% of the Thai population are followers of Islam. There are close to 3500 mosques in Thailand – over 170 in Bangkok alone. Of these mosques, the majority are associated with the Sunni branch of Islam.

The majority of Muslims in Thailand live in the southern provinces, though there are pockets in Bangkok and central and northern Thailand. In the southernmost provinces the Muslims are ethnic Malays, while northern Thailand's Muslims are Yunnanese descendants. The form of Islam found in southern Thailand is mixed with elements of Malay culture and animism.

The southernmost provinces of Yala, Pattani and Narathiwat contain the country's largest Muslim majority and have long been geographically and culturally isolated to the mainstream society. These provinces were independent sultanates that were conquered by the Bangkok-based kings. During the ultra-nationalist era in the 1940s, this region responded with separatist resistance, later becoming a sanctuary for communist and insurgent activities in the 1980s. Violence flared again in the early 2000s and has persisted. Most observers classify the conflict as an ethno-nationalist struggle.

Thai Muslim women function in society as actively as their Buddhist counterparts. Headscarves are prevalent but not mandatory; sometimes a visitor only realises that someone is a Muslim when they decline an offering of pork at the dinner table. The popular view of the Thai monarch as godlike is heresy for a monotheistic religion like Islam, though many Thai Muslims respect and even love the king and do not voice open criticism.

Other Minorities

Thailand's minority groups include small percentages of Vietnamese, Khmer, Mon, Semang (Sakai), Moken ('people of the sea' or 'sea gypsies'), Htin, Mabri, Khamu and a variety of hill peoples. Ethnic minorities in the mountainous regions of northern Thailand are known as *chow kŏw* (mountain people). Each minority has its own language, customs, mode of dress and spiritual beliefs.

Meal preparation, floating market

STOCKPHOTO MANIA/SHUTTERSTOCK ©

Thai Cuisine

Thai food – one of the country's most famous exports – balances spicy, sweet, sour and salty flavours in complex combinations. Ingredients are fresh, flavours are assertive and the sting of the beloved chilli triggers an adrenaline rush. Price doesn't affect the quality of Thai food: you can enjoy a meal at a street stall with as much relish as you will in an upscale restaurant.

Rice

In the morning Thais rise with two fundamental smells: rice being cooked and the burning joss sticks that are offered in household shrines. The start of the new day means another opportunity to eat, and eating in Thailand means eating rice (the Thai word 'to eat' is *gin kôw*, literally 'to eat rice').

Rice can be steamed, fried, boiled in a soup, formed into noodles or made into a dessert. In its steamed form it is eaten with a spoon or, in the case of *kôw něe·o* (sticky rice), eaten with the hands. The classic morning meal is a watery rice soup (either *jóhk* or *kôw đôm*) that is the ultimate comfort food, the equivalent of oatmeal on a cold day. The next meal of the day will probably be a stir-fry or curry, typically served over rice. In the evening in provincial towns, everyone heads to the night market to see and be seen and to eat more rice.

Pàt gà·prow

WACHIWIT/GETTY IMAGES ©

Noodles

When rice just won't do there is another, albeit rice-derived, alternative: *gŏo·ay đĕe·o* (rice noodles). Day or night, city or village, *gŏo·ay đĕe·o* is the original Thai fast food, served by itinerant vendors or from humble shopfronts. It demonstrates Thais' penchant for micro-managing flavours. You choose the kind of noodle and the kind of meat and you flavour it yourself with a little fish sauce, sugar, vinegar and chillies; don't shy away from the sugar.

There are three basic kinds of rice noodles – *sên yài* (wide), *sên lék* (thin) and *sên mèe* (thinner than thin) – as well as *bà·mèe,* which is a curly noodle made from wheat flour and egg. Most of these only appear in noodle soups but a few are used in various stir-fries, such as *pàt tai* (thin rice noodles stir-fried with dried or fresh shrimp, tofu and egg).

Head to the morning market for a bowl of *kà·nŏm jeen* (rice noodles doused in a thin curry). This dish is piled high with strange pickled and fresh vegetables that will make you feel as if you've grazed on the savannah and swum through the swamp. *Kà·nŏm jeen* is usually served at rickety wooden tables shared with working-class women dressed in market clothes.

Curry

The overseas celebrity of Thai cuisine, *gaang* (curry) is a humble dish on home turf. At roadside stands, especially in southern Thailand, big metal pots contain various curry con-coctions of radioactive colours. When you ask vendors what they have, they'll lift the lids and name the type of meat in each: for example *gaang gài* (curry with chicken) or *gaang plah* (shorthand for sour fish curry). In Bangkok, street-side vendors and small shops will display their curry-in-a-hurry in buffet-style trays. In either case, you point to one and it will be ladled over rice. Use a spoon to scoop it up and push the lime leaves to the side – they aren't edible.

All curries start with a basic paste that can include ingredients such as ground corian-der seed, cumin seed, garlic, lemongrass, kaffir lime, galangal, shrimp paste and chillies (either dried or fresh). Most visitors know their curries by their colour, mainly red (from dried red chillies) and green (from fresh green chillies). Green curry is a classic central Thailand dish.

Regional Cuisines

Over the past 20 years there has been so much migration within Thailand that many of the once region-specific dishes have been incorporated into the national cuisine.

Northern Thai

True to its Lanna character, northern Thai cuisine is more laid-back – the flavours are mellow and the influences have migrated over the mountains from Myanmar and China. Northern cuisine is enamoured with pork, from *sâi òo·a* (local-style sausages) to *kăap mŏo* (pork rind). The Burmese influence has imparted the use of turmeric and ginger (though some could argue that northern Burmese food was influenced by Chinese) into the curry pastes used in *gaang hang·lair* (rich pork stew).

Northern flavours favour sour notes. Pickled vegetables are loaded on top of the signature noodle dishes of *kôw soy* (wheat-and-egg noodles with a thick coconut red curry) and *kà·nŏm jeen nám ngée·o* (rice noodles served with a curry broth made with pork and tomatoes); shallots and lime wedges are common seasoning garnishes. Northern Thailand shares Isan's love of *kôw nĕe·o*, which is often served in rounded bamboo baskets and accompanies such dishes as *nám prík òng* (a chilli paste made with ground pork and tomato).

Southern Thai

Southern Thai food draws from the traditions of seafaring traders, many of whom were Muslims from India or ethnic Malays. Indian-style flat bread (known as roti) often competes with rice as a curry companion or is drizzled with sugar and sweetened condensed milk as a market dessert. Turmeric imparts its telltale yellow hue to *kôw mòk gài* (chicken biryani) and southern-style fried chicken.

The curries here are flamboyant, with dry-roasted spice bases prepared in the Indian fashion and featuring lots of locally produced coconut milk. Shaved, milked, strained and fresh, the coconut is a kitchen mainstay. Fresh seafood is plentiful. Plump squid is grilled and served on a stick with an accompanying sweet-and-spicy sauce. Whole fish are often stuffed with lemongrass and limes and barbecued over a coconut-husk fire.

Northeastern Thai

Northeasterners are known for their triumvirate dishes: *sôm·đam* (spicy green papaya salad), *kôw nĕe·o* and *gài yâhng* (grilled chicken). In the morning, open-coal grills are loaded up with marinated chicken. Alongside the grill is a large mortar and pestle in which *sôm·đam* is prepared. In go strips of green papaya, sugar, chillies, fish sauce, green beans, tomatoes, dried shrimps and a few special requests: peanuts to make it *sôm·đam* Thai, or field crabs and *plah ráh* (fermented fish sauce) to make it *sôm·đam* Lao (referring to the ethnic Lao who live in northeastern Thailand). The vendor pounds the ingredients together with the pestle to make a musical 'pow-pow-pow' sound that is sometimes used as an onomatopoetic nickname.

What to Drink

Thai beers, such as Singha (pronounced 'sing'), are hoppy lagers which are often mixed with ice to keep them cool and palatable. Fruit shakes are refreshing on a hot day and are served with a pinch of salt to help regulate body temperature. Sweet iced coffee and tea are popular street-stall drinks. Thais get their drink on with rice whisky mixed with ice, soda water and a splash of Coke.

Mural depicting the life of Buddha

Arts & Architecture

Thais' refined sense of beauty is reflected in their artistic traditions, from Buddhist sculpture to temple architecture. Monarchs were the country's great artistic patrons; their funeral monuments were ornate stupas, and handicrafts were developed specifically for royal use. Religious artwork continues to dominate the artistic space but has been adapted to the modern multimedia context.

Religious Art

Temples are the country's artistic repositories, where you'll find ornate murals depicting Hindu-Buddhist mythology and Buddha sculptures. The country is most famous for its graceful and serene Buddhas that emerged during the Sukhothai era. Always instructional in intent, temple murals often depict the *Jataka* (stories of the Buddha's past lives) and the *Ramakian* (Thai version of the Hindu epic *Ramayana*). Reading the murals requires both knowledge of these religious tales and an understanding of the murals' spatial relationship. Most murals are divided into scenes, in which the main theme is depicted in the centre with resulting events taking place above and below the central action. Usually in the corner of a dramatic tableau are independent scenes of Thai village life: women carrying bamboo baskets, men fishing or a festive get-together.

Thailand's Artistic Periods

The development of Thai religious art and architecture is broken into different periods defined by the patronage of the ruling capital. A period's characteristics are seen in the depiction of the Buddha's facial features, the top flourish on the head, the dress, and the position of the feet in meditation. Another signature is the size and shape of the temples' *chedi* (stupas) – telltale characteristics are shown in the pedestal and the central bell before it begins to taper into the uppermost tower.

Period	Temple & Chedi Styles	Buddha Styles	Examples
Dvaravati period (7th-11th centuries)	Rectangular-based *chedi* with stepped tiers	Indian-influenced with a thick torso, large hair curls, arched eyebrows to represent a flying bird, protruding eyes, thick lips and a flat nose	Phra Pathom Chedi, Nakhon Pathom; Lopburi Museum, Lopburi; Wat Chama Thawi, Lamphun
Srivijaya period (7th-13th centuries)	Mahayana-Buddhist-style temples; Javanese-style *chedi* with elaborate arches	Indian influenced: heavily ornamented, humanlike features and slightly twisted at the waist	Wat Phra Boromathat, Chaiya; Wat Phra Mahathat Woramahawihaan and National Museum, Nakhon Si Thammarat
Khmer period (9th-11th centuries)	Hindu-Buddhist temples; corn-cob-shaped *prang*	Buddha meditating under a canopy of the seven-headed *naga* and atop a lotus pedestal	Phimai, Nakhon Ratchasima; Phanom Rung, Surin
Chiang Saen-Lanna period (11th-13th centuries)	Teak temples; square-based *chedi* topped by gilded umbrella; also octagonal-base *chedi*	Burmese influences with plump figure, round, smiling face and foot-pads facing upwards in meditation pose	Wat Phra Singh, Chiang Mai; Chiang Saen National Museum
Sukhothai period (13th-15th centuries)	Khmer-inspired temples; slim-spired *chedi* topped by a lotus bud	Graceful poses, often depicted 'walking'; no anatomical human detail	Sukhothai Historical Park
Ayuthaya period (14th-18th centuries)	Classical Thai temple with three-tiered roof and gable flourishes; bell-shaped *chedi* with tapering spire	Ayuthaya-era king, wearing a gem-studded crown and royal regalia	Ayuthaya Historical Park
Bangkok-Ratanakosin period (19th century)	Colourful and gilded temple with Western-Thai styles; mosaic-covered *chedi*	Reviving Ayuthaya style	Wat Phra Kaew, Wat Pho and Wat Arun, Bangkok

Contemporary Art

Adapting traditional themes and aesthetics to the secular canvas began around the turn of the 20th century, as Western influence surged in the region. In general, Thai painting favours abstraction over realism and continues to preserve the one-dimensional perspective of traditional mural paintings. Italian artist Corrado Feroci is often credited with being

Jim Thompson House (p48)

the father of modern Thai art. He was first invited to Thailand by Rama VI in 1924 and built Bangkok's Democracy Monument, among other European-style statues. Feroci founded the country's first fine arts institute in 1933, a school that eventually developed into Silpakorn University, Thailand's premier training ground for artists. In gratitude, the Thai government made Feroci a Thai citizen, with the Thai name Silpa Bhirasri.

In recent years, there's been a growing sense that art is starting to move beyond purely intellectual, political or even artsy circles and into the mainstream. The number of galleries in Bangkok and elsewhere has increased immensely, and in 2017, Kamin Lertchaiprasert was asked to create art that would decorate the trains of Bangkok's Skytrain/BTS network. In 2018, Thailand hosted its first biennale, the Bangkok Art Biennale. The next edition is scheduled to take place in 2020.

The Modern Buddha

In the 1970s Thai artists began to tackle the modernisation of Buddhist themes through abstract expressionism. Leading works in this genre include the mystical pen-and-ink drawings of Thawan Duchanee. Montien Boonma used the ingredients of Buddhist merit-making, such as gold leaf, bells and candle wax, to create abstract temple spaces within museum galleries.

Protest & Satire

In Thailand's quickly industrialising society, many artists watched as rice fields became factories, forests became asphalt and the spoils went to the politically connected. During the student activist days of the 1970s, the Art for Life Movement was the banner under which creative discontents rallied against the military dictatorship and embraced certain aspects of communism and workers' rights. Sompot Upa-In and Chang Saetang are two important artists from that period. An anti-authority attitude continues today. Photographer Manit Sriwanichpoom is best known for his 'Pink Man on Tour' series, in which he depicted artist Sompong Thawee in a pink suit and with a pink shopping cart amid Thailand's most iconic attractions, suggesting that Thailand's cultural and natural spaces were for sale. He has since followed up this series with other socially evocative photographs poking fun at ideas of patriotism and nationalism.

During the political turmoil of the past decade, artists channelled first-person experiences into multimedia installations. Tanks, guns, violence and protest imagery are woven together to express outrage, grief, anxiety and even apathy in the collective memory during the protest-coup-election era. Vasan Sitthiket created a collection of colourful but chaotic collages in the series descriptively called *Hypocrisy* Chulayarnnon Siriphol's short film *A Brief History of Memory* recounts one woman's experience of violent street protests.

Public Art

In this hierarchical society, artistic innovation is often stifled by the older generation who holds prestige and power. In the 1990s there was a push to move art out of the dead zones of the museums and into the public spaces, beyond the reach of the cultural authoritarians. An artist and art organiser, Navin Rawanchaikul, started his 'in-the-streets' collaborations in his home town of Chiang Mai and then moved his big ideas to Bangkok, where he filled the city's taxi cabs with art installations, a show that literally went on the road.

His other works have had a way with words, such as the mixed-media piece *We Are the Children of Rice (Wine)* in 2002 and his rage against the commercialisation of museums in his epic painting entitled *Super (M)art Bangkok Survivors* (2004), which depicts famous artists, curators and decision-makers in a crowded Paolo Veronese setting. The piece was inspired by the struggles the Thai art community had in getting the new contemporary Bangkok art museum to open without it becoming a shopping mall in disguise.

Handicrafts

Thailand's handicrafts live on for the tourist markets, and some have been updated by chic Bangkok designers.

Ceramics The best-known ceramics are the greenish Thai-style celadon, and central Thailand's *ben·jà·rong* (five colour).

Lacquerware Northern Thailand is known for this handicraft inherited from Burma.

Textiles The northeast is famous for *mát·mèe* cloth – a thick cotton or silk fabric woven from tie-dyed threads. Each hill tribe has a tradition of embroidery; Chiang Mai and Chiang Rai are popular handicraft centres.

Pop Fun

True to the Thai nature, some art is just fun. The works of Thaweesak Srithongdee are pure pop. He paints flamboyantly cartoonish human figures woven with elements of traditional Thai handicrafts or imagery. In a similar vein, Jirapat Tatsanasomboon depicts traditional Thai figures in comic-book-style fights or in sensual embraces with Western icons. In *Hanuman Is Upset!* the monkey king chews up the geometric lines of Mondrian's famous gridlike painting. Thai-Japanese artist Yuree Kensaku creates cartoon-like paintings with pop-culture references.

Sculpture

Although lacking in commercial attention, Thai sculpture is often considered to be the strongest of the contemporary arts: not surprising considering the country's relationship with Buddha figures. Moving into nonreligious arenas, Khien Yimsiri is the modern master creating elegant human and mythical forms out of bronze. Kamin Lertchaiprasert explores the subject of spirituality and daily life in his sculptural installations, which often include a small army of papier-mâché figures. His exhibit *Ngern Nang* (Sitting Money) included a series of figures made of discarded paper bills from the national bank and embellished with poetic instructions on life and love.

Theatre & Dance

Traditional Thai theatre consists of dance-dramas, in which stories are acted out by masked or costumed actors. Traditional theatre was reserved for royal or religious events but, with the modernisation of the monarchy, the once-cloistered art forms have lost their

Kŏhn masked dance-drama performers

patrons and gone into decline. Classical Thai dance, on the other hand, has survived quite well in the modern era and is still widely taught in schools and universities.

Kŏhn & Lí·gair

Kŏhn is a masked dance-drama depicting scenes from the *Ramakian*. The central story revolves around Prince Rama's search for his beloved Princess Sita, who has been abducted by the evil 10-headed demon Ravana and taken to the island of Lanka.

Most often performed at Buddhist festivals by troupes of travelling performers, *lí·gair* is a gaudy, raucous theatrical art form thought to have descended from drama rituals brought to southern Thailand by Arab and Malay traders. It contains a colourful mixture of folk and classical music, outrageous costumes, melodrama, slapstick comedy, sexual innuendo and up-to-date commentary.

Classical & Folk Dance

Inherited from the Khmer, classical dance was a holy offering performed by the earthly version of *apsara* (heavenly maidens blessed with beauty and skilled in dance, who are depicted in graceful positions in temple murals and bas-reliefs). But traditional dancing enjoyed its own expressions in the villages and defined each region. In some cases the dances describe the rice-planting season, while others tell tales of flirtations. During local festivals and street parades, especially in the northeast, troupes of dancers, ranging from elementary-school age to college age, will be swathed in traditional costumes, ornate headdresses and white-powder make-up to perform synchronised steps accompanied by a marching band.

Music

Classical Thai music features a dazzling array of textures and subtleties, hair-raising tempos and pastoral melodies. The classical orchestra is called the *pèe·pâht* and can include as few as five players or more than 20. Among the more common instruments is the *pèe,* a woodwind instrument that has a reed mouthpiece; it is heard prominently at Thai-boxing matches. The *rá·nâht èhk,* a bamboo-keyed percussion instrument resembling the xylophone, carries the main melodies. The slender *sor,* a bowed instrument with a coconut-shell soundbox, is sometimes played solo by street buskers.

If you take a cab in Bangkok, you're likely to hear Thailand's version of country music: *lôok tûng* (literally 'children of the fields'). Lost love, tragic early death and the plight of the hard-working farmers are popular themes sung plaintively over a melancholy accompaniment. More upbeat is *mŏr lam,* a folk tradition from the rural northeast that has been electrified with a fast-paced beat. Step into a shopping mall or a Thai disco and you'll hear the bouncy tunes of Thai pop (also dubbed 'T-pop'). The ageing hippies from the protest era of the 1970s and 1980s pioneered *pleng pêu·a chee·wít* (songs for life), which feature in the increasingly hard-to-find Thai country bars. The 1990s gave birth to an alternative pop scene – known as 'indie'.

Architecture

Temples

The most striking examples of Thailand's architectural heritage are the Buddhist temples (*wát*), which dazzle in the tropical sun with wild colours and soaring rooflines. Thai temples are compounds of different buildings serving specific religious functions. The most important structures include the *uposatha* (*bòht* in central Thai, *sĭm* in northern and northeastern Thai), which is a consecrated chapel where monastic ordinations are held, and the *wí·hăhn,* where important Buddha images are housed.

A classic component of temple architecture is the presence of one or more *chedi* (stupas), a solid mountain-shaped monument that pays tribute to the enduring stability of Buddhism. *Chedi* come in myriad styles, from simple inverted bowl-shaped designs imported from Sri Lanka to the more elaborate octagonal shapes found in northern Thailand. Many are believed to contain relics (often pieces of bone) belonging to the historical Buddha. Some *chedi* also house the ashes of important kings and royalty. A variation of the stupa inherited from the Angkor kingdom is the corn-cob-shaped *prang,* a feature in the ancient Thai temples of Sukhothai and Ayuthaya.

Traditional Homes

Traditional Thai homes were adapted to the weather, the family and artistic sensibilities. These antique specimens were humble dwellings consisting of a single-room wooden house raised on stilts. More elaborate

Temple Symbols

The architectural symbolism of Thai temples relies heavily on Hindu-Buddhist iconography. *Naga,* the mythical serpent that guarded Buddha during meditation, appears on handrails at temple entrances. A silhouette of the birdlike *chôr fáh* adorns the tip of the roof. Three-tiered roofs represent the triple gems of Buddhism: the Buddha, the *dhamma* (teachings) and the *sangha* (Buddhist community). The lotus, a reminder of religious perfection, decorates temple gates and posts, verandah columns and spires of Sukhothai-era *chedi,* and often forms the pedestal for images of the meditating Buddha. Lotus buds are used solely for merit-making.

Bangkok's Postmodern Mountain Range

Bangkok is a crowded, chaotic collection of skyscrapers that punctuates the sky with gravity-defying majesty. During the mid-1980s building boom, Thai architects flirted with whimsy and form over function. The best example of the era is the famous Robot Building on Th Sathon Tai in Bangkok.

The building boom came to a sudden halt after the Asian financial crisis of the 1990s, leaving the skyline littered with unfinished buildings. The iconic Sathorn Unique Tower remains derelict even today, and has become an unofficial tourist attraction.

The most striking profile in Bangkok's skyline is currently cut by the post-apocalyptic King Power Mahanakhon Building, which at 314m is the city's tallest skyscraper.

homes, for the village chief or minor royalty for instance, might link a series of single rooms by elevated walkways. Since many Thai villages were built near rivers, the elevation provided protection from flooding during the annual monsoon. During the dry season the space beneath the house was used as a hideaway from the heat of the day, an outdoor kitchen or as a barn for farm animals. Later this all-purpose space would shelter bicycles and motorcycles.

Once plentiful in Thai forests, teak was always the material of choice for wooden structures and its use typically indicates that a house is at least 50 years old. Rooflines in central, northern and southern Thailand are steeply pitched and often decorated at the corners or along the gables with motifs related to the *naga*, a mythical water serpent long believed to be a spiritual protector of Tai cultures throughout Asia. In Thailand's southern provinces it's not unusual to come upon houses of Malay design, using high masonry pediments or foundations rather than wooden stilts. Residents of the south also sometimes use bamboo and palm thatch, which are more plentiful than wood. In the north, the homes of community leaders were often decorated with an ornate horn-shaped motif called *galare,* a decorative element that has become shorthand for old Lanna architecture. Roofs of tile or thatch tend to be less steeply pitched, and rounded gables – a feature inherited from Myanmar – can also be found further north.

Contemporary Architecture

Thais began mixing traditional architecture with European forms in the late 19th and early 20th centuries, as exemplified by certain buildings of the Grand Palace. The port cities of Thailand, including Bangkok and Phuket, acquired fine examples of Sino-Portuguese architecture – buildings of stuccoed brick decorated with an ornate facade – a style that followed the sea traders during the colonial era. In Bangkok this style is often referred to as 'old Bangkok' or Ratanakosin. In the 1960s and 1970s the European Bauhaus movement shifted contemporary architecture towards a stark functionalism. During the building boom of the mid-1980s, Thai architects used high-tech designs such as ML Sumet Jumsai's famous Robot Building on Th Sathon Tai in Bangkok. In the new millennium, shopping centres and hotels have reinterpreted the traditional Thai house through an industrial modernist perspective, creating geometric cubes defined by steel beams and glass curtains.

Erawan National Park (p80)

MIGEL/SHUTTERSTOCK ©

Environment & Wildlife

Thailand clings to a southern spur of the Himalaya in the north, cradles fertile river plains at its core and tapers between two shallow seas fringed by coral reefs. Its shape is likened to an elephant's head, with the Malay Peninsula representing the trunk. Spanning 1650km and 16 latitudinal degrees from north to south, Thailand is one of the most environmentally diverse countries in Southeast Asia.

Northern Thailand

Northern Thailand is fused to Myanmar, Laos and southern China through the southeast-trending extension of the Himalayan mountain range known as the Dawna-Tenasserim. The tallest peak is Doi Inthanon (measured heights vary from 2565m to 2576m), which is topped by a mixed forest of evergreen and swamp species, including a thick carpet of moss. Monsoon forests comprise the lower elevations and are made up of deciduous trees, which are green and lush during the rainy season but dusty and leafless during the dry season. Teak is one of the most highly valued monsoon forest trees but it now exists only in limited quantities and is illegal to harvest. The cool mountains of northern Thailand are considered to be some of the most accessible and rewarding birding destinations in

White-handed gibbon, Khao Yai National Park

KUNTALEE RANGNOI/GETTY IMAGES ©

Asia and are populated by montane species and migrants with clear Himalayan affinities, such as flycatchers and thrushes.

Central Thailand

In the central region the topography mellows into a flat rice basket, fed by rivers that are as revered as the national monarchy. Thailand's most exalted river is the Chao Phraya, which is formed by the northern tributaries of the Ping, Wang, Yom and Nan – a lineage as notable as any aristocrat's. The river delta spends most of the year in cultivation, changing with the seasons from fields of emerald-green rice shoots to golden harvests. This region has been heavily sculpted by civilisation: roads, fields, cities and towns have transformed the landscape into a working core. In the western frontier, bumping into the mountainous border with Myanmar is a complex of forest preserves that cover 17,800 sq km – the largest protected area in Southeast Asia and a largely undisturbed habitat for endangered elephants and tigers.

Northeastern Thailand

The landscape of Thailand's northeastern region is occupied by the arid Khorat Plateau rising some 300m above the central plain. This is a hardscrabble land where the rains are meagre, the soil is anaemic and the red dust stains as stubbornly as the betel nut chewed by the local grandmothers. The dominant forest is dry dipterocarp, which consists of deciduous trees that shed their leaves in the dry season to conserve water. The region's largest forest preserve is Khao Yai National Park, which, together with nearby parks, has been recognised as a Unesco World Heritage Site. The park is mainly arid forest, a favourite of hornbills and more than 300 other bird species. There is a small population of wild elephants in the park but development around the perimeter has impacted important wildlife corridors.

Southern Thailand

The kingdom's eastern rivers dump their waters and sediment into the Gulf of Thailand, a shallow basin off the neighbouring South China Sea. In the joint of the fishhook-shaped gulf is Bangkok, surrounded by a thick industrial zone that has erased or polluted much of the natural environment. The extremities of the gulf, both to the east and to the south, are more characteristic of coastal environments: mangrove swamps form the transition between land and sea and act as the ocean's nursery, spawning and nurturing fish, bird and amphibian species. Thailand is home to nearly 75 species of these salt-tolerant trees that were once regarded as wastelands and were vulnerable to coastal development.

The long slender 'trunk' of land that runs between the Gulf of Thailand and the Andaman Sea is often referred to as the Malay Peninsula. This region is Thailand's most tropical: rainfall is plentiful, cultivating thick rainforests that stay green year-round. Malayan flora and fauna predominate and a scenic range of limestone mountains meanders from land to sea. On the west coast, the Andaman Sea is an outcropping of the larger Indian Ocean and home to astonishing coral reefs that feed and shelter thousands of varieties of fish and act as breakwaters against tidal surges. Many of the coral-fringed islands are designated marine national parks, limiting – to some degree – coastal development and boat traffic. The 2010 global coral bleaching phenomenon (in which El Niño weather conditions contributed to warmer sea temperatures) killed or damaged significant portions of Thailand's reefs.

Environmental Trivia

○ Thailand is equivalent in area to the size of France.

○ Bangkok sits at about N14° latitude, level with Madras, Manila, Guatemala City and Khartoum.

○ The Mekong rivals the Amazon River in terms of biodiversity.

○ Thailand is home to venomous snakes, including the pit viper and the king cobra.

○ Thailand's limestone formations are a soft sedimentary rock created by shells and coral from an ancient sea bed 250 to 300 million years ago.

National Parks & Protected Areas

With 15% of the kingdom's land and sea designated as park or sanctuary, Thailand has one of the highest percentages of protected areas of any Asian nation. There are more than 100 national parks, plus more than 1000 'nonhunting areas', wildlife sanctuaries, forest reserves, botanic gardens and arboretums. Thailand began its conservation efforts in 1960 with the creation of a national system of wildlife sanctuaries under the Wild Animals Reservation and Protection Act, followed by the National Parks Act of 1961. Khao Yai National Park was the first wild area to receive this new status. Despite promises, official designation as a national park or sanctuary does not guarantee protection from development or poaching. Local farmers, hunters and moneyed interests often circumvent conservation efforts. Enforcement of environmental regulations lacks political will and proper funding. Foreign visitors are often confused by resort development in national parks despite their protected status. In some cases private ownership of land pre-dated the islands' protected status, while in other cases rules are bent for powerful interests.

Mekong River

Defining the contours of Thailand's border with Laos is the Mekong River, Southeast Asia's artery. The Mekong is a workhorse, having been dammed for hydroelectric power, and a mythmaker, featuring in local peoples' folktales and festivals. The river winds in and out of the steep mountain ranges to the northeastern plateau where it swells and contracts according to seasonal rainfall. In the dry season, riverside farmers plant vegetables in the muddy floodplain, harvesting the crop before the river reclaims its territory. Scientists have identified the Mekong River as having impressive biodiversity. As many as 1000 previously unidentified species of flora and fauna have been discovered in the last decade in the Mekong region (which includes Vietnam, Laos and Cambodia).

Air Pollution

On 13 March 2019, the air quality in Chiang Mai was officially rated the world's worst. A combination of farmers burning waste to clear land for the next harvest in the region sparked forest fires, resulting in Chiang Mai being blanketed in a dangerous haze. Forest fires and agricultural burning have long created a haze over northern Thailand between January and May each year, but air pollution is now a problem across the kingdom. In January 2019, all 437 of Bangkok's public schools were forced to close for two days because of choking smog. Air pollution in Bangkok is mostly the result of emissions from factories and the nearly 10 million vehicles that clog the capital's roads.

The government has made improving air quality a priority, with measures such as enforced factory closures, car-pooling and better waste management being mulled over. But with no formal legislation mandating clean air, the situation might just get worse before it gets better.

Environmental Issues

Thailand has put enormous pressure on its ecosystems as it has industrialised. Natural forest cover now makes up about 28% of land area, compared to 70% some 50 years ago. Thailand's coastal region has experienced higher population and economic growth than the national average and these areas suffer from soil erosion, water pollution and degradation of coral reef systems. Seasonal flooding is a common natural occurrence in some parts of Thailand due to the nature of the monsoon rains. But high-level floods have increased in frequency and severity. The record-busting 2011 flooding was one of the world's costliest natural disasters. Of the country's 77 provinces, 65 were declared flood disaster zones; there were 815 deaths and an estimated US$45.7 billion worth of damage.

In 2013 a pipeline unloading an oil tanker off the coast of Rayong spilled 50,000L of crude into the sea, coating the western side of Ko Samet. While the outward condition of beaches quickly recovered with the use of dispersants, experts say there may be considerable long-term effects of the spill on both human health and the marine ecosystem.

Energy Consumption

As Southeast Asia's second-largest energy consumer (Indonesia ranks first in the region), Thailand is looking to increase and diversify its energy supply and production, by expanding oil and gas resources or developing alternative fuel sources, including nuclear. Currently, three quarters of Thailand's energy derives from natural gas. Thailand also produces biofuels, including ethanols from molasses and cassava, and biodiesel from palm oil. Power generation, agriculture and industrial activity account for the largest proportion of the country's greenhouse gas emissions.

Thailand is aiming to boost its production of renewable energy, with a target of generating 6000 MW from solar energy by 2036. The country's first large-scale solar farm in Lopburi started producing power in 2013. There is also great potential for increasing energy-from-waste production.

Hmong women near Chiang Mai (p187)

Responsible Travel

Thais are a warm and friendly people who generally welcome foreign visitors and appreciate efforts to understand their culture and society. There are numerous volunteer organisations for travellers who are keen on contributing, and they can be a rewarding way to learn more about Thailand, its people and the environment.

Cultural Etiquette

The monarchy and religion (which are interconnected) are treated with extreme deference in Thailand. Thais avoid criticising or disparaging the royal family for fear of offending someone or, worse, being charged with a violation of the country's very strict lèse-majesté laws, which carry a jail sentence.

Buddha images are sacred objects. Thais consider it bad form to pull a silly pose in front of one for a photo, or to clamber upon them (in the case of temple ruins). Instead they would show respect by performing a *wâi* (a prayer-like gesture) to the figure no matter how humble it is. As part of their ascetic vows, monks are not supposed to touch or be touched by women. If a woman wants to hand something to a monk, the object is placed within reach of the monk or on the monk's 'receiving cloth'.

From a spiritual viewpoint, Thais regard the head as the highest and most sacred part of the body and the feet as the dirtiest and lowest. Many of the taboos associated with the feet have a practical derivation as well. Traditionally Thais ate, slept and entertained on the floor of their homes with little in the way of furniture. To keep their homes and eating surfaces clean, the feet (and shoes) contracted a variety of rules.

Shoes aren't worn inside private homes and temple buildings, both as a sign of respect and for sanitary reasons. Thais can kick off their shoes in one fluid step and many lace-up shoes are modified by the wearer to become slip-ons. Thais also step over – not on – the threshold, which is where the spirit of the house is believed to reside. On some buses and 3rd-class trains, you'll see Thais prop their feet up on the adjacent bench, and while this isn't the height of propriety, do notice that they always remove their shoes before doing so. Thais also take off their shoes if they need to climb onto a chair or seat.

Thais don't touch each others' heads or ruffle hair as a sign of affection. Occasionally you'll see young people touching each others' heads, which is a teasing gesture, maybe even a slight insult, between friends.

Thais hold modesty in personal dress in high regard, though this is changing in recent times among the younger generation. The importance of modesty extends to the beach as well. Except for urbanites, most provincial Thais swim fully clothed. For this reason, sunbathing nude or topless is not acceptable and in some cases may even be illegal. Remember that swimsuits are not proper attire off the beach; wear a cover-up in between the sand and your hotel.

Tourism

Most forms of tourism have a positive effect on the local economy in Thailand, providing jobs for young workers and business opportunities for entrepreneurs. In addition, many travellers look for opportunities to spend their money where it might be needed, either on charitable causes or activities that preserve traditional ways of life. Thailand has successfully benefited from this trend by promoting village craft programs and homestays. It is increasingly easy for foreign tourists to engage with small-scale tourism projects that offer an insight into traditional ways of life.

Overtourism

According to the Ministry of Tourism & Sports, Thailand was visited by a record 38.3 million people in 2018, including over 10 million from China. Those staggering numbers are likely to continue to increase in the near future, with some estimates predicting that 60 million people will be visiting Thailand annually by 2030.

Parts of the country are already suffering adversely from high visitor volumes, with tourist infrastructure stretched to the limit. Anyone visiting Chiang Mai, Ko Samui or Phuket during the peak winter tourist season (December to February) can't help but notice the press of people at the airports and on the streets and beaches. There is also a negative impact on the environment, especially on small but busy islands, where maintaining adequate fresh water supplies and disposing of waste is an increasing struggle. Ecosystems are threatened as more and more hotels and resorts are built.

The Thai tourist authorities and government are already taking steps to protect the most environmentally fragile areas. Maya Bay in Ko Phi-Phi, the location for the Leonardo DiCaprio movie *The Beach* and a must-see stop for many visitors to the island, has been closed since June 2018, following reports that up to 50% of its coral was dead. The experiment has been a success, with marine biologists reporting that the coral reefs are regenerating, and reef sharks and ghost crabs have returned to the bay. Maya Bay is now likely to stay shut until 2021 and it is likely that some of the other most popular destinations on Thailand's islands will be temporarily closed, or restricted, in the future.

Visitors can play their part in reducing the effects of overtourism. Apart from being careful with trash, one obvious option is to avoid the most-visited destinations. There is much more to Thailand than just Bangkok, Chiang Mai, Phuket or Ko Samui. By deciding to visit less-frequented destinations, not only will you have more elbow room, but you'll get to see a more authentic Thailand and help boost the economy in regions that have yet to benefit from the tourism boom.

Responsible Diving

The popularity of Thailand's diving industry places immense pressure on fragile coral sites. To help preserve the ecology, adhere to these simple rules:

● Avoid touching living marine organisms, standing on coral or dragging equipment (such as fins) across reefs. Coral polyps can be damaged by even the gentlest contact.

● When treading water in shallow reef areas, be careful not to kick up clouds of sand, which can easily smother the delicate reef organisms.

● Take great care in underwater caves where your air bubbles can be caught within the roof and leave previously submerged organisms high and dry.

● Join a coral clean-up campaign that's sponsored by dive shops.

● Don't feed the fish or allow your dive operator to dispose of excess food in the water. The fish become dependent on this food source and don't tend to the algae on the coral, causing harm to the reef.

Elephant Encounters

Throughout Thai history, elephants have been revered for their strength, endurance and intelligence, working alongside their mahouts harvesting teak, transporting goods through mountainous terrain or fighting ancient wars.

Many of the elephants' traditional roles have either been outsourced to machines or outlawed, leaving the 'domesticated' animals and their mahouts without work. Some mahouts turned to begging on the streets in Bangkok and other tourist centres, but most elephants find work in Thailand's tourism industry. Their jobs vary from circus-like shows and elephant camps giving rides to tourists to 'mahout-training' schools, while sanctuaries and rescue centres provide modest retirement homes for animals that are no longer financially profitable to their owners.

Essential Etiquette – Dos

Stand respectfully for the royal and national anthem They are played on TV and radio stations as well as in public and government places.

Smile a lot It makes everything easier.

Bring a gift if you're invited to a Thai home Fruit, drinks or snacks are acceptable.

Take off your shoes When you enter a home or temple building.

Dress modestly for temple visits Cover to the elbows and ankles and always remove your shoes when entering any building containing a Buddha image.

Sit in the 'mermaid' position inside temples Tuck your feet beside and behind you.

Give and receive politely Extend the right hand out while the left hand gently grips the right elbow when handing an object to another person or receiving something.

It costs about 30,000B (US$1000) a month to provide a comfortable life for an elephant, an amount equivalent to the salary of Thailand's upper-middle class. Welfare standards within the tourism industry are not standardised or subject to government regulations, so it's up to the conscientious consumer to encourage the industry to ensure safe conditions for elephants.

With more evidence than ever available to support claims by animal welfare experts that elephant rides and shows are harmful to these gentle giants, who are often abused to force them to perform for humans, a small but growing number of sanctuaries offer more sustainable interactions, such as observing retired and rescued elephants.

Lonely Planet does not recommend riding on elephants or viewing elephant performances. We also urge visitors to be wary of organisations that advertise as being a conservation centre but actually offer rides and performances.

Hill-Tribe Hiking

Though marginalised within mainstream society, Thailand's hill-dwelling minorities remain a strong tourism draw, with large and small businesses organising 'trekking' tours (these can range from proper hikes to leisurely walks) to villages for cultural displays and interactions. It is unclear whether this truly helps alleviate the poverty of the hill peoples, but a small percentage of the profits from trekking does filter down to individual families within minority villages, giving them a small source of income that might prevent urban migration.

In general, the trekking business is now more socially conscious than in past decades. Most companies tend to limit the number of visits to a particular area to lessen the impact of outsiders on the daily lives of ordinary villagers. But the industry still has a long way to go. It should be noted that trekking companies are Thai owned and employ Thai guides. Many ethnic-minority people lack full citizenship and, without an identification card, are unable to qualify for a Tourism Authority of Thailand (TAT) tour-guide licence, which makes it hard for them to find work with trekking companies.

Trekkers should also realise that hill peoples maintain their own distinct cultural identity and many continue their animistic traditions, which define social taboos and conventions. If you're planning on visiting hill-peoples villages on an organised trek, talk to your guide about acceptable behaviour.

Responsible Trekking

● Always ask for permission before taking photos of minority peoples, especially at private moments inside their dwellings. Many traditional belief systems regard photography with suspicion.

● Show respect for religious symbols and rituals. Don't touch totems at village entrances or sacred items hanging from trees. Don't participate in ceremonies unless invited.

● Avoid encouraging the practice of begging, especially among children. Talk to your guide about donating to a local school instead.

● Avoid public nudity and be careful not to undress near an open window where village children might be able to peep in.

● Don't flirt with members of the opposite sex unless you plan on marrying them.

● Don't drink or do drugs with villagers; altered states sometimes lead to culture clashes.

● Smile at villagers even if they stare at you. Ask your guide how to say 'hello' in the local language.

Avoid public displays of affection, which in some traditional systems are viewed as offensive to the spirit world.

Don't interact with the villagers' livestock, even the free-roaming pigs; they are valuable possessions, not entertainment. Also avoid interacting with jungle animals, which in some belief systems are viewed as visiting spirits.

Don't litter.

Adhere to the same feet taboos that apply to Thai culture. Don't step on the threshold of a house, prop your feet up against the fire or wear your shoes inside.

Homestays

A homestay is one of the best ways to experience Thailand's rural culture, not to mention a means of ensuring that your baht are going directly to locals. Homestays differ from guesthouses in that visitors are welcomed into a family's home, typically in a small village that isn't on the tourist trail. Accommodation can be simple: a mat or foldable mattress on the floor, but you might get a private room with a shared bathroom. Rates include lodging, meals with the family and cultural activities that highlight the region's traditional way of life, from rice farming to silk weaving. English fluency varies, so homestays are also an excellent way to sharpen up your Thai-language skills.

Essential Etiquette – Don'ts

Get a tattoo of the Buddha Nor display one you already have. It is considered sacrilegious.

Criticise the monarchy The monarchy is revered and protected by defamation laws – more so now than ever.

Prop your feet on tables or chairs Feet are considered dirty and people have to sit on chairs.

Step on a dropped bill to prevent it from blowing away Thai money bears a picture of the king. Feet + monarchy = grave offence.

Step over someone or their personal belongings As feet are considered unclean, don't do this.

Tie your shoes to the outside of your backpack They might accidentally brush against someone: gross.

Touch a Thai person on the head It is considered rude, not chummy.

Touch monks Step out of the way when passing one, and don't sit next to them on public transport.

Volunteering

There are myriad volunteer organisations in Thailand to address both the needs of the locals and visitors' desires to help. A regularly updated resource for grassroots-level volunteer opportunities is Volunteer Work Thailand (www.volunteerworkthailand.org). Be aware, though, that so-called 'voluntourism' has become a big business and that not every organisation fulfils its promise of meaningful experiences. It is essential that you do your own thorough research before agreeing to volunteer with any organisation.

A number of NGOs undertake local conservation efforts and run rescue and sanctuary centres for wild animals that have been adopted as pets or veterinarian clinics that tend to the domesticated population of dogs and cats. At centres and sanctuaries that rely on volunteer labour, your hard work is often rewarded with meaningful interactions with the animals.

Northern Thailand, especially Chiang Mai and Chiang Rai, has a number of volunteer opportunities working with disadvantaged hill-tribe groups. There are also many volunteer teaching positions in northeastern Thailand, the country's agricultural heartland.

Young monk accepting offerings

When looking for a volunteer placement, it is essential to investigate what your chosen organisation does and, more importantly, how it goes about it. If the focus is not primarily on your skills and how these can be applied to help local people, that should ring alarm bells. Any organisation that promises to let you do any kind of work, wherever you like, for as long as you like, is unlikely to be putting the needs of local people first.

For any organisation working with children, child protection is a serious concern, and organisations that do not conduct background checks on volunteers should be regarded with extreme caution. Experts recommend a three-month commitment for volunteering with children. Visit www.thinkchildsafe.org for more information.

Colourful shopfronts, Phuket Town (p138)

KEVIN HELLON/SHUTTERSTOCK ©

Survival Guide

Directory A–Z

Accessible Travel

Thailand has better facilities for travellers with access needs than any Southeast Asian country, other than Singapore. However, high kerbs, uneven and crowded footpaths and nonstop traffic make Thai cities difficult to navigate for those with a vision or mobility impairment. In Bangkok, many streets must be crossed via pedestrian bridges accessed by steep stairways. In any town or city, wheelchair users who are willing to take the risk and have nerves of steel will find it easier to take to the road. Ramps and other access points for wheelchairs to buildings, pavements and tourist sites are patchy. However, a lack of infrastructure is often made up for by the helpfulness of Thai people.

At Suvarnabhumi Airport in Bangkok facilities for disabled travellers are good. Wheelchairs and electric carts are available, lifts service all levels and accessible toilet facilities are clean and well maintained. The rail link from the airport to the city is well adapted for travellers with access needs, including elevators with Braille buttons and voice announcements, and wheelchair-accessible ticket machines and gates. Most international flights use air-bridges, which isn't always the case for domestic flights at Bangkok's Don Mueang Airport or other regional airports around Thailand. It's therefore important to advise your airline at the time of booking if you use a wheelchair or need assistance.

Buses and boats stop barely long enough even for the fully mobile, and long-distance trains and provincial stations are a bit of a lottery for access. In the capital, BTS Skytrain is accessible for wheelchair users, with elevators at all stations except Saphan Taksin. Every MRT metro station has lifts and wheelchair access. Both BTS and MRT staff are extremely helpful.

Note that many taxis in Thailand run on natural gas, with the gas tank located in the boot (trunk), which limits the space available for a wheelchair or mobility aid Fully wheelchair-accessible taxis are only available in Bangkok and Hua Hin and have to be booked in advance. There are none in Chang Mai. The Bangkok Metropolitan Authority has a handful of vehicles, mainly for locals; call ☎1555 during office hours for availability, or contact Wheelchair Taxi Thailand (www.transport-disabled-bangkok.weebly.com).

Most midrange and top-end hotels have accessible rooms, but standards vary widely, so make sure your needs are met by requesting information and/or photos. Most budget hotels and guesthouses, as well as many boutique hotels, lack accessible facilities, but most will be happy to meet your needs if you are able to be adaptable or have low access needs.

Many Thai towns and cities have at least one modern shopping mall, and this is where to head for hassle-free

Accessible Travel Resources

Download Lonely Planet's free Accessible Travel guides from https://shop.lonelyplanet.com/products/accessible-travel-online-resources-2019. Long-time Chang Mai resident and wheelchair user Dominique maintains a useful website: www.thailandehandicap.com.

The following tour operators specialise in accessible tours to and accommodation in Thailand, and have their own adapted vehicle(s):

Gehandicapten (☎31 36 537 6677; http://gehandicapten.com)

Wheelchair Holidays Thailand (☎66 8 1375-0792; www.wheelchairtours.com)

Wheelchair Thailand Tours (http://wheelchair-thailand-tours.weebly.com)

shopping and eating, as well as an accessible toilet.

Accommodation

Thailand offers a wide variety of accommodation, from cheap and basic to pricey and luxurious. Where spoken English might be limited, it is handy to know the difference between *hôrng pát lom* (room with fan) and *hôrng aa* (room with air-con).

Bargaining

Thais respect a good haggler. Always let the vendor make the first offer, then ask 'Can you lower the price?'. This usually results in a discount. Now it's your turn to make a counter-offer. Always start low, but don't bargain unless you're serious about buying. If you're buying several of an item, you have much more leverage to request and receive a lower price. It helps immeasurably to keep the negotiations relaxed and friendly.

Customs Regulations

You do not have to fill in a customs form on arrival unless you have imported goods to declare. In that case you can get the proper form from Thai customs of-

Climate

Bangkok

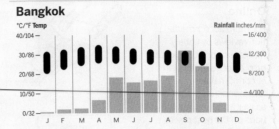

Chiang Mai

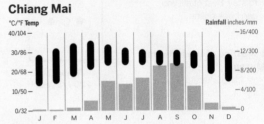

Phuket

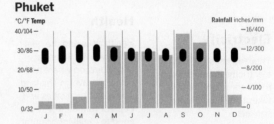

ficials at your point of entry. The **Customs Department** (✆nationwide 02 667 6000; www.customs.go.th) maintains a helpful website with specific information about regulations for travellers. Thailand allows the following items to enter duty-free:

○ reasonable amount of personal effects (clothing and toiletries)

○ professional instruments

○ 200 cigarettes

○ 1L of wine or spirits

Thailand prohibits the import of the following items:

○ firearms and ammunition (unless registered in advance with the police department)

○ illegal drugs

○ pornographic media

When leaving Thailand, you must obtain an export licence for any antique reproductions or newly cast Buddha images. This takes time (at least four days); submit two front-view photos of the object(s), a photocopy of your passport, the purchase receipt and the object(s) in question to

Book Your Stay Online

For more accommodation reviews by Lonely Planet authors, check out http://hotels.lonelyplanet.com/Thailand. You'll find independent reviews, as well as recommendations on the best places to stay. Best of all, you can book online.

the **Office of the National Museum** (Map p58; 4 Th Na Phra That, National Museum, Bangkok; ⊙9am-4pm Tue-Fri; ⛴Chang Pier, Maharaj Pier).

Electricity

Thailand uses 220V AC electricity. Power outlets most commonly feature two-prong round or flat sockets.

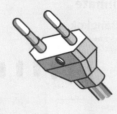

Type C
220V/50Hz

Type A
220V/50Hz

Health

Health risks and the quality of medical facilities vary depending on where and how you travel in Thailand. The majority of cities and popular tourist areas have good to excellent hospitals. However, travel to remote rural areas can mean less adequate medical care.

Our health advice is a general guide and does not replace the advice of a doctor trained in travel medicine.

Before You Go

Pack medications in clearly labelled original containers and obtain a signed and dated letter from your physician describing your medical conditions, medications and syringes or needles. If you have a heart condition, bring a copy of your electrocardiogram (ECG) taken just prior to travelling.

In Thailand you can buy many medicines over the counter without a doctor's prescription, but it can be difficult to find the exact medication.

Insurance

Don't travel without health insurance – accidents can and do happen. Most hospitals require an upfront guarantee of payment (from yourself or your insurer) prior to admission. Enquire before your trip about payment of medical charges and retain all documentation (medical reports, invoices etc) for claim purposes.

Recommended Vaccines

The Centers for Disease Control and Prevention (www.cdc.gov) has a traveller's health section that contains recommendations for vaccinations. The only vaccine required by international regulations is yellow fever. Proof of vaccination will only be required if you have visited a country in the yellow-fever zone (specifically countries in Africa or South America) within the six days prior to entering Thailand.

In Transit

Deep-vein thrombosis (DVT) occurs when blood clots form in the legs during long trips chiefly because of prolonged immobility. Though most blood clots are reabsorbed uneventfully, ome may break off and ravel through the blood vessels to the lungs, where they an cause life-threatening omplications.

The chief symptom of DVT is swelling or pain of the foot, ankle or calf, usually but not always on one side. When a blood clot travels to the lungs, it may cause chest pain and difficulty in breathing. Travellers with any of these symptoms should immediately seek medical attention.

To prevent the development of DVT on long flights you should walk about the cabin, and drink plenty of fluids (nonalcoholic).

Jet lag is common when crossing more than five time zones. It results in insomnia, fatigue, malaise or nausea. To avoid jet lag, drink plenty of fluids (nonalcoholic) and eat light meals. Upon arrival, seek exposure to natural sunlight and readjust your schedule. Some people find melatonin helpful.

In Thailand

Infectious Diseases

Dengue Fever

This mosquito-borne disease is increasingly problematic in Thailand, especially in the cities. As there is no vaccine, it can only be prevented by avoiding mosquito bites. The mosquito that carries dengue is a daytime biter, so use insect-avoidance measures at all times. Symptoms include high fever, severe headache (especially behind the eyes),

---

Medical Checklist

Recommended items for a personal medical kit include the following, most of which are available in Thailand.

- antifungal cream, eg Clotrimazole
- antibacterial cream, eg Muciprocin
- antihistamine, eg Cetrizine and Promethazine
- antiseptic, eg Betadine
- antispasmodic, eg Buscopan
- DEET-based insect repellent
- oral rehydration solution for diarrhoea
- diarrhoea 'stopper' (eg Loperamide)
- antinausea medication
- alcohol-based hand gel or wipes
- ibuprofen or another anti-inflammatory
- indigestion medication
- paracetamol
- sunscreen, sunglasses and hat

---

nausea and body aches (dengue was previously known as 'breakbone fever'). Some people develop a rash (which can be very itchy) and experience diarrhoea.

There is no specific treatment, just rest and paracetamol – do not take aspirin or ibuprofen as they increase the risk of haemorrhaging. See a doctor to be diagnosed and monitored.

Dengue can progress to the more severe and life-threatening dengue haemorrhagic fever, but this is very uncommon in tourists. The risk of this increases substantially if you have previously been infected with dengue and are then infected with a different serotype.

Hepatitis A

The risk of hepatitis A in Bangkok is decreasing, but there is still significant risk in most of the country. This food- and waterborne virus infects the liver, causing jaundice (yellow skin and eyes), nausea and lethargy. There is no specific treatment for hepatitis A. All travellers to Thailand should be vaccinated against hepatitis A.

Hepatitis B

The only sexually transmitted disease (STD) that can be prevented by vaccination, hepatitis B is spread by body fluids, including sexual contact. In some parts of Thailand up to 20% of the

Tap Water

Although it's deemed potable by the authorities, Thais don't drink the tap water and neither should you. Stick to bottled or filtered water during your stay.

population are carriers of hepatitis B, and usually are unaware of this. The long-term consequences can include liver cancer, cirrhosis and death.

HIV

HIV is now one of the most common causes of death in people under the age of 50 in Thailand. Always practise safe sex, and avoid getting tattoos or using unclean syringes.

Influenza

Present year-round in the tropics, influenza (flu) symptoms include high fever, muscle aches, runny nose, cough and sore throat. Flu is the most common vaccine-preventable disease contracted by travellers and everyone should consider vaccination. There is no specific treatment, just rest and paracetamol. Complications such as bronchitis or middle-ear infection may require antibiotic treatment.

Malaria

There is an enormous amount of misinformation concerning malaria. Malaria is caused by a parasite transmitted by the bite of an infected mosquito. The most important symptom of malaria is fever, but general symptoms such as headache, diarrhoea, cough or chills may also occur – the same symptoms as many other infections. A diagnosis can only be made by taking a blood sample.

Most parts of Thailand visited by tourists, particularly city and resort areas, have minimal to no risk of malaria, and the risk of side effects from taking antimalarial tablets is likely to outweigh the risk of getting the disease itself. If you are travelling to high-risk rural areas (unlikely for most visitors), seek medical advice on the right medication and dosage for you.

Measles

This highly contagious viral infection is spread through coughing and sneezing and remains prevalent in Thailand. Measles starts with a high fever and rash and can be complicated by pneumonia and brain disease. There is no specific treatment. Ensure you are fully vaccinated.

Rabies

This disease, fatal if left untreated, is spread by the bite or lick of an infected animal – most commonly a dog or monkey. You should seek medical advice immediately after any animal bite and commence post-exposure treatment. Having a pretravel vaccination means the postbite treatment is greatly simplified.

STDs

Sexually transmitted diseases most common in Thailand include herpes, warts, syphilis, gonorrhoea and chlamydia. People carrying these diseases often have no signs of infection. Condoms will prevent gonorrhoea and chlamydia, but not warts or herpes. If after a sexual encounter you develop any rash, lumps, discharge or pain when passing urine, seek immediate medical attention. If you have been sexually active during your travels, have an STD check on your return home.

Typhoid

This serious bacterial infection is spread through food and water. It gives a high and slowly progressive fever, severe headache and may be accompanied by a dry cough and stomach pain. It is diagnosed by blood tests and treated with antibiotics. Vaccination is recommended for all travellers spending more than a week in Thailand, or travelling outside of the major cities. Be aware that vaccination is not 100% effective, so you must still be careful with what you eat and drink.

Traveller's Diarrhoea

Traveller's diarrhoea is by far the most common problem affecting travellers. In over 80% of cases, traveller's diarrhoea is caused by a bacteria (there are numerous potential culprits) and responds promptly to treatment with antibiotics.

Here we define traveller's diarrhoea as the passage of more than three watery bowel movements within 24 hours, plus at least one other symptom such as vomiting, fever, cramps, nausea or feeling generally unwell.

Treatment consists of staying well hydrated; rehydration solutions such as Gastrolyte are the best for this. Antibiotics such as Norfloxacin, Ciprofloxacin or Azithromycin will kill the bacteria quickly. Seek medical attention if you do not respond to an appropriate antibiotic. Loperamide is just a 'stopper' that only treats the symptoms. It can be helpful, for example, if you have to go on a long bus ride. Don't take Loperamide if you have a fever, or blood in your stools.

Environmental Hazards

Jellyfish Stings

Box jellyfish stings are extremely painful and can even be fatal. There are two main types of box jellyfish – multi-tentacled and single-tentacled.

Multi-tentacled box jellyfish are present in Thai waters – these are the most dangerous and a severe envenomation can kill an adult within two minutes. They are generally found along sandy beaches near river mouths and mangroves during the warmer months.

Stings from single-tentacled box jellyfish seem

Rare But Be Aware

Avian Influenza Most of those infected have had close contact with sick or dead birds.

Filariasis A mosquito-borne disease that is common in the local population; practise mosquito-avoidance measures.

Hepatitis E Transmitted through contaminated food and water and has similar symptoms to hepatitis A. Follow safe eating and drinking guidelines.

Japanese B Encephalitis Viral disease transmitted by mosquitoes, typically occurring in rural areas. Vaccination is recommended.

Meliodosis Contracted by skin contact with soil. The symptoms are very similar to those experienced by tuberculosis (TB) sufferers. It can be treated with medications.

Strongyloides A parasite transmitted by skin contact with soil; common in the local population. It is characterised by an unusual skin rash. It can be treated with medications.

Typhus Murine typhus is spread by the bite of a flea or mite. Symptoms include fever, muscle pains and a rash. Doxycycline will prevent it.

minor at first; however, severe symptoms such as back pain, nausea, vomiting, sweating and difficulty in breathing can develop between five and 40 minutes later.

The only way to prevent these stings is to wear protective clothing.

Heat

For most people it takes at least two weeks to adapt to the hot climate. Prevent swelling of the feet and ankles as well as muscle cramps caused by excessive sweating by avoiding dehydration and excessive activity in the heat of the day.

Heatstroke requires immediate medical treatment.

Symptoms come on suddenly and include weakness, nausea, a hot dry body with a body temperature of more than 41°C, dizziness, confusion, loss of coordination, fits and eventually collapse and loss of consciousness.

Insect Bites & Stings

● Bedbugs live in the cracks of furniture and walls and then migrate to the bed at night to feed on humans. You can treat the itch with an antihistamine.

● Ticks are contracted when walking in rural areas. If you've been bitten by a tick and a rash develops at the site of the bite or elsewhere, along with fever or muscle aches, see a doctor. Doxy-cycline prevents tick-borne diseases.

● Leeches are found in humid rainforests. They do not transmit disease, but their bites are often itchy for weeks afterwards and can easily become infected. Apply an iodine-based antiseptic to the bite to help prevent infection.

● Bee and wasp stings mainly cause problems for people who are allergic to them. Anyone with a serious allergy should carry an in-jection of adrenaline (eg an EpiPen) for emergencies.

Parasites

Numerous parasites are common in local popula-tions in Thailand, but most of these are rare in travel-lers. To avoid parasitic infec-tions, wear shoes and avoid eating raw food, especially fish, pork and vegetables.

Skin Problems

Prickly heat is a common skin rash in the tropics, caused by sweat being trapped under the skin. Treat by taking cool showers and using powders.

Two fungal rashes commonly affect travel-lers. The first occurs in the groin, armpits and between the toes. Treatment involves keeping the skin dry, avoiding chafing and using an antifungal cream such as Clotrimazole or Lamisil. The fungus *Tinea versicolor* causes small

and light-coloured patches, most commonly on the back, chest and shoulders. Consult a doctor.

Cuts and scratches become easily infected in humid climates. Immediate-ly wash all wounds in clean water and apply antiseptic. If you develop signs of infec-tion, see a doctor. Coral cuts can easily become infected.

Snakes

Though snake bites are rare for travellers, there are more than 85 species of venom-ous snakes in Thailand. Wear boots and long pants if walking in an area that may have snakes.

The Thai Red Cross pro-duces antivenom for many of the poisonous snakes in Thailand.

Sunburn

Even on a cloudy day, sunburn can occur rapidly. Use a strong sunscreen (at least factor 30+), making sure to reapply after a swim, and always wear a wide-brimmed hat and sunglass-es outdoors. If you become sunburnt stay out of the sun until you have recovered, apply cool compresses and take painkillers for the discomfort. One-percent hy-drocortisone cream applied twice daily is also helpful.

Children's Health

Consult a doctor who spe-cialises in travel medicine prior to travel to ensure your child is appropriately prepared. A medical kit

designed specifically for children includes liquid medicines for children who cannot swallow tablets. Azithromycin is an ideal paediatric formula used to treat bacterial diarrhoea, as well as ear, chest and throat infections.

Good resources include Lonely Planet's *Travel with Children* and, for those spending longer away, Jane Wilson-Howarth's *Your Child's Health Abroad*.

Women's Health

● There have been out-breaks of the Zika virus in Thailand, although not for a couple of years. Check the International Association for Medical Assistance to Travellers (www.iamat.org) website for updates on the situation.

● Sanitary products are readily available in Thai-land's urban areas.

● Bring adequate supplies of your personal birth-control option, which may not be available.

● Heat, humidity and anti-biotics can all contribute to thrush, which can be treated with antifungal creams and Clotrimazole. A practical alternative is one tablet of fluconazole (Diflucan).

● Urinary-tract infections can be precipitated by dehy-dration or long bus journeys without toilet stops; bring suitable antibiotics for treatment.

Insurance

A travel-insurance policy to cover theft, loss and medical problems is an excellent idea. Be sure that your policy covers ambulances or an emergency flight home. Some policies specifically exclude 'dangerous activities', which can include scuba diving, motorcycling and even trekking. A locally acquired motorcycle licence is not valid under some policies. You may prefer a policy that pays doctors or hospitals directly rather than you having to pay on the spot and claim later. If you have to claim later, make sure you keep all documentation.

Worldwide travel insurance is available at www.lonelyplanet.com/travel-insurance. You can buy, extend and claim online any time – even if you're already on the road.

Internet Access

Wi-fi is almost standard in hotels, guesthouses and cafes. Signal strength deteriorates in the upper floors of a multistorey building; request a room near a router if wi-fi is essential. Cellular data networks continue to expand and increase in capability.

Language & Signs

Tourist towns are well stocked with English speakers, though bus drivers, market vendors and taxi drivers are less fluent, so it helps to know how to order food and count in Thai.

Thailand has its own script. Street signs are transliterated into English, but there is no standard system so spellings vary widely. Not all letters are pronounced as they appear ('Ph' is an aspirated 'p' not an 'f').

Legal Matters

In general Thai police don't hassle foreigners, especially tourists. They usually go out of their way to avoid having to speak English with a foreigner, especially regarding minor traffic issues. Thai police do, however, rigidly enforce laws against drug possession. Do be aware that some police divisions, especially on the Thai islands, might view foreigners and their legal infractions as a money-making opportunity.

If you are arrested for any offence, the police will allow you the opportunity to make a phone call, either to your embassy or consulate in Thailand if you have one, or to a friend or relative if not. There's a whole set of legal codes governing the length of time and the manner in which you can be detained before being charged or put on trial, but a lot of discretion is left to the police. In the case of foreigners the police are more likely to bend these codes in your favour. However, as with

police worldwide, if you don't show respect you will make matters worse.

Thai law does not presume an indicted detainee to be either guilty or innocent but rather a 'suspect', whose guilt or innocence will be decided in court. Trials are usually speedy.

The **tourist police** (24hr 1155) can be very helpful in cases of arrest. Although they typically have no jurisdiction over the kinds of cases handled by regular cops, they may be able to help with translations or with contacting your embassy. You can call the hotline to lodge complaints or to request assistance with regards to personal safety.

LGBT+ Travellers

Thai culture is relatively tolerant of both male and female homosexuality. There is a fairly prominent LGBT+ scene in Bangkok, Pattaya and Phuket, all three of which hold annual gay pride events. With regard to dress and mannerisms, the LGBT+

Practicalities

o **Newspapers** English-language newspapers include the *Bangkok Post* (www.bangkokpost.com), the business-heavy *Nation* (www.nationmultimedia.com) and *KhaoSod English* (www.khaosodenglish.com), the English-language service of a mainstream Thai newspaper. Weeklies such as the *Economist* and *Time* are sold at news stands.

o **Radio** There are more than 400 AM and FM radio stations. Many smaller radio stations and international services are available to stream over the internet.

o **TV** Six VHF TV networks carry Thai programming, plus TrueVision cable with international programming. Digital programming has increased programming.

community are generally accepted without comment. However, public displays of affection – whether heterosexual or homosexual – are frowned upon.

It's worth noting that, perhaps because Thailand is still a relatively conservative place, lesbians generally adhere to rather strict gender roles. Overtly 'butch' lesbians, called *tom* (from 'tomboy'), typically have short hair, and wear men's clothing. Femme lesbians refer to themselves as *dêe* (from 'lady'). Visiting lesbians who don't fit into one of these categories may find themselves met with confusion.

Thailand passed the Gender Equality Act in 2015, the country's first law to provide protection from unfair gender discrimination. But while transgender and third gender people are quite visible in Thailand, they continue to face discrimination in the workplace and

when dealing with branches of the government. Many transgender people find their employment options limited to the entertainment or sex industries.

Utopia (www.utopia-asia. com) posts lots of Thailand information for LGBT+ travellers.

Money

Most places in Thailand prefer transactions in cash. Credit cards are accepted by travel agents, and in up-market hotels, restaurants, shopping malls and stores. Note that the availability of electronic transaction facilities diminishes as you move further away from urban centres.

ATMs

Debit and ATM cards issued by a bank in your home country can be used at

ATMs around Thailand to withdraw cash (in Thai baht only) directly from your account back home. ATMs are extremely ubiquitous throughout the country and can be relied on for the bulk of your spending cash. Most ATMs allow a maximum of 20,000B in withdrawals per day.

The downside is that Thai ATMs charge a 220B foreign-transaction fee on top of whatever currency conversion and out-of-network fees your home bank charges. Before leaving home, shop around for a bank account that has free international ATM usage and reimburses fees incurred at other institutions' ATMs.

Changing Money

Banks or private money changers offer the best foreign-exchange rates. When buying baht, US dollars is the most accepted currency, followed by British pounds, euros and Chinese yuan. Most banks charge a commission and duty for each travellers cheque cashed. Current exchange rates are posted at exchange counters.

Credit & Debit Cards

Credit and debit cards can be used for purchases at many shops, hotels and restaurants. The most commonly accepted cards are Visa and MasterCard. American Express is typically only accepted at high-end hotels and restaurants.

Contact your bank and your credit-card provider before you leave home and notify them of your upcoming trip so that your accounts aren't suspended due to suspicious overseas activity.

Tipping

Tipping is not generally expected in Thailand, though it is appreciated. The exception is loose change from a large restaurant bill – if a meal costs 488B and you pay with a 500B note, some Thais will leave the change. It's a way of saying 'I'm not so money grubbing as to grab every last baht'. At many hotel restaurants and more upmarket eateries, a 10% service charge will be added to your bill.

Opening Hours

Banks and government offices close for national holidays. Some bars and clubs close during elections and certain religious holidays when alcohol sales are banned. Shopping centres have banks that open late.

Banks 8.30am–4.30pm Monday to Friday; ATMs 24hr

Bars 6pm–midnight or 1am

Clubs 8pm–2am

Government offices 8.30am–4.30pm Monday to Friday; some close for lunch

Restaurants 8am–10pm

Shops 10am–7pm

Photography

Be considerate when taking photographs of locals. Learn how to ask politely in Thai and wait for an embarrassed nod. In some of the regularly visited minority areas, be prepared for the photographed subject to ask for money in exchange for a picture. Some hill peoples will not allow you to point a camera at them.

Post

Thailand has a very efficient postal service (www. thailandpost.co.th) and local postage is inexpensive. Typical provincial post offices open from 8.30am to 4.30pm weekdays and 9am to noon on Saturdays. Larger main post offices in provincial capitals may also be open for a half-day on Sunday. You will need to show your passport to send anything.

Most provincial post offices will sell DIY packing boxes. Don't send cash or other valuables through the mail.

Public Holidays

Government offices and banks close their doors on the following public holidays:

1 January New Year's Day

February (date varies) Makha Bucha; Buddhist holy day

6 April Chakri Day; commemorating the founder of the Chakri dynasty, Rama I

13–15 April Songkran Festival

1 May Labour Day

4 May Coronation Day

May (date varies) Royal Ploughing Ceremony

May/June (date varies) Visakha Bucha; Buddhist holy day

3 June Her Majesty the Queen's Birthday

28 July King Maha Vajiralongkorn's Birthday

July/August (date varies) Asanha Bucha; Buddhist holy day

12 August Queen Sirikit's Birthday/Mother's Day

13 October Late King Bhumibol's Memorial Day

23 October Chulalongkorn Day

5 December Late King Bhumibol's Birthday/Father's Day

10 December Constitution Day

31 December New Year's Eve

Safe Travel

Thailand is generally a safe country to visit, but it's smart to exercise caution, especially when it comes to dealing with strangers (both Thais and foreigners) and travelling alone.

Drug Possession

It is illegal to buy, sell or possess opium, heroin, cocaine, amphetamines, methamphetamine, ecstasy,

Smoking

Smoking is strictly banned in restaurants, bars, public transport and indoor public areas (although it still takes place in some bars). Many establishments such as hotels, restaurants and cafes have a clearly designated open-air smoking area. Locals can routinely be seen smoking on roads, but it's not encouraged.

hallucinogenic mushrooms or marijuana. Possession can result in one or more years of prison time. Attempting to cross a border with drugs carries higher sanctions, including the death penalty.

Scams

Bangkok is a hotspot for long, involved frauds that dupe travellers into thinking they've made a friend and are getting a bargain, when in fact they are getting ripped off. All offers of free shopping or sightseeing help from strangers should be ignored. They will invariably take a commission from your purchases.

Touts

In Bangkok, some túk-túk drivers and other new 'friends' often take new arrivals on city tours. These almost always end up in high-pressure sales situations at silk, jewellery or handicraft shops.

Touts also steer customers to certain guesthouses that pay a commission. Travel agencies are notorious for talking newly arrived tourists into staying at inconveniently located, overpriced hotels thanks to commissions. Some travel agencies masquerade as TAT, the government-funded tourist information office.

Websites

The following government websites offer travel advisories and information on current hotspots.

Australian Department of Foreign Affairs (www.smartraveller.gov.au)

British Foreign Office (www.gov.uk/foreign-travel-advice)

Canadian Department of Foreign Affairs (www.dfait-maeci.gc.ca)

New Zealand Foreign Affairs & Trade (www.safetravel.govt.nz)

US State Department (www.travel.state.gov/traveladvisories)

Taxes & Refunds

Thailand has a 7% value-added tax (VAT) on many goods and services. Mid-range and top-end hotels and restaurants might also add a 10% service tax. The two combined are known as 'plus plus', or '++'.

You can get a refund on VAT paid on shopping, though not on food or

hotels, as you leave the country. For how-to info, visit http://vrtweb.rd.go.th.

Telephone

The telephone country code for Thailand is 66 and is used when calling the country from abroad. All Thai telephone numbers are preceded by a '0' if you're dialling domestically (the '0' is omitted when calling from overseas). If the initial '0' is followed by a '6', an '8' or a '9' then you're dialling a mobile phone.

Mobile Phones

The easiest option for making calls in Thailand is to buy a local SIM card. Make sure that your mobile phone is unlocked before travelling.

Important Phone Numbers

Thailand country code	☎66
Bangkok city code	☎02
Mobile numbers	☎06, 08, 09
Operator-assisted international calls	☎100
Free local directory assistance	☎1133

Time

Thailand is seven hours ahead of GMT/UTC. Times are often expressed according to the 24-hour clock.

Toilets

The Asian-style squat toilet is becoming less common in Thailand. Sit-down toilets are becoming more prevalent wherever foreign tourists can be found.

If you encounter a squat, here's what you should know. Straddle the two foot pads and face the door. To flush, use the plastic bowl to scoop water out of the adjacent basin and pour it into the toilet bowl. Some places supply a small pack of toilet paper at the entrance (5B), otherwise bring your own stash or wipe the old-fashioned way with water.

Many septic systems may not be designed to take toilet paper. In such cases there will be a waste basket where you're supposed to place used toilet paper and feminine hygiene products. Many toilets also come with a small spray hose – Thailand's version of the bidet.

Tourist Information

The government-operated tourist information and promotion service, **Tourism Authority of Thailand** (TAT; nationwide call centre 1672; www.tourismthailand.org), was founded in 1960 and produces excellent pamphlets

on sightseeing. The TAT head office is in Bangkok and there are regional offices throughout the country; check the website for contact information.

Visas

Thailand has visa-exemption agreements with 64 countries (including European countries, Australia, New Zealand and the USA). Nationals from these countries can enter Thailand at no charge without pre-arranged documentation. Depending on nationality, these citizens are issued a 14- to 90-day visa exemption. Note that for some nationalities, less time (15 days rather than 30 days) is given if arriving by land rather than air. Check the **Ministry of Foreign Affairs** (02 203 5000; www.mfa.go.th; 443 Th Si Ayuthaya, Bangkok) website for more details. Citizens of an additional 19 countries are eligible for visa-on-arrival, which allows for stays of up to 15 days.

Women Travellers

Women travellers face relatively few problems in Thailand. It is respectful to cover up if you're going deep into rural communities, entering temples or going to and from the beach. But on the whole, local women dress

in a variety of different styles (particularly in cities) without being stared at or frowned upon.

Keep Thai etiquette in mind during social interactions. Women who aren't interested in romantic encounters should not presume that the Thai men they encounter always have platonic motives. A Thai man could feel a loss of face if conversation, flirting or other attention is directed towards him and then diverted to another person. In extreme cases (or where alcohol is involved), this could result in an unpleasant situation or even lead to violence.

Attacks and rapes do sometimes occur, and women are at greater risk when they are alone at night or in isolated locations. Stay alert if returning home alone from a bar, and avoid accepting rides from strangers late at night.

Transport

Getting There & Away

Flights and tours can be booked online at www.lonelyplanet.com/bookings.

Air

Airports with international connections include the following:

Suvarnabhumi International Airport (02 132 1888; www.airportthai.co.th; Samut Prakan) The country's main air terminal is located in Samut Prakan, 30km east of Bangkok and 110km from Pattaya. The airport's name is pronounced *sù·wan·ná·poom*.

Don Mueang International Airport (02 535 1192; www.airportthai.co.th; Don Mueang) Located 25km north of central Bangkok, Don Mueang was retired from service in 2006 only to reopen later as the city's de facto budget and domestic hub.

Phuket International Airport (076 632 7230; www.phuketairportonline.com) With several domestic and international destinations.

Chiang Mai International Airport (053 922000; www.chiangmaiairportonline.com) International destinations include many Asian and Southeast Asian cities.

Chiang Rai International Airport (Mae Fah Luang International Airport; 053 798000; www.chiangraiairportthai.com) International destinations include Kunming, China.

Samui International Airport (www.samuiairportonline.com) International destinations include Singapore.

Krabi International Airport International destinations include Doha, Kuala Lumpur, Singapore and a few cities in China.

Land

Thailand shares land borders with Cambodia, Laos, Malaysia and Myanmar. Land travel between all of these countries can be done at sanctioned border crossings. With improved highways and new bridges, it has become easier to travel from Thailand to China via Laos.

Getting Around

Air

Hopping around the country by air continues to be affordable. Most routes originate from Bangkok (both Don Mueang and Suvarnabhumi International Airports), but Chiang Mai, Chiang Rai, Hat Yai, Ko Samui, Phuket and Udon Thani all have a few routes to other Thai towns.

Domestic Airlines

AirAsia (nationwide 02 515 9999; www.airasia.com) From Don Mueang to Chiang Mai, Chiang Rai, Krabi, Phuket and Udon Thani; from Chiang Mai to Krabi and Phuket.

Bangkok Airways (nationwide 1771; www.bangkokair.com) From Suvarnabhumi to Chiang Mai, Chiang Rai, Ko Samui, Krabi and Phuket; from Chiang Mai to Ko Samui and Phuket.

Nok Air (nationwide 1318; www.nokair.com) From Don Mueang to Chiang Mai, Chiang Rai, Krabi, Phuket and Udon

Thani; from Chiang Mai to Udon Thani.

Orient Thai (nationwide 02 229 4100; www.flyorientthai.com) From Don Mueang to Phuket.

Thai Lion Air (nationwide 02 529 9999; www.lionairthai.com) From Don Mueang to Chiang Mai, Chiang Rai, Krabi and Phuket.

Thai Smile (nationwide 02 118 8888; www.thaismileair.com) From Suvarnabhumi to Chiang Mai, Chiang Rai, Krabi, Phuket and Udon Thani; from Chiang Mai to Phuket.

Bicycle

Lack of infrastructure and dangerous roads mean that cycling isn't generally recommended as a means of transport for the casual tourist. Exceptions are the guided bicycle tours of Bangkok and some other large cities that stick to rural routes.

Boat

The true Thai water transport is the *reu·a hăhng yow* (long-tail boat), so-called because the propeller is mounted at the end of a long driveshaft extending from the engine. Long-tail boats are a staple of transport on rivers and canals in Bangkok and neighbouring provinces, and between islands.

Between the mainland and small, less-touristed islands, the standard craft is a wooden boat, 8–10m long, with an inboard engine, a wheelhouse and a simple roof to shelter passengers and cargo. To more popular destinations, faster hovercraft (jetfoils) and speedboats are the norm.

Bus & Minivan

The bus network in Thailand is prolific and reliable. The Thai government subsidises the Transport Company (*bò·rí·sàt kŏn sòng*), usually abbreviated to Baw Khaw Saw (BKS). Every city and town in Thailand linked by bus has a BKS station, even if it's just a patch of dirt by the side of the road.

Be aware of bus scams and other common problems. We do not recommend using bus companies that operate directly out of tourist centres, such as Bangkok's Th Khao San, because of repeated instances of theft and commission-seeking stops.

For an increasing number of destinations, minivans are superseding buses. Minivans are run by private companies and because their vehicles are smaller, they can depart from the market (instead of the out-of-town bus stations) and in some cases will deliver passengers directly to their hotel.

Car & Motorcycle

Hire

Cars, 4WDs and vans can be hired in most major cities and airports from local companies as well as all the usual international chains.

Climate Change & Travel

Every form of transport that relies on carbon-based fuel generates CO_2, the main cause of human-induced climate change. Modern travel is dependent on aeroplanes, which might use less fuel per kilometre per person than most cars but travel much greater distances. The altitude at which aircraft emit gases (including CO_2) and particles also contributes to their climate change impact. Many websites offer 'carbon calculators' that allow people to estimate the carbon emissions generated by their journey and, for those who wish to do so, to offset the impact of the greenhouse gases emitted with contributions to portfolios of climate-friendly initiatives throughout the world. Lonely Planet offsets the carbon footprint of all staff and author travel.

Local companies tend to have cheaper rates, but the quality of their fleets varies. Check the tyre tread and general upkeep of the vehicle before committing.

Motorcycles can be hired in major towns and tourist centres from guesthouses and small businesses. For daily hires most businesses will ask that you leave your passport as a deposit. Before hiring a motorcycle, check the vehicle's condition and ask for a helmet (which is required by law).

Road Rules & Hazards

Thais drive on the left-hand side of the road – most of the time! Other than that, just about anything goes, in spite of road signs and speed limits.

The main rule to be aware of is that right of way goes to the bigger vehicle – this is not what it says in the Thai traffic laws, but it's the reality. Maximum speed limits are 50km/h on urban roads and 80km/h to 100km/h on most highways – but on any given stretch of highway you'll see various vehicles travelling as slowly as 30km/h and as fast as 150km/h.

In Bangkok traffic is chaotic, roads are poorly signposted and motorcycles and random contraflows mean you can suddenly find yourself facing a wall of cars coming the other way.

Outside of the capital, the principal hazard when driving in Thailand, besides the general disregard for traffic laws, is having to contend with so many different types of vehicles on the same road – trucks, bicycles, túk-túk and motorcycles. This danger is often compounded by the lack of working lights. In village areas the vehicular traffic is lighter but you have to contend with stray chickens, dogs and water buffaloes.

Dangerous Roads

Thailand's roads are dangerous. In 2018, they were the deadliest in Southeast Asia and the seventh-deadliest in the world, according to the World Health Organization. Several high-profile bus accidents involving foreign tourists have prompted some Western nations to issue travel advisories for highway safety due to disregard for speed limits, reckless driving and long-distance bus drivers' use of stimulants.

Fatal bus crashes make headlines, but nearly 75% of vehicle accidents in Thailand involve motorcycles. Less than half of the motorcyclists in the country wear helmets and many tourists are injured riding motorcycles because they don't know how to handle the vehicles and are unfamiliar with local driving conventions.

Insurance

Thailand requires a minimum of liability insurance for all registered vehicles on the road. The better hire companies include comprehensive coverage for their vehicles — usually defined as a 'super collision damage waiver'. Always verify that a vehicle is insured for liability before signing a rental contract; you should also ask to see the dated insurance documents.

Local Transport

City Bus & Sŏrng·tăa·ou

Bangkok has the largest city-bus system in the country. The etiquette for riding public buses is to wait at a bus stop and hail the vehicle by waving your hand palm-side downward. You typically pay the fare once you've taken a seat or, in some cases, when you disembark.

Elsewhere, public transport is provided by *sŏrng·tăa·ou* ('two rows'; a small pick-up truck outfitted with two facing benches for passengers). They sometimes operate on fixed routes, just like buses, but they may also run a shared taxi service where they pick up passengers going in the same general direction. In tourist centres, *sŏrng·tăa·ou* can be chartered just like a regular taxi, but you'll need to negotiate the fare beforehand. You can usually hail a *sŏrng·tăa·ou* anywhere along its route and pay the fare when you disembark.

Mass Transit

Bangkok is the only city in Thailand to have an above-ground (BTS) and underground light-rail (MRT) public transport system. Both are being expanded, with new stations and lines set to open in the next few years.

Taxi

Bangkok has the most formal system of metered taxis, although other cities have growing 'taxi meter' networks. In some cases, fares are set in advance or require negotiation.

App-based taxi hailing initiatives are also available, especially in bigger cities and major tourist destinations. The most popular app-based service is Grab (www.grab.com), which bought out Uber in Southeast Asia in 2018. Other services include All Thai Taxi (www.allthaitaxi.com).

Motorcycle Taxi

Many cities in Thailand have *mor·đeu·sai ráp jâhng*, motorcycle taxis that can be hired for short distances. If you're empty-handed or travelling with a small bag, they can't be beaten for transport in a pinch.

In most cities, you'll find motorcycle taxis clustered near street intersections, as well as at bus and train stations. Usually, the drivers wear numbered orange, yellow or green vests. You'll need to establish the price beforehand.

Săhm·lór & Túk-túk

Săhm·lór (also spelt *săamláw*) are three-wheeled pedicabs that are typically found in small towns where traffic is light and old-fashioned ways persist.

The modern era's version of the human-powered săhm·lór is the motorised túk-túk (pronounced *dúk dúk*). They're small utility vehicles, powered by screaming engines (usually LPG-powered) with a lot of flash and sparkle.

With either form of transport the fare must be established by bargaining before departure. In tourist centres, túk-túk drivers often grossly overcharge foreigners, so have a sense of how much the fare should be before soliciting a ride. Hotel staff are helpful in providing reasonable fare suggestions.

Train

Thailand's train system connects the four corners of the country and is a scenic, if slow, alternative to buses for the long journey north to Chiang Mai or south to Surat Thani.

The 4500km rail network is operated by the **State Railway of Thailand** (SRT; 🖉nationwide 1690; www. railway.co.th) and covers four main lines: northern to Chiang Mai, southern to Sungai Kolok, northeastern to Nong Khai or Ubon Ratchathani, and eastern to Aranya Prathet, on the border with Cambodia. All long-distance trains originate from Bangkok's Hualamphong Train Station.

Train stations have printed timetables in English, though this isn't always the case for smaller stations.

Classes

The SRT operates trains in three classes – 1st, 2nd and 3rd – but each class varies considerably depending on whether you're on an ordinary, rapid or express train.

1st class Private, two-bunk cabins define the 1st-class carriages, available only on rapid, express and special-express trains.

2nd class The seating arrangements in a 2nd-class, nonsleeper carriage are similar to those on a bus, with pairs of padded seats, usually recliners, facing in one direction. On 2nd-class sleeper cars, pairs of seats face one another and convert into two fold-down berths. There are air-con and fan 2nd-class carriages.

3rd class A typical 3rd-class carriage consists of two rows of bench seats divided into facing pairs. Each bench seat is designed to seat two or three passengers. Express trains do not carry 3rd-class carriages at all. Commuter trains in the Bangkok area are all 3rd class.

Costs

Fares are determined on a base price with surcharges added for distance, class and train type (special express, express, rapid, ordinary). Extra charges are added if the carriage has air-con and for sleeping berths (either upper or lower).

Reservations

Advance bookings can be made from one to 60 days before your intended date of departure. You can make bookings in person from any train station. Train tickets can also be purchased at travel agencies, which usually add a service charge to the ticket price. If you're making an advance reservation from outside the country, contact a licensed travel agent.

It is advisable to make advance bookings for long-distance sleeper trains between Bangkok and Chiang Mai, or from Bangkok to Surat Thani, as seats fill up quickly.

For short-distance trips you should purchase your ticket at least a day in advance for seats (rather than sleepers).

Partial refunds on tickets are available depending on the number of days prior to your departure that you arrange a cancellation. These arrangements can be handled at the train station booking office.

Language

There are different ways of writing Thai in the Roman alphabet – we have chosen one method below. The hyphens indicate syllable breaks within words, and some syllables are further divided with a dot to help you pronounce them. Thai is a tonal language – the accent marks on vowels represent these low, mid, falling, high and rising tones.

Note that after every sentence, men add the polite particle *káp*, and women *ká*.

To enhance your trip with a phrasebook, visit **lonelyplanet.com**. Lonely Planet iPhone phrasebooks are available through the Apple App store.

Basics

Hello.
สวัสดี   sà-wàt-dee

How are you?
สบายดีไหม   sà-bai dee măi

I'm fine.
สบายดีครับ/ค่า   sà-bai dee kráp/kâ (m/f)

Excuse me.
ขออภัย   kŏr à-pai

Yes./No.
ใช่/ไม่   châi/mâi

Thank you.
ขอบคุณ   kòrp kun

You're welcome.
ยินดี   yin dee

Do you speak English?
คุณพูดภาษา   kun pôot pah-săh
อังกฤษได้ไหม   ang-grìt dâi măi

I don't understand.
ผม/ดิฉัน ไม่เข้าใจ   pŏm/dì-chăn mâi kôw jai (m/f)

How much is this?
เท่าไร   tôw-rai

Can you lower the price?
ลดราคาได้ไหม   lót rah-kah dâi măi

Accommodation

Where's a hotel?
โรงแรมอยู่ที่ไหน   rohng raam yòo têe năi

Do you have a single/double room?
มีห้องเดี่ยว/   mee hôrng dèe·o/
เตียงคู่ไหม   đee·ang kôo măi

Eating & Drinking

I'd like (the menu), please.
ขอ (รายการ   kŏr (rai gahn
อาหาร) หน่อย   ah-hăhn) nòy

What would you recommend?
คุณแนะนำอะไรบ้าง   kun náa-nam à-rai bâhng

That was delicious.
อร่อยมาก   à-ròy mâhk

Cheers!
ไชโย   chai-yoh

Please bring the bill/check.
ขอบิลหน่อย   kŏr bin nòy

I don't eat ...
ผม/ดิฉัน ไม่กิน ...   pŏm/dì-chăn mâi gin . . .
(m/f)

eggs	ไข่	kài
fish	ปลา	þlah
nuts	ถั่ว	tòo·a
red meat	เนื้อแดง	néu·a daang

Emergencies

I'm ill.
ผม/ดิฉันป่วย   pŏm/dì-chăn þòo·ay (m/f)

Help!
ช่วยด้วย   chôo·ay dôo·ay

Call a doctor!
เรียกหมอหน่อย   rêe·ak mŏr nòy

Call the police!
เรียกตำรวจหน่อย   rêe·ak đam·ròo·at nòy

Where are the toilets?
ห้องน้ำอยู่ที่ไหน   hôrng nám yòo têe năi

Directions

Where's (a market/restaurant)?
(ตลาด/ร้านอาหาร)   (đà-làht/ráhn ah-hăhn)
อยู่ที่ไหน   yòo têe năi

What's the address?
ที่อยู่คืออะไร   têe yòo keu à-rai

Could you please write it down?
เขียนลงให้ได้ไหม   kĕe·an long hâi dâi măi

Can you show me (on the map)?
ให้ดู (ในแผนที่)   hâi doo (nai păan têe)
ได้ไหม   dâi măi

Behind the Scenes

Acknowledgements

Climate map data adapted from Peel MC, Finlayson BL & McMahon TA (2007) 'Updated World Map of the Köppen-Geiger Climate Classification', *Hydrology and Earth System Sciences*, 11, 1633–44.

Illustrations pp40–1, pp44–5 by Michael Weldon.

Cover photograph: Ko Khao Phing Kan, Phuket; mikolajn/Shutterstock ©

This Book

This 3rd edition of Lonely Planet's *Best of Thailand* guidebook was curated by Anirban Mahapatra and researched and written by Anirban, Tim Bewer, David Eimer, Ashley Harrell, Tharik Hussain, Michael Kohn, Daniel McCrohan and Olivia Pozzan. This guidebook was produced by the following:

Destination Editor Tanya Parker

Senior Product Editors Kate Chapman, Kathryn Rowan

Regional Senior Cartographer Diana Von Holdt

Product Editor Barbara Delissen

Book Designer Wibowo Rusli

Cartographer Julie Dodkins

Assisting Editors Nigel Chin, Victoria Harrison, Kate Morgan, Fionnuala Twomey, Anna Tyler, Brana Vladisavljevic

Cover Researcher Brendan Dempsey-Spencer

Thanks to Joel Cotterell, Bruce Evans, Anne Mulvaney, Jenna Myers, Monique Perrin, Gabriela Sanchez Acosta, Simon Sanford

Send Us Your Feedback

We love to hear from travellers – your comments keep us on our toes and help make our books better. Our well-travelled team reads every word on what you loved or loathed about this book. Although we cannot reply individually to postal submissions, we always guarantee that your feedback goes straight to the appropriate authors, in time for the next edition. Each person who sends us information is thanked in the next edition, the most useful submissions are rewarded with a selection of digital PDF chapters.

Visit lonelyplanet.com/contact to submit your updates and suggestions or to ask for help. Our award-winning website also features inspirational travel stories, news and discussions.

Note: We may edit, reproduce and incorporate your comments in Lonely Planet products such as guidebooks, websites and digital products, so let us know if you don't want your comments reproduced or your name acknowledged. For a copy of our privacy policy visit lonelyplanet.com/privacy.

Index

Symbols & Map Key

Look for these symbols to quickly identify listings:

- ◉ Sights
- ✈ Activities
- ✿ Courses
- ◉ Tours
- ✪ Festivals & Events
- ✖ Eating
- ◉ Drinking
- ★ Entertainment
- ⊕ Shopping
- ❶ Information & Transport

These symbols and abbreviations give vital information for each listing:

🌱 Sustainable or green recommendation

FREE No payment required

- ☎ Telephone number
- ⊘ Opening hours
- Ⓟ Parking
- ⊖ Nonsmoking
- ✺ Air-conditioning
- @ Internet access
- 🛜 Wi-fi access
- ⊠ Swimming pool
- 🚌 Bus
- 🚢 Ferry
- 🚋 Tram
- 🚆 Train
- 📖 English-language menu
- 🥗 Vegetarian selection
- 👪 Family-friendly

Find your best experiences with these Great For... icons.

 Art & Culture

 Beaches

 Budget

 Cafe/Coffee

🚲 Cycling

 Detour

 Drinking

Entertainment

✨ Events

👪 Family Travel

🍽 Food & Drink

 History

 Local Life

 Nature & Wildlife

 Photo Op

 Scenery

 Shopping

 Short Trip

 Sport

 Walking

 Winter Travel

Sights

- 🏖 Beach
- 🐦 Bird Sanctuary
- 🛕 Buddhist
- 🏰 Castle/Palace
- ✝ Christian
- ☯ Confucian
- 🕉 Hindu
- ☪ Islamic
- 卍 Jain
- ✡ Jewish
- ❶ Monument
- 🏛 Museum/Gallery/ Historic Building
- 🏚 Ruin
- ⛩ Shinto
- 🪯 Sikh
- ☯ Taoist
- 🍇 Winery/Vineyard
- 🦁 Zoo/Wildlife Sanctuary
- ◉ Other Sight

Points of Interest

- ⊙ Bodysurfing
- ⊙ Camping
- ⊖ Cafe
- 🛶 Canoeing/Kayaking
- ● Course/Tour
- 🤿 Diving
- 🍷 Drinking & Nightlife
- ✖ Eating
- 🎭 Entertainment
- ♨ Sento Hot Baths/ Onsen
- 🛍 Shopping
- ⛷ Skiing
- 🛏 Sleeping
- 🤿 Snorkelling
- 🏄 Surfing
- 🏊 Swimming/Pool
- 🚶 Walking
- 🏄 Windsurfing
- ✿ Other Activity

Information

- 🏦 Bank
- 🏛 Embassy/Consulate
- ➕ Hospital/Medical
- @ Internet
- 👮 Police
- ✉ Post Office
- ☎ Telephone
- 🚻 Toilet
- ❶ Tourist Information
- • Other Information

Geographic

- 🏖 Beach
- ⋈ Gate
- 🏠 Hut/Shelter
- 🗼 Lighthouse
- 🔭 Lookout
- ▲ Mountain/Volcano
- 🌴 Oasis
- 🌳 Park
-)(Pass
- 🏞 Picnic Area
- 🏞 Waterfall

Transport

- ✈ Airport
- Ⓑ BART station
- ⊗ Border crossing
- Ⓣ Boston T station
- 🚌 Bus
- 🚠 Cable car/Funicular
- 🚲 Cycling
- ⛴ Ferry
- Ⓜ Metro/MRT station
- 🚝 Monorail
- Ⓟ Parking
- ⛽ Petrol station
- Ⓢ Subway/S-Bahn/ Skytrain station
- 🚕 Taxi
- 🚂 Train station/Railway
- 🚋 Tram
- Ⓤ Underground/ U-Bahn station
- • Other Transport

Ashley Harrell

After a brief stint selling day-spa coupons door-to-door in south Florida, Ashley decided she'd rather be a writer. She went to journalism grad school, convinced a newspaper to hire her, and started covering wildlife, crime and tourism, sometimes all in the same story. Fueling her zest for storytelling and the unknown, she travelled widely and moved often, from a tiny NYC apartment to a vast California ranch to a jungle cabin in Costa Rica, where she started writing for Lonely Planet. From there her travels became more exotic and further flung, and she still laughs when paychecks arrive.

Tharik Hussain

Born in Sylhet, Bangladesh, but raised in east London, Tharik is a freelance travel writer, author, journalist and occasional broadcaster who specialises in Muslim cultures. Tharik has travelled across the globe in search of forgotten Islamic heritage and has written about this for the BBC, Lonely Planet, Al Jazeera and Arab News amongst others. He has a Masters in Islamic Studies and has previously lived in Jeddah, Saudi Arabia. Tharik is also a cultural consultant and a member of the British Guild of Travel Writers.

Michael Kohn

Michael has been working as a travel writer for over a decade. In 2003 he jumped in headfirst with Lonely Planet by taking on the Uzbekistan and Kazakhstan chapters of the *Central Asia* guidebook. Since then he has been exploring some of the remoter corners of Asia and the Middle East for Lonely Planet, while also reporting the news for international media outlets. His Lonely Planet titles include *Sri Lanka, Tibet, Mongolia, Israel & the Palestinian Territories* and *Trans-Siberian Railway*. Michael's particular area of interest is Mongolia, where he has covered the news for Bloomberg, the BBC and others. During his time in Mongolia he wrote *Lama of the Gobi,* a biography of the 19th-century poet-monk Danzanravjaa, and *Dateline Mongolia,* a personal memoir about his time spent working as a reporter in Ulaanbaatar.

Daniel McCrohan

With a Greek father, a Spanish grandfather, an Irish grandmother and a Chinese wife, Daniel has always looked beyond his English homeland for influence and inspiration. He's been travelling the world, on-and-off, for 25 years, and has been writing Lonely Planet guidebooks (42 and counting) for more than a decade. He specialises in China and India, but has travelled extensively throughout Thailand, forming a special bond over the years with Isan, a region he loves for its history, its wildlife parks and its almost total lack of tourists. Follow his adventures on Twitter (@danielmccrohan) or at danielmccrohan.com.

Olivia Pozzan

Olivia's travel-writing career was born from a life of travel and adventure. Her unusual knack for attracting adventure has seen her caving in Oman, expedition racing in Morocco, and trekking mountain ranges from the Himalayas to the Alps. Her veterinary career has seen her working on remote cattle stations in outback Australia, vetting on a camel expedition in the heart of Australia, darting lions in South Africa and working for an Arabian prince in the Middle East. With so much raw material at her fingertips, writing was a natural progression. Her articles and books have been published worldwide. For Lonely Planet, Olivia has covered regions in the Middle East, Italy, Thailand and Australia. Olivia is passionate about animal welfare and has led volunteer veterinary aid projects to Cambodia. When not travelling to the world's most exotic places, she lives the beach lifestyle on Australia's beautiful Sunshine Coast where she is a freelance writer and practicing veterinarian.

Our Story

A beat-up old car, a few dollars in the pocket and a sense of adventure. In 1972 that's all Tony and Maureen Wheeler needed for the trip of a lifetime – across Europe and Asia overland to Australia. It took several months, and at the end – broke but inspired – they sat at their kitchen table writing and stapling together their first travel guide, *Across Asia on the Cheap*. Within a week they'd sold 1500 copies. Lonely Planet was born.

Today, Lonely Planet has offices in Tennessee, Dublin, Beijing and Delhi, with a network of over 2000 contributors in every corner of the globe. We share Tony's belief that 'a great guidebook should do three things: inform, educate and amuse'.

Our Writers

Anirban Mahapatra

Anirban is a travel writer, photographer and filmmaker who has authored multiple editions of Lonely Planet's bestselling *India* guidebook, as well as several regional handbooks. He has written and curated Lonely Planet guidebooks on Bangladesh, Sri Lanka and Bhutan, designed content models and held author workshops for Lonely Planet and made videos and documentaries for international television networks, corporates and ministries under the Government of India. When not travelling the world, he lives in Kolkata and Bangkok, where he reads up on Buddhism, listens to the blues and plans his next adventure.

Tim Bewer

While growing up, Tim didn't travel much. He has spent most of his adult life making up for this, and has since visited over 80 countries, including most in Southeast Asia. After university he worked briefly as a legislative assistant before quitting capitol life to backpack around West Africa. It was during this trip that the idea of becoming a freelance travel writer and photographer was hatched, and he's been at it ever since. He has lived in Khon Kaen, Thailand, since 2007 and blogs at Tim's Thailand (www.timsthailand.com). He also tweets (@TimBewer) a lot about Thailand.

David Eimer

David has been a journalist and writer ever since abandoning the idea of a law career in 1990. After spells working in his native London and Los Angeles, he moved to Beijing in 2005, where he contributed to a variety of newspapers and magazines in the UK. Since then, he has travelled and lived across China and in numerous cities in Southeast Asia, including Bangkok, Phnom Penh and Yangon. He has been covering China, Myanmar and Thailand for Lonely Planet since 2006.

More Writers

STAY IN TOUCH LONELYPLANET.COM/CONTACT

IRELAND Digital Depot, Roe Lane (off Thomas St), Digital Hub, Dublin 8, D08 TCV4, Ireland

 twitter.com/ lonelyplanet

 facebook.com/ lonelyplanet

 instagram.com/ lonelyplanet

 youtube.com/ lonelyplanet

 lonelyplanet.com/ newsletter